EFFECTIVE TEACHING IN CORRECTIONAL SETTINGS

EFFECTIVE TEACHING IN CORRECTIONAL SETTINGS

Prisons, Jails, Juvenile Centers, and Alternative Schools

By

ROBERT G. THOMAS

California Men's Colony
San Luis Obispo

and

R. MURRAY THOMAS

University of California
Santa Barbara

CHARLES C THOMAS · PUBLISHER, LTD.
Springfield · Illinois · U.S.A.

Published and Distributed Throughout the World by

CHARLES C THOMAS • PUBLISHER, LTD.
2600 South First Street
Springfield, Illinois 62704

© 2008 by CHARLES C THOMAS • PUBLISHER, LTD.

ISBN 978-0-398-07816-4 (hard)
ISBN 978-0-398-07817-1 (paper)

Library of Congress Catalog Card Number: 2008010871

With THOMAS BOOKS *careful attention is given to all details of manufacturing
and design. It is the Publisher's desire to present books that are satisfactory as to their
physical qualities and artistic possibilities and appropriate for their particular use.*
THOMAS BOOKS *will be true to those laws of quality that assure a good name
and good will.*

Printed in the United States of America
SM-R-3

Library of Congress Cataloging-in-Publication Data

Thomas, Robert G.
  Effective teaching in correctional settings : prisons, jails, juvenile centers, and
alternative schools / by Robert G. Thomas and R. Murray Thomas.
    p. cm.
  Includes bibliographical references and index.
  ISBN 978-0-398-07816-4 (hard) -- ISBN 978-0-398-07817-1 (pbk.)
  1. Prisoners--Education--United States. 2. Effective teaching--United States. I.
Thomas, R. Murray (Robert Murray), 1921- II. Title.
  HV8883.3.U5T46 2007
  365'.6660973--dc22
                                                                        2008010871

To Courtney and Devon

PREFACE

The dual purpose of this book is to identify problems faced by people who teach in correctional institutions and to propose solutions for those problems. The book is intended for three kinds of readers – those who contemplate a career in correctional education, those who are already in correctional education, and those who simply want to learn what teaching in a prison, jail, or juvenile facility is all about.

Two recent trends in American society suggest that such a book is needed. First, the populations of prisons, jails, and juvenile detention centers have continued to grow. Therefore, the number of potential learners in correctional institutions has been increasing year after year. Second, states and cities have been taking the expressions *correctional* and *rehabilitation* more seriously than ever before, so new plans are being offered for improving inmates' skills and attitudes rather than merely locking up lawbreakers.

The continuing-growth trend can be illustrated with data on adults incarcerated or under supervision in the United States over the past quarter century. The number of detainees (in prison or jail, or on probation or parole) in 1980 was 1,842,100. That number grew to 4,350,300 in 1990, to 6,445,100 in 2000, and to 7,056,000 in 2005. In effect, within 25 years the prison, jail, and supervised population increased 3.8 fold. The average annual growth was around 3.5% (Bureau of Justice Statistics, 2005).

An example of the trend toward increased correctional/rehabilitation practices is the California governor's 2006-07 budget request for $52.8 million to fund the development and expansion of "a wide range of programs designed to reduce recidivism, including education, rehabilitation, and treatment programs for inmates and parolees." The requested amount would increase to $79.3 million in 2007–08, and $95.3 million in 2008–09 (Legislative Analyst's Office, 2006).

Because of the rapid increase of inmates seeking educational opportunities in prisons, jails, and juvenile centers, the numbers of teachers must increase at a similar rate if those inmates' opportunities are to be available. The intent of this book is to help both new instructors as well as current ones perform their jobs effectively.

Now to the backgrounds of the book's primary authors who form a son-and-father team. The son, Robert G. Thomas (better known as *Rob*) has been an instructor over the past quarter century at the Central Coast Adult School in the California Men's Colony, a medium-security prison located in San Luis Obispo. He has taught five kinds of students, (a) ones in a program for the emotionally and physically disadvantaged, (b) ones operating at the upper-elementary level, (c) those acquiring junior-high-level academic skills, (c) ones preparing to pass GED (General Educational Development) tests, and (d) ones pursuing an associate-of-arts degree through a nearby community college. During the first 15 years of his tenure as an instructor, Rob was also a correctional officer. Prior to joining the Men's Colony faculty, he served as a counselor in a juvenile hall. His publications relating to correctional education have included articles in *The International Encyclopedia of Education* and in such professional periodicals as *Federal Probation* and *The Journal of Correctional Education*.

The father, R. Murray Thomas, is an emeritus professor of educational psychology at the University of California, Santa Barbara. His 50-year teaching career ranged from junior-high grades through university graduate schools. Books he has written that relate to the subject-matter of the present volume include *Violence in America's Schools*, *What Wrongdoers Deserve*, *Classifying Reactions to Wrongdoing*, *Prevent-Repent-Reform-Revenge*, *Teaching About the Law*, *The Problem of Learning Difficulties*, *Counseling and Lifespan Development*, and *Individual Differences in the Classroom*.

Colleen Laney-Kobata and Basil DuBois are two additional instructors at the Central Coast Adult School (California Men's Colony) who contributed very substantially to the contents of this book.

Colleen (B.A. in English, M.S. in educational administration) was a teacher of language-arts and GATE (Gifted and Talented Education) classes in a public junior high school before joining the Central Coast Adult School in the Men's Colony. During her 12 years at the Men's Colony, she has taught ELD (English language development) classes and courses for inmates operating at a primary-school level. She also served on the leadership team responsible for the Colony's WASC (Western Association of Schools and Colleges) accreditation and for standardized-test administration.

Basil (B.A. and Higher-Education Diploma in history and geography), throughout two decades at the Central Coast Adult School (Men's Colony), has taught high-school history, ABE2 and ABE3 classes (upper-elementary and junior-high-level courses), and directed the computer-assisted-instruction laboratory. In 2003, he was elected Teacher-of-the-Year for the Correctional Education Association's Region Seven.

Because Rob's, Colleen's, and Basil's experiences have been entirely with male inmates, most of the problem cases described throughout the book involve men and boys. However, many of those same problems are also found in correctional facilities for females, so most of the suggested solutions for male-inmate problems are applicable as well to incarcerated women and girls.

Other correctional educators whose aid with this book has been much appreciated include G. Cantwell, Lisa Gomez, Robert Green, John Long, Michael R. Miller, Patrick Moloney, Andy Nunez, Gilda Romans, Deborah Roberts, Deborah Tobola, and Jack Tuckey.

R.G.T.
R.M.T.

CONTENTS

PART III – POSTSCRIPT

EFFECTIVE TEACHING IN
CORRECTIONAL SETTINGS

Chapter 1

WHAT THE BOOK IS ABOUT

This book's contents have been drawn primarily from the experiences of three veteran correctional-education instructors, with those experiences supplemented by descriptions of successful educational programs in such publications as *The Journal of Correctional Education, Corrections Today Magazine, Criminal Justice, The Prison Journal,* and *Punishment & Society.*

The three instructors – Rob Thomas, Colleen Laney-Kobata, and Basil DuBois – teach in the California Men's Colony, a medium-security state prison. All three admit to a strong bias in favor of a career in correctional education. They truly enjoy their occupation. They have foregone opportunities to work elsewhere in order to continue teaching in a prison because of the rewards and challenges. Their greatest reward has come from witnessing the educational progress of inmates who had never before done well in school and who now – pleased with their new success – openly express their gratitude to their instructors. Also rewarding is the satisfaction derived from creating solutions to the daily problems that the teaching task poses. Furthermore, instructors in correctional settings are spared many of the discipline challenges that confront teachers in public and private schools outside of prisons and juvenile facilities. In contrast to schools in the general society, teachers in prisons and juvenile centers are not obliged to tolerate unruly, uncooperative students. And very rarely do instructors in prisons hear from meddling parents who try to intimidate teachers into providing those parents' sons and daughters unwarranted privileges.

However, teaching in a correctional institution is not problem-free. As in every school, there are difficulties to be solved each day. Some difficulties are the same as those faced in public and private schools outside of correctional institutions. Other problems are specific to prisons, jails, and juvenile centers.

This book (a) identifies both kinds of problems – ones found in all schools and ones particularly significant in correctional settings – and (b) illustrates ways the problems can be solved.

THE BOOK'S STRUCTURE

The 10 chapters that follow this initial chapter are presented in three parts.

Part I (Correctional-Education Backgrounds) introduces readers to the field of correctional education. Chapter 2 (The Nature of American Correctional Institutions) describes correctional efforts in America, including kinds of facilities, the inmate populations, and controversies over providing inmates educational opportunities. Chapter 3 (Types of Programs and Personnel) identifies kinds of educational and rehabilitation programs and describes varieties and sources of teachers and educational administrators.

Part II (Instructional Problems and Solutions) is composed of seven chapters that explore the teaching process in terms of perspectives, problems, and solutions. Each chapter is divided into two major sections – (a) perspectives and (b) problems and solutions.

Perspectives are vantage points from which to view the central topic of a chapter. For example, in Chapter 4 (Significant Student Characteristics) students are analyzed from eight perspectives – their abilities, learning disorders, age, gender, ethnicity, gang membership, length of imprisonment, and reasons for enrolling in educational programs. In Chapter 8 (Selecting Teaching Methods) the teacher's task is seen from the perspectives of nine teaching methods – lecturing, diagnostic teaching, diminishing help, class discussion, tutoring, small-group work, reading assignments, games, and individual projects.

The second section of every chapter is titled *problems and solutions*. Each problem is presented as a brief case study that includes (a) the nature of a particular problem, (b) factors affecting decisions about what a teacher might do, and (c) one or more proposed solutions.

Part III (Postscript) contains a single chapter (Correctional Education – A Likely Future) that summarizes key concepts from the previous 10 chapters and speculates about the state of correctional education in the years ahead.

THE NATURE OF TEACHERS' PROBLEMS

We imagine that readers may now wonder exactly what we mean by "problems that correctional-education teachers face." In other words, precisely what sorts of problems are addressed in the seven chapters of Part II? To satisfy such curiosity, we offer the following sample of 20 of the 56 problems whose solutions are proposed in Part II. Each case is in the form of an anecdote, with the parentheses at the end of the anecdote identifying which later chapter offers solutions to that dilemma.

Case 1. Mr. X, a 20-year-old prison inmate periodically pulled up his left sleeve in order to glance at his bare arm during a weekly spelling test. The instructor suspected that Mr. X had spelling words written on his arm (Chapter 10: Assessing Student Progress).

Case 2. The statewide curriculum-planning board sent a revised set of learning objectives to teachers of ELD (English-Language-Development or English-as-a-Second-Language) classes. The following example illustrates the form of the objectives.

> ELD/ELS students, in both speaking and writing, will learn to use standard English (a) verb tenses, (b) agreement between subject and predicate, and (c) contractions.

The problem for the ELD teacher was that of converting those general objectives into specific ones for the purpose of planning lessons. For instance, she had to decide which verb tenses should be taught, which sorts of agreement between subject and predicate should be emphasized, and which contractions qualify as "standard English" (Chapter 7: Specifying Learning Goals).

Case 3. During interviews with a researcher, a woman in a halfway house (in her transition from prison to the general community) expressed her disappointment with the impersonal attitude of the teacher of the General Educational Development (GED) class in which the woman was enrolled. She compared the present teacher unfavorably with a teacher from her elementary-school years, one who had shown sincere interest in the student as an individual and who had served as her esteemed mentor (Chapter 5: Assigning Students to Programs).

Case 4. When taking roll at the beginning of class, the instructor of an academic program noted that four students were absent (Chapter 6: Managing the Class).

Case 5. Shortly after a 19-year-old inmate advanced from a junior-high-level class to a class that prepared students for a General Educational Development (GED) certificate, he began disrupting the GED class by making critical remarks about the instructor. He openly charged her with failing to explain mathematics operations accurately, with mistaking the causes of historical events, and with voicing political opinions. He complained about the teacher to classmates, to the teacher's aide (an inmate), and to the correctional officers in charge of the inmate's dormitory. The teacher, highly distressed about the rebellious student, expressed her anguish to fellow teachers and to the supervisor of academic instruction (Chapter 5: Assigning Students to Programs).

Case 6. In a men's prison, an instructor was disappointed with the lackadaisical effort that numbers of class members put into their studies. He was convinced that they could progress more rapidly if they tried harder and more consistently (Chapter 8: Selecting Teaching Methods).

Case 7. When a teacher monitored a student's weekly progress in completing workbook assignments, the teacher noted that the student continually produced less work than the minimum amount expected. Another class member called the student "lazy" until the instructor warned the class that such words as "lazy, stupid, dumb, and goof-off" would not be tolerated (Chapter 4: Significant Characteristics of Students).

Case 8. A newly hired teacher in a men's prison was informed that he must conduct a security search of his classroom at the end of each day. However, since he had never performed a search, he was unsure about how to go about it (Chapter 6: Managing the Class).

Case 9. An instructor in a women's prison was notified that a member of her class had been diagnosed as schizophrenic (Chapter 4: Significant Characteristics of Students).

Case 10. The teacher of a prison class must fill out end-of-the-academic-quarter evaluations for 27 students. Only two students who were in the class at the start of the quarter were still there at the end, and the three students who were most recently enrolled had just been assigned to the class during the final week (Chapter 10: Assessing Student Progress).

Case 11. An offender, sent to prison for safecracking, enrolled in a correctional-education class where he learned to divide fractions, spell lists of words, and write complete sentences, but he would not have changed his attitude about breaking the law. When released on parole, he would be better educated, but still intent on opening other people's safes (Chapter 7: Specifying Learning Goals).

Case 12. At the beginning of the fiscal year, a teacher was informed that she would be given half the normal amount of money to purchase learning materials for the upcoming academic year (Chapter 9: Choosing and Creating Learning Materials).

Case 13. An instructor who spoke only a little Spanish was assigned to an English-as-a-second-language course in which the majority of students spoke Spanish and were just beginning to learn English (Chapter 8: Selecting Teaching Methods).

Case 14. The teacher of a GED class was asked to submit a list of the students he believed were adequately prepared to take the official General-Education-Development test battery (Chapter 10: Assessing Student Progress).

Case 15. The social climate of a prison was constantly marred by inmates of one ethnic group exchanging insults with inmates of other ethnic groups. The insults featured derogatory ethnic stereotypes (Chapter 4: Significant Characteristics of Students).

Case 16. An instructor was given the task of developing a program in which he was expected to teach both a junior-high-level class and a GED test-preparation course. The students were to attend class for half of their six-and-one-half-hour school day and spend the remaining time completing independent-study assignments. Therefore, the teacher needed to design the program in a way that would provide meaningful learning experiences both inside the classroom and outside during independent-study time, all the while ensuring that students worked diligently throughout the entire school day (Chapter 8: Selecting Teaching Methods).

Case 17. A 73-year-old inmate, serving a life sentence in a state prison, enrolled in a high-school-level class as a way to spend his days in constructive activity, but during class discussions he never volunteered an opinion. When the instructor asked him why, the elderly student said that other class members always spoke up before he could decide what to say and how to say it (Chapter 4: Significant Characteristics of Students).

Case 18. A 26-year-old inmate, enrolled in a prison upper-elementary-level class on the basis of entry-test scores, amazed the teacher with how well he performed on class assignments (Chapter 5: Assigning Students to Programs).

Case 19. A 49-year-old white male claimed to be attending school only because it was part of his mandated prison work/training program. He kept a low profile in class by sitting quietly at his desk, completing only the bare minimum number of required assignments. He appeared unconcerned about passing written tests, and he typically failed to give acceptable responses when called on to answer questions during whole-class activities. Although the inmate was well behaved, the instructor felt the fellow was not working up to his ability level (Chapter 8: Selecting Teaching Methods).

Case 20. In a men's prison, when students were leaving the classroom at lunchtime, one of them, in a rush to get out the door, banged another inmate hard against the door jam. The one who had been bumped immediately turned to knock his assailant across the room, and a fight broke out between the pair (Chapter 6: Managing the Class).

In summary, these 20 cases illustrate problems commonly met in correctional-education classes, with such cases and their solutions providing a major portion of this book's content.

CONCLUSION

One conviction on which this book has been founded is that teaching in a correctional setting can be a rewarding and challenging profession. A second conviction is that the rewards are greater and the challenges are conquered most readily by teachers who are well versed in how to cope with the problems met in correctional programs. The purpose of *Effective Teaching in Correctional Settings* is to offer insights into the world of correctional education and to help equip teachers with problem-solving skills.

PART I

CORRECTIONAL-EDUCATION BACKGROUNDS

Problems of teaching in correctional settings, and methods of solving those problems, can profitably be interpreted against a backdrop of information about the nature of the nation's penal institutions, their programs, and their personnel. The purpose of the two chapters in Part I is to provide such information.

Chapter 2 describes American correctional institutions in terms of (a) their types and purposes, (b) their populations, and (c) the controversy over whether they should offer prisoners educational opportunities.

Chapter 3 surveys types of educational programs and their personnel – teachers, administrators, teachers' assistants, and support staff.

Chapter 2

THE NATURE OF AMERICAN CORRECTIONAL INSTITUTIONS

As a background for understanding correctional education, this chapter offers a brief overview of prisons, jails, and juvenile-detention facilities in terms of (a) their types and purposes, (b) their populations, and (c) the controversy over whether they should offer prisoners educational opportunities.

TYPES AND PURPOSES

Two distinctions among prisons, jails, and juvenile facilities are in the kinds of inmate populations they hold and the sorts of government units that sponsor the institutions. Prisons are usually intended for law-breakers serving sentences longer than one year, while jails are for those confined for one year or less. Prisons are maintained either by the federal government or by states, whereas jails are supported by city, county, or town governments. Juvenile facilities are local establishments intended for children and adolescents found guilty of breaking the law. Each of these general types – prisons, jails, and juvenile facilities – can include subtypes based on different purposes and on key characteristics of their inmates.

In mid-1996, there were more than 1.6 million men and women in prisons and jails, nearly double the number confined in 1986. An additional 73,000 individuals were supervised by jail authorities outside of jail facilities in such programs as electronic monitoring, house detention, community service, or work release (Prison and jail inmates,

11

1996). By 2005 the total in prisons and jails had reached 2.2 million, representing an average annual 3.3 percent growth rate since 1996 (Prison statistics, 2005).

Prisons

Prisons are usually divided according to their levels of security as determined by the estimated likelihood of inmates' becoming violent or attempting to escape. For example, federal prisons are ranked by five levels, ranging from the most lenient to the most restrictive. The levels are labeled minimum security, medium security, close security, maximum security, and super-maximum security. State prisons are also graded in terms of security, with the number of levels often varying from one state to another.

Security levels differ from each other in their kinds of housing for inmates, the way inmates are administered, tactics used by corrections officers, and educational opportunities for inmates. In general, educational opportunities are greater in lighter-security facilities than in heavier-security prisons. The risk of physical danger to teachers is greater in heavy-security than in light-security settings.

Minimum Security

The least restrictive inmate environments are in places for offenders who are thought to pose little threat to the public. The inmates are usually ones found guilty of such nonviolent crimes as fraud and perjury. The residents are typically housed in dormitories with communal showers, toilets, and sinks. Prison buildings are surrounded by a fence that is watched by officers but not constantly patrolled. Sometimes inmates leave the premises, supervised by a guard, to work on public-service projects, such as cleaning up the community or conserving the natural environment.

Educational opportunities can include an array of academic and vocational classes within the facility, correspondence courses, and – in an increasing number of places – access to the computer Internet.

Medium Security

Medium-security prisons impose greater limits on inmates' freedom of movement than do minimum-security institutions. Prisoners assigned to such facilities have been committed for various kinds of crime – drug peddling, robbery, theft, forgery, and more – but they are regarded as unlikely to act violently during their imprisonment. Inmates typically occupy dormitories with bunk beds and lockers for individuals' belongings. Dormitories are regularly patrolled by officers and usually locked at night. The prison compound is surrounded by a pair of fences and sometimes includes surveillance towers manned by armed officers.

Close Security

Occupants of close-security prisons are ones considered more prone to violence than those in medium-security facilities. Inmates reside in one-person or two-person cells, which they can leave in order to wander about their cellblock, to exercise in the yard, to carry out work assignments, or to pursue education programs. To discourage attempts at escape, such facilities are usually surrounded by two fences of razor-sharp wire, often supplemented by a third electrified fence.

Maximum Security

Persistently uncooperative, aggressive, brutal prisoners are housed in individual cells whose doors are controlled from a central station. Because of the tendency of such inmates to get into altercations with fellow prisoners and officers, they are confined to their cells most of the day. Some prisons allow inmates more time out of their cells, but only under strict supervision and restraint.

Super-Maximum Security

The most confining prisons are designed to house inmates considered extremely dangerous. The federal government maintains two institutions of this sort, and a growing number of states are either designating sections of existing prisons as super-maximum facilities or are constructing new institutions for the most hostile lawbreakers.

Jails

Jails typically house three kinds of persons – (a) ones serving sentences of one year or less, (b) ones awaiting a court trial for an offense they allegedly committed, and (c) ones awaiting transfer to a different facility, such as a prison or a jail in a different county, city, or town.

The chance that jail inmates will have educational opportunities varies greatly from one place to another.

Juvenile Correctional Facilities

In the United States, the cases of accused lawbreakers under age 18 are usually tried in juvenile courts rather than in criminal courts for adults. Furthermore, juveniles convicted of crimes seldom serve their sentences in jails or prisons. Instead, they are placed in correctional centers intended specifically for those under age 18. Such facilities are of two general types – ones for the short-term housing of youths and ones for long-term residents. A third type of juvenile correctional facility is the alternative school.

The term *juvenile hall* or *detention center* or *detention home* commonly identifies a short-term correctional institution designed for youths who are between ages 8 and 17, after which they are considered to be adults. Juvenile halls are temporary holding stations for two sorts of minors – adolescents accused of delinquent acts and ones who have not committed crimes but are public wards judged to be incompetent to supervise themselves, or they have been victims of neglectful or abusive parents or guardians. Most juvenile halls separate wards from juvenile delinquents and relocate wards into more permanent care facilities as soon as possible.

In contrast to juvenile halls, *correctional institutions* or *commitment facilities* are places in which adolescents convicted of crimes are housed throughout the length of their sentences. The average length of stay for juveniles in publicly operated juvenile sites is about 6 months, but for youths detained in jails, juvenile halls, and other short-term facilities the average length of stay is just 37 days (Leone, Meisel, & Drakeford, 2002). By 2003, approximately 90 percent of the 109,225 youths in the nation's 2,861 residential juvenile centers were delinquents. The remaining 10 percent were wards (National Center for Juvenile Justice, 2006).

Both juvenile halls and commitment facilities usually provide educational services intended to prepare adolescents to be law-abiding members of society. The learning content and materials for inmates are the same as those in public schools.

A problem of particular concern in juvenile facilities is the large number of offenders who have disabilities that affect their learning potential. A survey early in the twenty-first century reported that the percentage of disabled youths in juvenile commitment centers ranged from a high of 70 percent in one state to a low of 10 percent in several others. The federal government's IDEA law (Individuals with Disabilities Education Act) defines children with disabilities as those who suffer "mental retardation, hearing impairments, including deafness, speech or language impairments, visual impairments including blindness, emotional disturbance, orthopedic impairments, autism, traumatic brain injury, other health impairments, specific learning disabilities, deaf/blindness, or multiple disabilities" (Leone, Meisel, & Drakeford, 2002). Thus, juvenile institutions are obligated to furnish educational services appropriate for such learners. However, provisions for the disabled are far short of the need.

Alternative schools that qualify as correctional institutions are maintained by many school districts to serve students who have not adapted well to regular public or private elementary and secondary schools. Such places may be identified by a variety of titles other than *alternative school*, such as *educational resource center*, *correctional school*, and *juvenile mentoring program*. Students who attend alternative schools are often referred to as *at-risk youths*, *struggling teens*, *delinquents*, or *dropouts*. Some are sent to an alterative facility for repeatedly breaking school rules about truancy, smoking, drug use, drinking, fighting, vandalism, and more. Others have been arrested for violating criminal laws and now attend an alternative school while on probation.

CORRECTIONAL INSTITUTIONS' POPULATIONS

Perhaps the most prominent characteristic of prisons, jails, and such offender-supervision programs as parole and probation has been the continuing growth of their populations. Even though crime rates over the 1990s decreased, the total of confined and supervised adult lawbreakers nationwide continued to rise at the rates shown in Table 2.1.

Over the quarter century from 1980 to 2005, the prison population increased 453 percent, jail inmates rose 406 percent, parolees grew by 359 percent, and probationers by 372 percent. When the four categories are combined, the overall increase of confined and supervised offenders was 383 percent. In each decade, the largest numbers of convicted adults were those under supervised probation. Around twice as many sentenced lawbreakers were in prisons than in jails, and there were slightly more supervised parolees than jail occupants.

Table 2.1

Numbers of Confined and Supervised Adult Offenders – 2005

Year	Incarcerated		Supervised		Total
	Prisons	Jails	Parole	Probation	
1980	319,598	183,988	220,438	1,118,097	1,842,100
1985	487,593	256,615	300,203	1,968,712	3,013,100
1990	743,382	405,320	531,407	2,670,234	4,350,300
1995	1,078,542	507,044	679,421	3,077,861	5,342,900
2000	1,316,333	621,149	723,898	3,826,209	6,445,100
2005	1,446,269	747,529	784,408	4,162,536	7,056,000

Source: Bureau of Justice Statistics, 2005

The pattern of change in numbers of juveniles in confinement has differed from that of adults. In 1997 there were 116,701 youths in the nation's 2,842 residential placement facilities. By 1999 the total had risen by 4 percent to 120,996, then dropped by 10 percent in 2003 to 109,225 (National Center for Juvenile Justice, 2006).

There are several reasons for the continuing rise in numbers of confined and supervised lawbreakers. One cause is the growth in the nation's general population. The larger the population, the more convicted criminals there will be. But there are other influences that cause the percentage of incarcerated individuals to outstrip the percentage of general population growth. The most significant of those influences has been stricter criminal laws passed by Congress, state legislators, county supervisors, and city councils. Zero-tolerance, tough-love, and three-strikes legislation has sent many thousands of individuals to prison and jail who, in the past, would have been dealt with in a different manner. A zero-tolerance law that sets a strict, unalterable sentence for a particular kind of crime removes judges' and juries' discretion to decide the consequences a lawbreaker should face for a crime committed under particular circumstances. A three-strikes law can automatically condemn a malefactor to a lifetime in prison for being convicted of three crimes – one or more of which might be of quite minor import. In effect, a growing quantity of criminal law allows no extenuating circumstances to be considered in deciding convicted law-breakers' fates.

Such strict sentencing practices over the past two decades have driven prison, jail, and juvenile-facility populations to ever-rising heights. In particular, according to the Federal Department of Justice, 52.7 percent of state prison inmates, 73.7 percent of jail inmates, and 87.6 percent of federal inmates were imprisoned for nonviolent offenses (drug abuse, petty crimes) which involved neither harm, nor the threat of harm, to a victim (Macallair, 2000).

Sasha Abramsky (2007, pp. xxvi-xxvii) noted that:

> In 1980 the incarceration rate was just over 200 per 100,000, somewhat higher than it had been in the 1970s, but still not too far off the historic norm. By 1990, however, it stood at 461 per 100,000. By 2000 it had risen to an astronomical 703 per 100,000. In the years since, it has gone up still further: by 2005, the Bureau of Justice Statistics was estimating that over 2.13 million people were living in the thousands of prisons and jails dotting the country. In absolute numbers, the United States went from being a country that incarcerated just under 475,000 people in 1980 to one with well over 2 million inmates. Nearly 5 million more were on either parole or probation. All told, by the end of 2004, 7 million Americans were under the supervision of one or another criminal-justice agency, up from 1.8 million a mere quarter century earlier. . . . If current trends continue, tens of millions of Americans will spend a significant portion of their adult life as prisoners.

Another factor contributing to the growing number of correctional-facilities' inmates has been a more diligent effort by the police to arrest offenders who have broken laws already on the books but laws that were never before aggressively enforced.

Not only has the difficulty of coping with more prisoners been increasing, but prospects for the future appear quite bleak. A study issued by the Pew Foundation in 2007 predicted that, without states' policy changes, by 2011 the cost of operating prisons will rise by at least $15 billion.

> Unless Montana, Arizona, Alaska, Idaho, and Vermont change their sentencing or release practices, they can expect to see their prison

systems grow by one third or more. Similarly, barring reforms, Colorado, Washington, Wyoming, Nevada, Utah, and South Dakota can expect their inmate populations to grow by about 25%. Connecticut, Delaware, and New York are projected to see no change in their prison populations. Maryland will see a 1% increase in prison population. (Report: U.S. prison growth, 2007)

Although imprisoned men will far outnumber women at a ratio of 14 to 1 over the 2007-2011 period, the number of women confined is expected to rise by 16 percent while the number of male inmates will increase by 12 percent.

The accelerating growth of prison and jail populations has resulted in the serious overcrowding of penal institutions, the early release of felons back into society because of the unprecedented number of new arrivals, and spiraling costs of locking up lawbreakers. In addition, the rising rate of individuals behind bars, coupled with a renewed effort by authorities to provide inmates educational opportunities, has exacerbated the need for more correctional teachers, particularly for highly qualified, dedicated teachers.

The critical need for schooling opportunities in penal institutions has been emphasized in a bulletin titled *Correctional Education* from the U.S. Department of Education.

> The most educationally disadvantaged population in the United States resides in our nation's prisons. Incarcerated adults have among the lowest academic skill levels and highest disability and illiteracy rates of any segment of our society – factors that likely contributed to their imprisonment. Upon completing their sentence, most inmates re-enter society no more skilled than when they left. Frustrated by a lack of marketable skills, burdened with a criminal record, and released without transitional services or supports, many return to illegal activities. Not surprising, statistics show that more than three-quarters of prisoners are recidivists caught in a cycle of catch-and-release. (Klein et al., 2004, p. 1)

THE CORRECTIONAL-EDUCATION CONTROVERSY

Within American society, endless debates – often animated by strong emotion – continue over the question of providing educational services for incarcerated lawbreakers. To understand the issues involved, consider the reasoning adduced by advocates of schooling for inmates in contrast to the reasoning offered by critics of education programs in penal institutions.

Correctional Education's Advocates

Proponents of education for inmates buttress their position with claims of cost effectiveness, reduced violence in penal institutions, the actualization of human potential, deserved human rights, and increased public safety.

Cost Effectiveness

Typical cost-effectiveness reasoning involves two propositions.

First proposition: Keeping lawbreakers locked up is very expensive. By 2001, the average annual cost per inmate in state prisons was $22,650. The amount varied markedly from one state to another, ranging from $44,379 in Maine to $8,128 in Alabama. The average cost in jails and federal prisons was similar to that in state prisons. The expense for housing prisoners over age 55 was twice that for housing younger ones, and the proportion of older inmates was increasing. The elderly suffer more serious illnesses and fall ill far more often than do the young. In addition, aged prisoners who are victims of aggressive younger prisoners or of guards sustain more lasting injuries than do young inmates (Stephan, 2004).

Second proposition: Millions of taxpayer dollars are saved when correctional education reduces the number of inmates who return to prison or jail. If this proposition is to be accepted, it must be supported with evidence that correctional-education does, indeed, lower recidivism. Around 95 percent of the nation's inmates eventually leave prison and, on the average, half of them return for violating parole or committing new crimes. The incidence of recidivism is not the same across the nation but varies markedly from one state to another. In the 1990s the proportion of released inmates who returned to jail or prison in California was 66 percent, in Florida 53 percent, in Illinois 38 percent, New York 56 percent, North Carolina 48 percent, and Texas 26 percent (Fischer, 2005).

But does correctional education actually lower the number of offenders who return to jail or prison? A host of research suggests that it does. A study of 3,200 prisoners in Maryland, Minnesota, and Ohio found a 29 percent reduction in re-incarceration rates for those who had received correctional education. In 1997 the Open Society Institute reported that inmates with at least two years of college education had only a 10 percent rearrest rate compared to 50 percent for the general population of inmates. Researchers at the women's maximum-security Bedford Hills Correctional Facility in New York reported a 7.7 percent recidivism rate among inmates who took in-prison college courses, as opposed to 29.9 percent among those who had not enrolled. Furthermore, the ones who had attended college classes were far less likely to violate parole (1.1%) than those who had not taken classes (17.8%). The researchers concluded that the reduced re-incarceration rate saves approximately $900,000 per 100 student prisoners over a two-year period (Fine, 2001; Prison break, 2002).

> Compared with the expense of re-incarceration, postsecondary prison education is a bargain. New York's program costs an estimated $2,500 per inmate annually, while incarcerating one individual for one year runs about $25,000. In April 2001 *Fortune* magazine cited a study that explored three decades of prison college education; it found that every dollar spent on education resulted in $1.71 in reduced crime costs. And in the late '90s the RAND Corporation reported that crime prevention was more cost-effective than building prisons and that education was the cheapest method. (Prison break, 2002)

It is also the case that the more formal education inmates receive, the less likely they will return to prison. From his survey of recidivism research, Stuart Henry reported that

> An Arizona Department of Adult Probation Study showed that probationers who received literacy training had a 35% rearrest rate compared with a control group that had 46% rearrest, and those who received a GED [passed high-school graduation-equivalent tests] had a rearrest rate of 24%. . . . [A Florida study] found that inmates who earn a GED are 8.7% less likely to recidivate than those who do not complete a program. . . . Inmates with at least two years college education have a 10% rearrest rate, compared to the national rate of 62%. A Texas study [found] that the overall recidivism rate for [college] degree holders in the Texas Department of Corrections between 1990-1991 was 15% compared to 60% for the national rate; and a two-year follow-up study showed that those with [two-year] associates degrees had a recidivism rate of 13.7%, those with [four-year] bachelor's degrees 5.6%, and those with master's degrees zero. (Henry, 2003)

However, evidence about which level of education leads to the greatest reduction in recidivism varies somewhat from one investigation to another. In contrast to the studies reported by Henry, research involving 14,000 inmates released from Texas prisons in 1991–1992 showed the greatest drop in recidivism was for offenders who had entered prison with the least education.

> Inmates at the lowest levels of educational achievement benefit most (as indicated by lower recidivism rates) from participation in academic programs. . . . It may be that participating in educational programs improves the self-image of the educationally disadvantaged and gives them new skills. In this study, participation in vocational programs showed smaller effects on re-incarceration rates [than engaging in academic programs]. (Adams et al., 1994)

In sum, a multiplicity of studies support the contention that offering inmates educational opportunities is an economical use of public funds.

Reduced Prison Violence

Observations of inmate behavior in penal facilities verify that institutions which offer educational programs for inmates have lower levels of violence and disruption than facilities without schooling opportunities. For example, at the Bedford women's prison in New York, researchers found that offering college courses altered "the prison environment, rendering it safer, more manageable, and characterized by fewer disciplinary incidents. Interviews with prison administrators, correctional officers, women in prison, and college faculty confirm that the presence of a college program enables the prison to run more smoothly on a day-to-day basis" (Fine, 2001).

After members of a class in "civility as a code of behavior" at Johns Hopkins University visited a maximum-security prison to talk with a group of inmates, one student remarked,

> I walked into that room with a lot of prejudices about convicts and prison and what these men would be like. But they were well-educated, thought-provoking, and civil people. Of course, they were all quick to point out that they were not typical of the prison population; they were the ones who had pursued their education in prison. They had, from what I could see, rehabilitated themselves through education. I walked away learning how integral education is to rehabilitation. (Rice, 1997)

Actualization of Human Potential

Many inmates come to jail or prison *functionally illiterate*, meaning that they cannot communicate satisfactorily enough to make their way through life without breaking the law. Functional literacy is not limited to reading, writing, and calculating effectively. It also includes speaking understandably, comprehending what others say, and complying with the "rules of the game." Those "rules" are society's expectations about how to behave in different contexts and roles – as a worker, family member, neighbor, and citizen. A lack of functional literacy can be the basic cause behind an offender breaking the law and ending up in a penal facility.

> Results of studies over the last two decades clearly indicate that offenders who were functionally illiterate upon entering the prison system may be successfully reintegrated into society if they participate in literacy programs during incarceration. . . . [In such programs] offenders develop the knowledge, skills, and attitudes needed to realize their potential and gain heightened self-awareness, a realistic and positive self-concept, a value system congruent with the larger society, and feelings of self commensurate with their potential abilities. . . . Functionally illiterate students are commonly unmotivated and demoralized, reflecting low self-esteem. The Council of Europe Select Committee of Experts on Education in Prison recently emphasized the key benefits of literacy programs in helping offenders develop a sense of responsibility, self-determination, an ability to manage stress, and an ability to counteract negative aspects of prison life. (Correctional Service of Canada, 2006)

A high rate of both legal and illegal immigration in the United States means that large numbers of penal-institution inmates lack English-language skills. Handicapped in their effort to find legitimate jobs, they turn to criminal activities. Or their failure to understand English may lead them to break laws inadvertently. Consequently, studying English as a second language while incarcerated can help them avoid breaking laws after their release.

In summary, correctional education can contribute to individuals actualizing their potential for living self-satisfying, crime-free lives.

Deserved Human Rights

The typical position that human-rights organizations adopt about inmates' access to schooling is reflected in such documents as the United Nations Declaration of Human Rights.

> Everyone has the right to education. Education shall be free, at least in the elementary and fundamental stages. Elementary education shall be compulsory. Technical and professional education shall be made generally available, and higher education shall be equally accessible to all on the basis of merit. (United Nations, 1948)

As a signatory to this declaration, the United States Government is obligated to ensure that its commitment to universal schooling is implemented throughout the populace, including among jail, prison, and juvenile offenders. In 1990 the general assembly of the Human Rights Education Associates – an international non-governmental organization that supports human rights learning – applied that commitment specifically to inmates in a statement of *Basic Principles for the Treatment of Prisoners.*

> Except for those limitations that are demonstrably necessitated by the fact of incarceration, all prisoners shall retain the human rights and fundamental freedoms set out in the Universal Declaration of Human Rights. . . . All prisoners shall have the right to take part in cultural activities and education aimed at the full development of the human personality. (Human Rights Education Associates, 1990)

Consequently, proponents of correctional education argue that formal learning opportunities for inmates are dictated by widely recognized human-rights principles.

Public Safety

If educational programs in jails, prisons, and juvenile centers reduce recidivism and equip released inmates to gain the self-confidence, social attitudes, and skills needed for leading satisfying law-abiding lives, then those programs have increased public safety.

Correctional-Education Critics

In opposition to the arguments adduced by advocates of correctional education, critics base their objections on several reasons, including claims about (a) what offenders deserve, (b) the effectiveness of punishment, and (c) the fair distribution of favors.

Just Desserts

An ancient concept of justice that is still widely held today is the talionic principle (*lex talionis*) which, in its strictest interpretation, holds that an inflicted punishment should correspond in degree and in kind to the offense of the wrongdoer. In other words, people should get what their misbehavior justly deserves. A biblical Old Testament version of this belief requires that "If any mischief follow, then thou shalt give life for life, eye for eye, tooth for tooth, hand for hand, foot for foot, burning for burning, wound for wound, stripe for stripe" (*Holy Bible*, 1611, Exodus 21:23–25).

And the New Testament reiterates the talionic policy with "Whatsoever a man sowest, that shall he also reap" (*Holy Bible*, 1611, Galatians 6:7)

Thus, matching an offense with a punishment involves retaliating with the same act as the original transgression, such as executing the murderer and confiscating the property of the thief. In the sense of exactly matching the offense, this strict version of the talionic principle can reasonably be applied to only certain types of misconduct. *Lex talonis* seems hardly a fitting response to rape, forgery, fraud, or the peddling of dangerous drugs. Therefore, a revised form of the principle is what advocates of just deserts usually intend. The revised version requires the transgressor to experience a measure of pain, loss, and inconvenience equal to that suffered by the victim of the crime, even though the kind of punishment is not identical to the original crime. Thus, punitive damages assessed in trials are meant to fulfill this principle from the viewpoint of society in general, while pain-and-suffering damages are intended to achieve the same effect from the perspective of persons directly harmed by the offense. Likewise, for people incarcerated for lawbreaking, the length of their sentence is intended to reflect the seriousness of their wrongdoing – a few months in jail for petty theft, a lifetime behind prison bars for murder.

Therefore, providing inmates educational opportunities is not an appropriate from of just deserts, because educational opportunities are rewards, not punishments.

Punishment Works

The great popularity of believing that punishment is an effective deterrent to misconduct is attested by public opinion polls, by most parents' treatment of their children, and by the laws legislators pass. Furthermore, crime-prevention research supports that belief. Punishment, and the threat of punishment, does serve to reduce crime – but only to a degree. That's because people's fear of being punished is only one factor that might prevent them from breaking laws. In other words, the reasons that people commit crimes are usually complex, including individuals' economic condition, emotional state, intelligence (ability to predict consequences), feelings of adequacy, health, companions, family background, school success, willingness to risk punishment, and more. Hence, believing that fear of punishment is a powerful deterrent is an expectation – or a hope – not well supported by facts. If it were an effective deterrent, 60 percent of prison inmates and 80 percent of juvenile offenders who, after being released from confinement, would not be caught committing more crimes and again be locked up.

The history of crime-prevention legislation over the past four decades shows a double shift in politicians' attitudes about what works best to reduce crime. The shift has been (a) from an earlier favorable view of rehabilitation to (b) confidence in punishment as a preventive and to (c) a recent gradual return of confidence in rehabilitation programs that have education at their core. Pete Shuler has described the first two stages of this history.

> Until the mid-1990s, the majority of politicians embraced the concept of prison as a place for rehabilitation and reform. In 1965 Congress passed legislation that explicitly permitted prisoners to apply for Pell grants, need-based financial aid for college students. States followed suit by allowing inmates to apply for similar state-sponsored funding. By 1982, due to this widespread support, more than 350 programs of higher education were available to prisoners in 45 states.
>
> In 1994, however, this reformist ideology faded, replaced with the doctrine of prison as punishment. Despite overwhelming statistical evidence that education in general and post-secondary education in particular dramatically reduce recidivism . . . Congress stripped prisoners of the right to apply for Pell grants.
>
> States again followed suit. In 1997 the Ohio legislature banned pris-

oners from applying for Ohio Instruction Grants and Student Choice Grants. As a result of this one-two, federal-state punch, nearly all prison-based higher education programs folded. (Shuler, 2004)

Stefan LoBuglio, recognizing that lawmakers and much of the general public believe that punishing criminals by confinement is the best way to go, has suggested that proponents of correctional education can profitably refocus their reasoning by accepting incarceration as a suitable form of punishment and then stressing the value of teaching inmates constructive life routines.

> Rather than pushing for rehabilitation as an alternative to the correctional goals of incapacitation and punishment or asserting the rights of inmates to these programs, supporters of correctional education might argue more effectively that inmates should be held responsible for a weekly regimen, comparable in time and energy with that of working citizens, and that this regimen will best prepare them to reintegrate into society. Correctional education and treatment programs can and should help "normalize" the correctional experience and teach socially productive skills. (LoBuglio, 2001)

In summary, punishment does work to a limited degree. But other things work better. Inmates' participation in educational programs while incarcerated is apparently the best of those other things.

Unjust Expenditures

The aspect of correctional education that legislators and a segment of the public found particularly objectionable in the early 1990s was the policy of furnishing college courses to prison inmates. Critics asked, "What's fair about paying the college tuition and textbook costs for incarcerated criminals when there are law-abiding but financially struggling youths in the general society who cannot afford to go to college? Why should criminals be rewarded when far more worthy individuals outside of prisons are being denied a chance for higher education?"

These were the compelling questions that motivated members of Congress in 1994 to deny penal-institution inmates the Pell grants that were intended to help low-income Americans finance college studies. A typical response of correctional-education proponents to the removal of such grants has been that (a) funding college studies saves taxpayer money by reducing recidivism and (b) inmates don't deserve privileged treatment – that's not their "right" – but all of society benefits by giving them "access to educational resources available to everyone else" (Fine, 2001).

CONCLUSION

The evidence about the outcomes of educational opportunities for prison, jail, and juvenile-center inmates convinces us that quality correctional education is an extremely wise investment for American society – not just financially but also as a way to enhance public safety and promote the constructive, humane treatment of individuals who have broken the law. In effect, correctional education is a good deal. Skilled, dedicated teachers help make it so. We are persuaded that correctional education deserves to be expanded and its quality improved.

Chapter 3

LEARNING OPPORTUNITIES AND EDUCATIONAL PERSONNEL

Whereas Chapter 2 sketched general characteristics of penal institutions and of controversies over education for inmates, Chapter 3 advances one step closer to the teaching problems and solutions in Part II by describing types of learning opportunities and types of educational personnel in jails, prisons, and juvenile facilities.

TYPES OF LEARNING OPPORTUNITIES

For convenience of analysis, educational opportunities in penal settings can be divided between two types – informal and formal.

Informal Channels

Informal opportunities are offered through media that inmates can visit on their own initiative without anyone guiding them. Such is the case with books and periodicals, radio, television, movies, videos, theatrical performances, voluntary attendance at lectures (secular and religious), and opportunities to converse with fellow inmates and visitors.

Penal institutions vary markedly in the availability of informal media and in the conditions governing their use. Common informal sources that are of educational value include institutions' libraries, newspapers and newsletters, radio and television programs, and religious sects' meetings.

Formal Programs

Formal learning opportunities are ones planned and directed by educational personnel or by supervisors of work sites. The term *correctional education* typically identifies programs conducted by professional educators. Those programs are the ones of primary interest throughout this book. In addition to such opportunities, correctional institutions typically include work assignments for inmates – the chance to hold a job within the jail, prison, or juvenile center. Although work assignments are not designed primarily to teach inmates an entire trade, they do offer a chance to learn how to do specific jobs. The following discussion first addresses kinds of correctional-education programs, then considers the educational role of work assignments.

Formal learning programs are found in each kind of correctional institution – jails, prisons, and juvenile facilities.

Jail programs. Formal schooling in jails can range from no programs at all to rather elaborate ones. An example of a modest set of offerings is the plan in Ingham County (Michigan) where (a) one instructor teaches inmates who have tested below a ninth-grade level of language usage, (b) another instructor helps high-school-level inmates prepare for GED (General Educational Development) tests, and (c) an instructional aide supervises a computer laboratory where inmates at all levels of competence can study academic subjects through a wide variety of software (Wiggelsworth, 2007).

A more ambitious plan is found in the Boulder County (Colorado) classes for jail residents. In the following list, the number in brackets following each program type indicates the annual average enrollment of students who continue in the program. Many additional inmates who enter classes drop out or are transferred from the jail.

- Learning-to-Read Program (LTR) Basic literacy instruction to improve reading and writing as provided by volunteers from the public library [15].
- English as a Second Language (ESL) Instruction in rudimentary English for all non-English-speaking inmates provided by student instructors from the University of Colorado International English Center [45].
- Adult Basic Education (ABE) Remedial instruction by the jail's education director for grades 1–8 [60].
- GED Preparation & Testing. Instruction by the jail's education

director for grades 9–12, preparing inmates to pass the General Educational Development exam [35].
- College-Level Correspondence Courses. Supervised by the education director. (Boulder County Sheriff's Department, 2007)

Prison programs. The percentages of the main types of education programs in U.S. prisons by the year 2000 are shown in Table 3.1.

Table 3.1
Prison Education Programs – 2000

Percentage of prisons with any:	Federal Prisons	State Prisons	Private Prisons
Educational program	100.0%	91.2%	87.6%
Adult basic education	97.4	80.4	61.6
Adult secondary education	98.7	83.6	70.7
Vocational training	93.5	55.7	44.2
College coursework	80.5	26.7	27.3
Special education*	59.7	39.6	21.9
Study release**	6.5	7.7	28.9

* Course work for inmates with learning disabilities
** Inmates temporarily released to attend classes in community schools

Source: Klein et al., 2004, p. 8.

Because prisons hold far more inmates and for longer periods of time than do jails, prisons' educational provisions are typically more elaborate than those of jails. The objectives, teaching methods, teaching materials, and evaluation techniques are planned by professional educators and are implemented by teachers, educational administrators, and support staff (teaching assistants, secretaries, counselors).

Programs are usually divided into three types – academic, vocational, and special. Each type can assume a variety of forms, as demonstrated by the following examples.

Academic classes. Schooling in a typical minimum-security or medium-security prison consists of a series of classes in clusters similar to the levels in school systems outside the prison – ranging from the elementary grades through high school. Between 20 and 30 students study in a regular classroom under the tutelage of a professional teacher, often assisted by one or two inmates as teacher aides. The following is a representative set of academic courses.

- Adult Basic Education I (ABE1) – Primary grades 1–3

- Adult Basic Education II (ABE2) – Upper-elementary grades 4–6
- Adult Basic Education III (ABE3) – Junior-high grades 7–9
- General Educational Development (GED) – high school grades 10–12 (preparation for a high-school-equivalent-diploma test battery)
- English Language Development (ELD) or English as a Second Language (ESL) – for non-English-speaking inmates
- Developmentally Disabled (DD) – a program for inmates with a mental or physical disorder, such as cerebral palsy or mental retardation, acquired before adulthood and usually lasting throughout life

Prisons also frequently offer college-level courses, either by correspondence or by instructors from a nearby college or university conducting classes in the prison's education complex.

Vocational classes. The aim of vocational programs is to equip inmates with the skills of particular occupations. The kinds of vocations and the specificity of the preparation vary markedly from one state to another and from one prison to another. The range of vocations for which students may prepare is illustrated by the following list of past and present offerings in the prisons of California's Department of Corrections and Rehabilitation. At any one time, a number of such programs will be available in any particular state prison.

Air Engine Mechanics, Air Frame Mechanics, Animal Grooming, Auto Mechanics, Automotive Body Repair, Baking, Barbering/ Haircutting, Building Maintenance
Cabinet Making, Carpentry, Commercial Diving, Cosmetology, Culinary Arts, Dental Technology, Diesel Mechanics, Dry Cleaning, Drywall Construction
Electrical Construction/Repair, Electronics, Eyewear Manufacturing Fiberglass/Plastics Technology, Floor Covering, Food Service, Garment Making, Graphic Arts for Publishing
Health Care Assisting, Heating/Air Conditioning, Horse Training, Information Technology and Programming, Janitorial Services, Machine Shop, Masonry, Meat Cutting, Mechanical Drawing, Meteorology
Office Services, Offset Printing Technology, Plumbing Construction/ Repair, Radiological Technology, Sheet Metal, Shoe Repair, Silk-Screen Printing, Small Engine/Motorcycle Mechanics, Stock Keeping/Ware-housing, Technical Illustration, Upholstery, Welding.

Special classes. Learning opportunities for offenders with limited English-language skills and ones with disabilities (sight, hearing, speech, medical health conditions) have increased in recent years. Many correctional facilities also offer such non-academic services as substance-abuse counseling and life-skills training to help inmates reintegrate into society upon their release.

Self-Instructional plans. Inmates sometimes are furnished materials that enable them to learn on their own. One version of self-instruction provides individuals workbooks in their cells, with occasional help from a visiting teacher. Another version uses a computer-assisted-instruction laboratory with lessons on computer software designed for individualized remedial, intermediate, and advanced instruction in language, mathematics, reading, writing, and keyboarding.

Juvenile-detention programs. As noted in Chapter 2, facilities for juveniles who have been arrested are of two basic kinds — those for temporarily holding youths (juvenile halls) and those for youths serving long-term sentences (juvenile detention facilities). Each kind usually provides formal education.

An example of a juvenile-hall program is the one in Kent County (Michigan), a 69-bed facility that offers regular school classes funded and staffed by the Grand Rapids Board of Education with five full-time academic teachers, one part-time art teacher, three teacher aides, two support staff, and two tutors for remedial math and reading. Schooling operates throughout the year with regular 40-minute class periods Monday through Thursday and life-and-social-skills classes on Friday (Juvenile detention, 2007).

Inmates' Work Assignments

In addition to formal educational opportunities, three kinds of work are often available to prison inmates. One kind engages prisoners in maintenance tasks intended to keep the prison neat and operating smoothly — sweeping, washing windows, serving food in the dining room, washing dishes, gardening, and the like. A second kind offers jobs in prison industries that produce goods and services.

> In 2000, 53% of state and federal prisoners (48% state, 100% federal) who were eligible and able to work had a work assignment. The type and required skill level of work conducted by people in prison varied. The vast majority was assigned to general maintenance positions

(39% state prisoners; 83% federal prisoners). Smaller numbers worked in correctional industry programs (6% and 23%) and in farming or agricultural work assignments (3% and 0.2%). Work assignments are less common in jails – not surprising given the short length of stay for many inmates. About one quarter of people in jail have institution-based jobs. (Re-Entry Policy Council, 2004)

Prison industries serve four purposes – (a) give inmates constructive ways to use their time, thereby helping them stay out of trouble, (b) teach vocational skills and work habits (getting to work on time, working steadily, doing the job well, getting along with workmates), (c) enable inmates to earn spending money, and (d) furnish products useful in the prison and elsewhere. The nature of such industries is suggested by the following examples drawn from a variety of penal institutions.

- Bindery – 3-ring and spiral binders, notebooks, display cards
- Metal-fabrication center – license plates, lockers, vehicle accessories
- Furniture factory – office furniture, storage, communication centers
- Laundry – wet and dry cleaning
- Optical laboratory – eyeware
- Garment industry – institutional clothing, fire-protection gear
- Food products industry – eggs, milk, packaged meats
- Bedding factory – mattresses, pillows
- Footwear factory – men's and women's shoes and boots
- Stationery center – binders, conference folios
- Cleaning-products center – bar soap, janitorial detergents
- Glove factory – work gloves, driver gloves, fire-fighter gloves
- Sign and decal center – highway signs, organization decals

The Re-Entry Policy Council reported that:

The general maintenance positions filled by most people in prison or jail are less likely than jobs in prison industries to provide participants with marketable skills that will lead to successful careers. The jobs that are believed to be most effective at providing skills are those that produce goods and services sold in the commercial market. But only a small percentage of prisoners can participate in such work due to a limited number of slots. For example, the Prison Industry Enhancement (PIE) program, which operates in 572 state (482), federal (68), and private (22) facilities, includes partnerships with private companies to provide jobs for people in prison or jail. However, the PIE programs provide space for only about three-tenths of one percent of the state prison population. (Re-Entry Policy Council, 2004)

Although the supervisors of prison industries are not trained as instructors, they nevertheless serve an instructional function since supervisors teach inmates how to do their jobs properly. Suggestions in this book's Part II about how to solve such problems can be helpful to prison-industries personnel, because supervisors face many of the problems that confront teachers in correctional-education classes.

A third category of jobs in prisons consists of clerical positions (including the job of teaching assistant) that utilize the better-educated inmates as clerks who perform such functions as typing reports, processing paperwork, and filing non-confidential documents. Such jobs are available in housing units, medical and education departments, prison-industries, education classes, and administrative offices of religious leaders.

TYPES OF EDUCATIONAL PERSONNEL

The main people directly responsible for the quality of education in correctional settings are teachers, administrators, and teaching assistants.

Sources of Teachers and Administrators

Among people who are hunting for careers, not many clamor to teach in jails, prisons, and juvenile facilities. In effect, the job of teaching in correctional settings is not a prestigious, highly-sought-after occupation. Therefore, the pool from which instructors can be drawn is limited. Furthermore, the members of any profession differ from each other in a variety of ways – in skills and knowledge, diligence, initiative, energy, decision-making ability, ambition, goals, emotional stability, and more. Consequently, from the viewpoint of instructional efficiency, teachers in jails, prisons, and juvenile centers form a diverse collection, with some of them truly excellent, some rather mediocre, and others quite inept. Of course, the same is true of teachers in regular public and private schools.

There are several common sources of teachers and administrators, including

- People who have retired from public or private schools and wish to remain in the education profession by taking a job in a prison, jail, or juvenile center.
- Transfers from other correctional facilities.
- Individuals seeking a teaching position in a region whose market for teaching and administrative jobs is saturated, so accepting a correctional-education post is the next-best alternative.
- People who served as jail or prison guards, clerical staff, or in some other capacity, and subsequently earned teaching or administrative credentials.
- Teacher-education programs' graduates who choose to work in a correctional program as a mission, dedicating themselves to serving a population of learners who were not successful students in the past and now need to prepare for a crime-free life after their release.

Traits of Good Teachers

There are various sources of information about – or opinions about – teaching practices that promote students' success in correctional settings. As might be expected, some of those practices are important in virtually all sorts of schools, whereas others are especially important in prisons, jails, and detention centers.

Our own experience suggests that successful practices in nearly any type of school result from teachers'

- Displaying a sure command of the subject matter being taught.
- Recognizing the differences among students that influence how effectively each one learns and, as far as is feasible, attempting to adjust instruction to those differences. In other words, teachers seek to individualize instruction.

Additional teacher traits particularly important in correctional settings include

- Being firm, yet fair, in addressing student disciplinary issues.
- Being consistent in responding to students from one occasion to another.
- Demonstrating a friendly attitude toward students.

- Exhibiting a sincere, enthusiastic interest in the schooling progress of each student.
- Using proper grammar and language when speaking to students.
- Providing positive support and encouragement.
- Demonstrating respect toward all students and expecting an equal level of respect from them.

Teaching Assistants

A common practice in correctional institutions is to use the inmate population as the source of teaching assistants to serve as aides in education programs. A large amount of individualized and small-group instruction is needed in correctional-education classrooms because (a) class members typically display a wide range of skills and knowledge and (b) the membership of a class is constantly changing as inmates may enter and leave at any time. Therefore, inmate assistants who share instructional duties with the teacher are invaluable assets in correctional education.

A typical way teacher-aides are recruited and used can be illustrated with the California prison system. The typical classroom's teacher-student ratio is 1-to-27, with the students displaying varying levels of knowledge and skills in mathematics, English language usage, and English reading comprehension. Consequently, a substantial amount of class time is spent in small-group and individualized instruction. Teaching assistants are particularly useful in tutoring individuals or small groups, scoring tests, correcting workbook exercises, performing clerical duties, and providing classroom janitorial services.

Instructors recruit assistants from the general inmate population, using such criteria as (a) a high overall TABE – Test of Adult Basic Education – score (with 12.9 as the highest grade-level-equivalent score), (b) an occupational background related to education or business, (c) a congenial personality, (d) a willingness to help other people, (d) a prison record of good behavior, and (e) a solid work ethic (diligent, accurate, prompt).

Inmates interested in applying for a teacher-aide position can announce their intention to their correctional counselor who refers them to the education department. Or an inmate can submit an application and background résumé directly to the education office. Instructors can also rely on recommendations from other teachers, their own former assistants, and their current or former students. Some institutions limit the number of years an aide may work for the same instructor, with the limit intended to reduce the chance that the relationship between the instructor and the assistant will become too close.

In the process of selecting a teacher-aide, an instructor is wise to inspect a candidate's institutional record-file to discover the nature of the inmate's disciplinary and work history. This caution is particularly important for female instructors in male institutions, because offenders who engaged in extreme violence during the commission of a crime or who have a record of sexual assault are usually disqualified as assistants for women teachers.

CONCLUSION

Prisons are the correctional institutions that offer the widest range of formal and informal educational opportunities to inmates, with jails and juvenile detention centers providing a far more limited array of options from which to choose. The programs that appear to be most effective in preparing offenders for a constructive, crime-free life upon their release are academic classes, vocational courses, and prison industries.

The people most essential for operating formal educational programs are teachers, administrators, and the teacher assistants drawn from the inmate population. Although some college and university criminal-justice departments include programs for training correctional-education personnel, most teachers and administrators in prisons, jails, and juvenile facilities come from the general population of educators. They arrive on the job without any specialized preparation for the tasks they will face. Thus, one purpose of this book is to provide a portion of the needed preparation.

PART II

INSTRUCTIONAL PROBLEMS
AND SOLUTIONS

Each of the seven chapters of Part II (a) offers perspectives from which to view the chapter's topics, (b) describes a range of problems faced by teachers in correctional institutions and (c) proposes solutions for those problems as based chiefly on the experience of three veteran correctional-education instructors, with their suggestions supplemented by options drawn from correctional-education journals.

The matters addressed in chapters 4 through 10 include: (4) identifying significant characteristics of students, (5) assigning students to learning programs, (6) managing a classroom, (7) selecting learning goals, (8) choosing instructional methods, (9) choosing and creating teaching materials, and (10) assessing student progress.

Throughout Part II, nearly all of the 56 problems and their solutions have been provided by three correctional-education instructors – Colleen Laney-Kobata, Basil DuBois, and Rob Thomas. As noted in this book's preface, all three have taught a variety of classes at the California Men's Colony (San Luis Obispo), which is a public prison operated by the California Department of Corrections and Rehabilitation.

During Colleen's 12 years at the Men's Colony, she has taught ELD (English-language-development or ESL – English-as-a-second-language) classes and courses for inmates who were operating at a primary-school level. She also served on the leadership team responsible for the Colony's WASC (Western Association of Schools and Colleges) accreditation and for standardized-test administration.

In Basil's two decades at the Men's Colony, he has taught high-school history, ABE2 and ABE3 classes (upper-elementary and junior-high-level courses), and directed a computer-assisted-instruction laboratory. In 2003, he was elected Teacher-of-the-Year for the Correctional Education Association's Region Seven.

Rob has been an instructor at the Men's Colony for 28 years. He has taught four kinds of students, (a) ones in a program for the emotionally and physically disadvantaged, (b) ones acquiring junior-high-level academic skills, (c) ones preparing to pass GED (General Educational Development) tests, and (d) ones pursuing an associate-of-arts degree through a nearby community college. Prior to joining the Men's Colony faculty, he served as a counselor in a juvenile hall.

Chapter 4

SIGNIFICANT CHARACTERISTICS
OF STUDENTS

Participants in the nation's correctional-education programs have only two things in common – all of the students have been convicted of crimes and all are now engaged in some form of organized education. Otherwise, correctional-education students differ from each other in many ways, with some of those ways significantly influencing how they are taught and how well they learn.

The purpose of the first section of this chapter is to inspect eight of those ways and to suggest how such differences may affect teachers' instructional methods and students' progress. The second section of the chapter (a) illustrates problems teachers encounter because of student characteristics and (b) suggests solutions for such problems.

EIGHT SIGNIFICANT CHARACTERISTICS

Eight influential student traits are abilities, learning disorders, age, gender, ethnicity, gang membership, length of imprisonment, and reasons that inmates enroll in educational programs.

Abilities

In the early twentieth century, psychologists began developing tests intended to measure people's intelligence, with *intelligence* conceived to be the general ability to acquire knowledge and solve problems. A scheme for scoring test results produced an *intelligence quotient* (IQ) in which a score of 100 was the average for the general population. Scores above 100 were earned by people who accurately answered more test questions than did the average person. The farther above 100 that a person scored, the smarter the person was thought to be. Likewise, the farther a person scored below 100, the less the individual was credited with mental ability. Labels were attached to different intelligence quotients. IQs between 90 and 110 were labeled *normal.* Individuals scoring below IQ 70 were judged to be *feebleminded* (divided among *idiots, imbeciles,* and *morons*). People earning an IQ between 120 and 130 were called *very bright* and ones above 150 or more were often deemed *geniuses.*

Still today, members of the general public often appear to accept this early notion of each person having a certain level of *general intelligence* that pervades all aspects of life. Each individual's performance in virtually all mental endeavors would therefore be expected to match his or her *intelligence.*

But since the 1930s and 1940s, the notion that people's mental ability is a single factor has been replaced by psychologists' proposal that it is better to recognize that people have different sorts of abilities. This is the belief that abilities are multiple factors influencing how people "think" and how well they perform the tasks they attempt. However, psychologists have not agreed on how to label those separate abilities or on how closely one ability is associated with another. For example, in 1938 a University of Chicago professor, Louis L. Thurstone, proposed that mental aptitude consisted of seven primary mental abilities that he named verbal comprehension, word fluency, number, spatial ability, associative memory, perceptual speed, and reasoning or induction. A person could be stronger in one of those abilities than in another. As an alternative to Thurstone's seven aptitudes, the creators of the Differential Aptitude Tests in 1947 divided mental skills into eight abilities − verbal reasoning, abstract reasoning, numerical abilities, mechanical reasoning, space relations, language usage, spelling, and perceptual speed and accuracy. A considerably more complex scheme was proposed in 1967 by J. P. Guilford at the University of Southern California. Guilford designed a three-dimensional view of human intellect that consisted of 120 specific abilities − a system later expanded to five dimensions, thus resulting in 150 abilities. A fourth option offered by Howard Gardner of Harvard University (1983, 1999) proposed that human intelligence is best viewed as consisting of seven types − linguistic, musical, logical-mathematical, spatial, bodily-kinesthetic, interpersonal, and intrapersonal. Gardner has also suggested that there may be even more factors, such as naturalistic (ability to discern patterns in nature), spiritual (recognition of life's sacred or religious features), and existential (concern about "ultimate issues" of existence). Which of the four psychologists' alternatives is closest to the truth is unclear. However, the idea that intelligence is a single, unified ability that determines a person's success in all facets of life seems no longer tenable.

Today a multi-factor theory of human intelligence or aptitude is the viewpoint best supported with empirical evidence. Thus, we suggest that such a conception is the most profitable one for correctional-education teachers to adopt. It should come as no surprise that any student may perform better in some areas of the curriculum than in others – math, English language, science, social studies, art, music, physical education, and various vocational specialties – as a result of both the individual's genetic inheritance and past experiences.

Learning Disorders

An important subcategory of *abilities* is that of *learning disorders*, *learning disabilities*, or *learning handicaps*. Such disorders can be frequent among inmates. For example, in their earlier school career, their learning difficulties may have caused them to succeed so poorly that they dropped out of school and turned to crime as a way of life. In addition, their disability may have reduced their skill in predicting the likely consequences of their acts. As a result, they were caught committing offenses that landed them jail.

Statistics from the US Dept. of Education indicate that 65% of inmates are illiterate.

The average prison inmate:
1. is functionally illiterate
2. probably learning disabled
3. never had a steady job
4. was a juvenile delinquent
5. abused substances
6. came from a dysfunctional home with a history of abuse
7. has not gone beyond the 10th grade, and
8. has an average IQ one standard deviation below the mean.

Fifteen percent of prison inmates score below 75 on the Wechsler

Scale of Adult Intelligence (Revised), indicating a substantially higher than average rate of mental retardation; and 70% have no skill or
trade education. (LoPinto, 2007)

Inmates' learning handicaps include such conditions as mental
retardation, attention deficit disorder (often accompanied by hyperac-
tivity), dyslexia (trouble with reading and writing), and dyscalculia
(trouble with calculating).

> The most common and best-known verbal learning disability is
> dyslexia, which causes people to have trouble recognizing or pro-
> cessing letters and the sounds associated with them. For this reason,
> people with dyslexia have trouble with reading and writing tasks or
> assignments.
> Some people with verbal learning disabilities may be able to read or
> write just fine but they have trouble with other aspects of language.
> For example, they may be able to sound out a sentence or paragraph
> perfectly, making them good readers, but they can't relate to the
> words in ways that will allow them to make sense of what they're
> reading (such as forming a picture of a thing or situation). And some
> people have trouble with the act of writing as their brains struggle to
> control the many things that go into it – from moving their hand to
> form letter shapes to remembering the correct grammar rules
> involved in writing down a sentence.
> People with nonverbal learning disabilities may have difficulty pro-
> cessing what they see. They may have trouble making sense of visu-
> al details like numbers on a blackboard. Someone with a nonverbal
> learning disability may confuse the plus sign with the sign for divi-
> sion, for example. Some abstract concepts like fractions may be dif-
> ficult to master for people with nonverbal learning disabilities.
> (Learning disabilities, 2007)

The likelihood that classes in correctional facilities will often include
inmates who suffer learning disorders means that teachers can profit
from recognizing symptoms of such disabilities' and know of ways to
help those students. How these tasks of recognition and aid may be
performed is illustrated later in this chapter among the sample problem cases.

Age

Imprisoned offenders can range in age from the time of puberty
until the end of old age – that is, from around age ten or twelve into

the nineties. Because students in correctional-education settings often represent a wide range of age levels, it is important for teachers to recognize how age is related to learning ability and memory over the lifespan. The following generalizations – each supported by research studies – can help teachers make suitable adjustments in their instructional methods and in their expectations for how students will likely perform at different ages. Each generalization is accompanied by suggestions about how the generalization might be applied to correctional education.

Lifespan Trends. For most people, learning speed and memory accuracy improve during adolescence to reach a peak in early adulthood, then gradually decrease with the passing decades until in a person's latter sixties the decline in speed and accuracy starts to accelerate into the nineties (Davis et al., 2003; Crook & West 1990; Youngjohn & Crook, 1993).

> Although learning performance tends on average to decline with age, all age groups can learn. Research studies have shown that learning performances can be improved with instructions and practice, extra time to learn information or skills, and relevance of the learning task to interests and expertise. It is well established that those who regularly practice their learning skills maintain their learning efficiency over their life span. (Aging facts, 2007)

Implications. For instructors, this information about lifespan trends holds several implications.

Teachers in juvenile facilities can recognize that the younger adolescents in their classes will still be in the process of developing the mental capacity to grasp complex, abstract concepts, so many younger teens will require more concrete explanations of terminology and processes (such as math functions) than will older youths. Thus, more pictorial material and physical demonstrations (as in teaching math, science, and grammar) are usually needed to convey concepts and procedures to the eleven-year-old than to the seventeen-year-old.

A class in a jail or prison can include inmates who range from age 18 into the eighties. In general, the younger ones can be expected to grasp new concepts and procedures quicker than the older ones, meaning that older class members may need more time both to learn new material and more time (as in test sessions, class discussions, and writing compositions) to recall and report what they had learned.

Individual Differences. The expression *all people are created equal* is a noble and highly desirable ideal when it is intended to mean that everyone deserves equal treatment before the law. However, in reality, it is clearly not true that *all people are created equal.* People are born with different genetic potentials for physical, intellectual, and emotional development. Likewise, the families in which they grow up differ in stability, in child-rearing skills, and in their capacity and willingness to furnish amenities for the growing child and youth – nourishing food, comfortable housing, respectable garb and grooming, and the like. Thus, the truth about life is that *all people are created unequal.* And because of these marked differences among individuals, if all are to have a fair chance to succeed in life, they cannot be treated equally, in the sense of being treated *all the same.* Instead, having a fair chance to succeed means people should be treated differentially in keeping with their varied abilities and needs.

Thus, there are significant differences among inmates of the same age in both their speed of learning and in the accuracy of their memories, with some individuals – at all times in their life – far less adept than others. Furthermore, some people maintain their learning and memory efficiency into old age far better than others. The ability to sustain intellectual efficiency is influenced by people's genetic inheritance, by their state of health, and by practice, with practice meaning the sorts of mental and psycho-motor tasks people pursue and how often and vigorously they engage in those tasks (Hultsch, Hertzog, & Dixon, 1990; Zelinski, Gilewski, & Schaie, 1993).

Implications. Inmates who seriously pursue learning while imprisoned are doing themselves the favor of slowing the decline in the speed and accuracy of their learning and remembering. Correctional-education instructors may help motivate students to work hard in class by informing them of this fact.

Teachers will be committing an error in judgment if they base their estimate of an inmate's learning ability on the inmate's age, even though learning speed and accuracy do decline with age, particularly after age sixty or seventy. Because of the differences among individuals, any particular inmate's learning efficiency can best be estimated – not on age – but by giving the individual several learning tasks to perform and then noting how quickly and accurately he or she accomplishes the tasks.

It is also appropriate for a teacher to accommodate the marked differences among individuals' learning speeds and accuracy by adjusting the teacher's and the students' expectations about how long it will take different learners to master concepts and skills. Conducting classes in a way that allows for such differences results in more students mastering knowledge and skills than is the case when everyone is expected to learn at the same speed and in the same manner. Ways of adapting instruction to learners' differences are illustrated in Chapter 8 (Selecting Teaching Methods) and Chapter 9 (Choosing and Creating Teaching Materials).

The Encoding Function. The term *encoding* refers to how a person stores new material in memory. Encoding is most efficient if the new material is associated in multiple ways with what is already in mind so that numerous neural connections are made between the new stimuli and the contents of the learner's long-term memory. When older people fail to remember things, a main reason for the failure is that they had not securely encoded or mastered the material in the first place, such material as the name of a new acquaintance, a phone number, a spelling list, or the meaning of *integer* or *adverb* or *judicial review* (Anderson, Craik, & Naveh-Benjamin, 1998; Price, Said, & Haaland, 2004).

Implications. There are several ways that teachers can improve students' recall of what they studied. One way is to have them initially over-learn the material by making multiple applications of the concept or skill – multiple math problems of the same kind, multiple sentences using the newly acquired word or part of speech, multiple discussions of causes of the Civil War, multiple problems involving the "water cycle" in science. Another way to foster secure encoding is to offer periodic review lessons involving the concept or skill in order to refresh and strengthen the pattern of neuron connections in the brain that represents the learned material.

Reaction Time. Some people fail to distinguish between memory loss and slow reaction time. Frequently, older individuals who are unable promptly to recall a name, date, word, or event are accused of having a poor memory when the real cause is a slow reaction time. Given enough time, the name or date will be recalled, so the memory was not lost. "When processing ordinary stimuli, adults do show large increases in response time with increasing age" (Aging facts, 2007).

Implications. When jail or prison inmates are allowed only limited minutes to finish a test or essay, the older ones – because of their slower recall time – are likely to earn lower scores than if they had been given unlimited time. This is also true of class or group discussions in which the older participants may fail to offer thoughtful remarks because they are no longer as quick-witted as the youthful members.

Gender

By 2006, 93 percent of prison inmates were men and 7 percent women, but the proportion of women offenders was rising more rapidly than the proportion of men. The female prison population increased by 2.6 percent and male population by 1.9 percent in 2005 (U.S. prison population, 2006).

Males and females are incarcerated in separate prisons, usually located far from each other.

Two ways that gender can affect correctional-education programs are in (a) the types of study programs offered and (b) the match between the gender of instructors and the gender of students.

Study programs. The most obvious difference between programs for men and for women is in prisons' vocational-education offerings that are often based on the typical gender-related job openings in the general society. Thus, men's prisons are more likely to offer classes in auto repair, carpentry, diesel mechanics, plumbing repair, and welding than are women's prisons. In contrast, women's prisons more often furnish courses in cosmetology, dental technology, culinary arts, and garment making. This can result in some inmates having no opportunity to prepare themselves for a vocation that has traditionally been considered less appropriate for their gender.

Instructor/student gender match. Some women teach in men's prisons, and some men teach in women's prisons, a situation that can result in at least two types of problems.

First, male inmates who have been raised in a male-dominated culture may resent a woman instructor being in charge of their class – deciding what students should learn, issuing instructions, and punishing reluctant learners. This can result in continual abrasive instructor/student interactions. The same may occur in women's prisons, where inmates may resent a male instructor who reminds them of being oppressed by domineering fathers, spouses, or employers in the past.

Second, a sexual attraction may develop between one or more male inmates and a woman instructor. Or in a correctional facility for women, the sexual attraction may involve one or more female inmates and a male instructor. If such inmates openly express their yearnings, the instructor can feel very uneasy and the quality of teaching can suffer. Or, if the instructor reciprocates the sexual attention, then the favoritism shown to the chosen inmate can be resented by other class members and may result in a tryst between instructor and inmate. Prison administrators will in no way tolerate even the slightest relationships of this sort.

Ethnicity and Gang Membership

In 1950, the nation's prison population consisted of 65 percent Caucasians (whites) and 35 percent ethnic minorities. By 2000, those figures had reversed – 65 percent of inmates were ethnic minorities and 35 percent were whites. In 2005, 8.1 percent of black males (about one of 13) were imprisoned compared to 2.6 percent of Hispanics and 1.1 percent of whites (Prison statistics, 2005). Among juveniles, 754 out of every 100,000 black males were in a correctional facility, as were 348 out of every 100,000 Hispanic males, and 190 out of every 100,000 whites males. The incarceration rates per 100,000 juvenile females were 214 for blacks, 209 for American Indians, 83 for Hispanics, 68 for whites, and 32 for Asians.

There is no clear agreement about the reasons behind the ethnic-group differences in incarceration rates. Some critics charge that the prejudicial treatment of minorities by both the police and the courts is a major cause of higher percentages of blacks, Indians, and Hispanics being locked up. In contrast, other analysts cite cultural traditions for a higher rate of law-breaking by members of some ethnic groups. But whatever the underlying reasons might be, the facts are clear. Far higher percentages of blacks, Hispanics, and Native Americans than of whites and Asians are in prisons and jails. When in jail or prison, inmates tend to associate most closely with members of their own ethnic group, and such groups often engage in conflicts that can disrupt the operation of the education program if ethnic antagonisms are carried into classrooms.

Problems of ethnic hostilities are usually greater when jail or a prison houses organized gangs. Nationwide, there are six major prison gangs – Aryan Brotherhood, Black Guerilla Family, La Nuestra Familia, Mexican Mafia, Ñeta Association, and Texas Syndicate. The first five in this list are known as "Traditional Prison Gangs" created by inmates in California during the 1960s and 1970s to protect themselves from hostile inmates who were usually from street gangs outside the prison. The Ñeta, which originated in Puerto Rico and spread to the United States, is found mainly in East Coast prisons that hold concentrations of Puerto Ricans and other Hispanics. Walker (2007) reports that such gangs "are known for their viciousness and violence and use this reputation to maintain power and control over other inmates."

A research team that studied prison conditions concluded that "Gang affiliation increases the likelihood of violent and other forms of misconduct, even after controlling for [individuals'] . . . previous history of violence and other background factors" (Gaes et al., 2001).

It is the case, however, that gangs frequently consider classrooms, like religious chapels, to be noncombatant zones, free from ethnic-group rivalries. Under such conditions, teachers are spared the need to cope with misconduct that results from ethnic disputes.

Ethnicity can sometimes be linked to religion, with one ethnic group seen as closely associated with a particular faith – Hispanics with Catholicism, Arabs with Islam, and blacks with Evangelical Protestantism or Islam. Thus, conflicts between ethnic groups may include derogatory comments about rival groups' supposed religious affiliations.

Length of Imprisonment

The length of time an inmate will be in an education program – and when the inmate will enter and leave the program – is determined to a great extent by conditions of the individual's confinement. Those conditions include:

- the length of the prison term originally set by the court in which the offender was tried,
- the amount of time that the original term is reduced by the inmate's good behavior and productive activity, such as enrolling in an education program,
- when the inmate arrived at the prison, jail, or detention center,
- when the inmate will be paroled or be released early because the facility is overcrowded,
- the availability of space in an education program,
- when the inmate will be transferred to a different facility, and

- when the inmate chooses to enter and leave the program.

Such factors cause great instability in the membership of jail, prison, or detention-center classes. In schools outside of penal institutions, most students enter class together in the autumn and leave together in early summer. In contrast, individuals in correctional-institutions enter and leave a class at any time of the year. Some will spend no more than a few weeks in a program, whereas others will spend a year or two. In effect, the entrance-and-exit process in correctional-education settings functions like a revolving door. Students are continually entering or leaving. For example, consider these attendance figures for a junior-high-level class in a minimum-security prison. The maximum number of students enrolled in the class at any one time was 32. Over a seven-year period (1995-2001), 647 students – an average of 92 per year – entered and exited the class (Thomas, 2003).

Not only do students enter and depart at odd times during the year, but teachers have little evidence on which to base an estimate of each new arrival's current knowledge and skill. The entrance tests used for determining the class level (literacy, elementary, junior high, senior high, college) to which a newcomer will be assigned do offer some information. But that information is considerably less than the cumulative record that students in schools outside of prisons bring with them as they annually advance from one grade to another.

Implications. For instructors, there are two important consequences of this flow of students in and out of class.

First, teachers need efficient methods of estimating each newcomer's current level of achievement in each subject-matter field – English language, math, science, social studies, life skills. Ways of doing this are described in Chapter 5 (Assigning Students to Classes) and Chapter 10 (Assessing Student Progress).

Second, teachers should adjust their instructional methods and materials as far as possible to fit the needs of each newcomer and, at the same time, meet the needs of the current class members. This is not an easy task. It requires more individualized instructional methods than are typically are found in public and private schools in the general society. Chapter 8 (Selecting Teaching Methods) and Chapter 9 (Choosing and Creating Teaching Materials) describe alternative ways of coping with the revolving door.

Reasons for Enrolling in a Program

When asked, students in correctional-education programs offer a variety reasons for their choosing to enter a program. Those reasons can affect how well students learn.

Differences among inmates' reasons can be illustrated with a questionnaire study of 27 students in a junior-high-level class and 27 in a senior-high-level class in a minimum-security state prison. The classes' instructor, on the basis of frequent past discussions with students, prepared a questionnaire listing (in random order) 15 potential reasons that inmates might offer for their choosing to join an academic program. When the questionnaire was administered during a class session, students were directed to place a zero before each of the 15 statements that was *not* a reason for them to enroll in the program. Then they were to rank the remaining reasons in terms of importance by placing a 1 before the most important, a 2 beside the next most important, and so on. At the bottom of the questionnaire, the respondents were invited to "List any other reasons you have for being in school."

Table 4.1
Reasons for Enrolling in an Education Program
(54 students)

Respondents		*Reasons*
N	*%*	
43	80	I want to earn a General Education Development (GED) diploma or high-school-equivalency degree
37	69	To improve the way my children see me and be a better role model for them
37	69	To be able to help my children with their school work
37	69	To improve my English language writing and speaking skills
34	63	To become eligible to enroll in a college or university
32	59	To get a better job when I get out of prison
30	56	To improve the way my family members look at me
28	54	To feel better about myself and overcome being seen as a school dropout
13	24	Because I have a good time when I am in class
14	25	Because the prison rules and officials require me to have a job or a school assignment
9	16	To get day-for-day work-incentive credit towards early release from my maximum prison term
9	16	Because my TABE (entrance-test) score is not high enough for me to get a regular prison job so I must go to school
2	4	For something to do to keep from getting bored
2	4	Because being in class is part of my Board-of-Prison-Terms program

The results of the study in Table 4.1 list the students' reasons from the most popular to the least popular (Thomas, 2007b).

In addition to choosing from among the 15 listed reasons, 9 students added to the list. Two wrote that they liked to learn something every day. Additional reasons were:

1. Because I want to be a good person
2. To be able to enroll in a biblical theology course
3. To try to excel in my life
4. To accomplish a goal I set before coming to prison
5. I really enjoy doing school work
6. To achieve my education for myself
7. Because I like being around the instructor – he's a gas

The students differed in the number of reasons they cited and in the importance they assigned to different reasons. The number of reasons offered ranged from 1 to 15, with an average of 6.

A somewhat similar pattern of motives was found in a study by Jeremiah Gee (2006) of students' intentions in a rural jail where inmates entered a GED program to (a) learn for the sake of learning (*cognitive control*), (b) pursue a certain end, such as a high-school-equivalency degree or good job upon release (*goal orientation*), (c) be around others and have something interesting to do (*activity orientation*), and (d) avoid negative stimuli, such as troubles in the exercise yard or dormitory (*avoidance posture*).

Nerd power. An incident in a male-prison's ABE3 (junior-high-level) class – and which led to a tradition that continued in the class – demonstrates the value many prisoners place on education. One day the teacher announced that a student had elevated his overall TABE (Test of Adult Basic Education) score from a fifth-grade level to an eleventh-grade level. Another student greeted the announcement with, "Man, you're a real nerd!" From that point forward, the entire class embraced the label "Nerd" as an honor for which to strive. The instructor thereupon established the *Nerd Society* and began bestowing the title *Official Nerd* on any student who achieved a minimum overall tenth-grade TABE score. Each so-honored student received a certificate proclaiming his status as a *nerd.* His name and TABE score were posted on the classroom's front wall beneath a large banner that read *Official Nerd Society* along with a picture of a graduation cap and diploma. The success of the ABE3 *Nerd Society* resulted in the practice of thus recognizing outstanding academic performance being adopted as well in the education program's GED (high-school-level) class.

Implications. We estimate that some students' reasons for enrolling in a class will serve as stronger motivation for concentrating on their studies than will other students' reasons. For example, we would guess that an individual who enrolled in order to earn a GED diploma, get a better job upon release from prison, and earn his family's respect would likely study more diligently than one who enrolled solely because he was required by prison authorities.

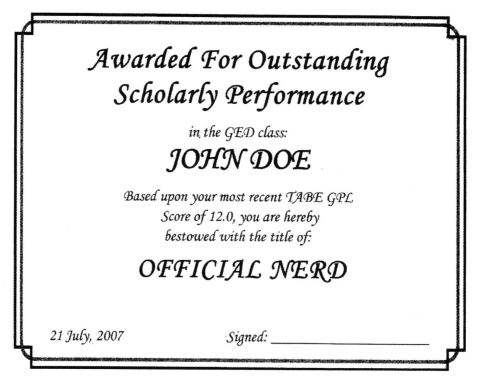

Awarded For Outstanding Scholarly Performance

in the GED class:
JOHN DOE

Based upon your most recent TABE GPL Score of 12.0, you are hereby bestowed with the title of:

OFFICIAL NERD

21 July, 2007   *Signed:* _____

Figure 4.1. Certificate for a Prison GED Class's Top Performers.

Next, with the foregoing student conditions in mind, we consider a series of problems that involve such conditions, and we inspect potential solutions offered by our three veteran correctional-education instructors.

PROBLEMS AND SOLUTIONS

Each of the cases described in this section is presented in three phases. First is the statement of the problem the teacher faces, second is an analysis of conditions related to the problem, and third is a proposed solution. The nine cases concern (a) an elderly inmate, (b) prisoners' cultural conflicts, (c) a student's low productivity, (d) an inmate's psychiatric disorder, (e) assigning credit for students' success, (f) requests for legal assistance, (g) offensive body odor, (h) hostile learners, and (i) rival gangs.

Slow Responder

The problem. A 73-year-old inmate, serving a life sentence in a state prison, enrolled in a high-school-level class as a way to spend his days in a constructive activity, but during class discussions he never volunteered an opinion. When the instructor asked him why, the elderly student said that other class members always spoke up before he could decide what to say and how to say it.

Analysis. It is possible that the elderly inmate's slow response time is at least partly a result of his advancing age. His hesitancy may also be influenced by bad experiences in the past with orally answering questions in public or by a lower level of logical-reasoning ability.

Solutions. Here are two of the instructor's options for including the older inmate in class discussions.

First, the instructor can ask particular students for their answer to a question or their opinion about the topic being discussed rather than allowing students to volunteer their opinions. However, the elderly inmate may be quite slow in generating a response, thereby resulting in a potentially embarrassing silence as he tries to think of what to say.

A second option involves the instructor telling the class, "I want to give everyone a chance to come up with an answer. So after I state a question, all of you are to write your answer and have it ready when we continue the discussion." This approach has the dual advantage of (a) ensuring that every class member pays close attention to the question and develops a response and (b) enabling the slower thinkers to participate actively in the discussion. The disadvantage is that the technique requires more time and interrupts the flow of the discussion more than would be the case if students could immediately offer their opinions orally.

Cultural Conflicts

The problem. The social climate of a prison was constantly marred by inmates of one ethnic group exchanging insults with inmates of other ethnic groups, insults featuring derogatory ethnic stereotypes.

Analysis. Conflicts between individuals who are from different ethnic or cultural groups often arise from (a) a lack of individuals' personal experience with a variety of members of groups other than their own or (b) having had only negative experiences with members of other groups. One way to combat the perpetuation of such stereotypes is to place individuals in situations that encourage them to understand members of other groups as individuals – some good, others bad, some pleasant, others unpleasant, some competent, others incompetent.

Solution. In an effort to promote positive interactions among members of different ethnic/cultural groups in a state prison, Pauline Geraci (2003) organized a multi-cultural book club whose volunteer members represented five cultural backgrounds – Asian, Hispanic, African, American Indian, and Caucasian (white). Geraci divided the members into four subgroups, each consisting of inmates from different cultural origins. Her purpose was to provide inmates

> a way to interact socially with other cultures in a non-threatening and open setting. I also wanted to promote reading . . . as well as writing, critical thinking, and literary discourse. I wanted to use literature as a way to create a safe environment in which students can bring their own lives and perspectives into the classroom. (Geraci, 2003)

The club met once a month so that each subgroup could discuss the book its members had chosen to read from a variety of novels the instructor provided. The suitability of the books for multicultural study is suggested by the following four titles.

- *La Maravilla* is about Beto, a fatherless nine-year-old boy living with his Spanish Catholic grandparents while searching for meaning amid the squatters and rusty Cadillacs of an impoverished Phoenix suburb.
- *Counting Coup* focuses on an Indian reservation girl's basketball team as its members strive to build constructive lives in the

midst of depressing social conditions – alcoholism, drug abuse, domestic violence, shoddy education, and low personal expectations that prevent the girls from reaching their potential, on and off the court. The book also describes joy, humor, and ethnic pride among the reservation populace.

- *Bodega Dreams* is set in New York City's Harlem and tells of Willie Bodega, former Young Lord, later a drug kingpin and Latino visionary, an "unforgettable blend of nobility and street, as if God never made up his mind whether to have Bodega be born a leader or a hood."
- *Tuesdays with Morrie* is about a journalist rediscovering a now-aged professor who had been a valued mentor to the journalist when he was in college twenty years earlier. The journalist describes the wisdom he gained while visiting the ailing mentor each Tuesday.

During the month in which each member read the book his subgroup had chosen, the member was required to keep a journal of his thoughts about the novel and how the content might relate to his own life. The journal notes became the basis of the subgroup's discussion at the next club meeting. At the end of the year, Geraci concluded that

> All in all, the multicultural book club was a success. I really valued students' talk, insight and interaction. The men learned to respond thoughtfully to these books in discussion and writing. I have learned that they can help each other learn and that their discussions and readings help them evaluate their past and their present and prepare them for the future.

She also offered advice and caveats for other correctional educators who contemplated starting a multicultural book club.

> Some teachers may not want to get students all stirred up. Multicultural literature many times contains obscenities, which should be considered if a teacher does not know how to deal with the students' reactions. Literature used in a multicultural book club also may contain topics such as drug usage, gangs, sexuality, and AIDS. Another issue is student interest in the text. If the student has trouble identifying with something or someone in the text, he may not like it. Several of my students reacted in this manner. I and the other students had to convince them they would like the text once they got into it more. Also, they were entitled to their [negative] opinion, but to belong to the club they had to participate whether or not they liked what they were reading. (Geraci, 2003)

Low Productivity

The problem. When the instructor monitored a junior-high-level student's weekly progress in completing workbook assignments, the instructor noted that the student continually produced less work than the minimum amount expected. Another class member called the student "lazy" until the instructor warned the class that such words as "lazy, stupid, dumb, and goof-off" would not be tolerated.

Analysis. Three plausible causes for the student's low production are (a) too little effort, (b) he is trying hard but lacks the ability to progress at the expected rate, or (c) his focus on schoolwork is disrupted by personal problems.

There are a number of methods for assessing the cause of a student's learning difficulties. One method is direct observation of his activities in the classroom. If he must be frequently reminded to stick to his assigned tasks or if he readily engages in idle conversation with classmates, chances are that he is simply not applying himself, has a short attention span, or suffers from distracting problems. If, however, he works steadily during class time, the problem may be limited learning ability.

A second way to analyze the student's difficulty is by interviewing him – asking questions that help distinguish among such causes as inadequate literacy skills, an insufficient knowledge base for the workbook assignment, or emotional issues. For example, the student can be asked to read aloud the directions for a page of the workbook, and then to show how he would apply those directions in completing the page's tasks.

Solutions. If the underlying problem appears to be the student's lack of motivation, the instructor can counsel him about the importance of applying himself in class so as to further his education. A second option is to offer a tangible reward for improving his study habits, such as lending him a set of headphones so he can enjoy listening to a computer compact-disc player. A third option is to apply punishment, such as withholding privileges if the student fails to work diligently.

On the other hand, should the instructor decide that the workbook materials are too advanced for the student, easier workbooks can be provided, or the inmate can receive one-to-one tutoring by the teacher or by an inmate teaching assistant. In extreme cases of students with inadequate background preparation, the best solution may be to reassign them to a lower-grade-level class.

However, if the learner's inadequate progress appears to result from his struggling with psychological problems, the teacher can verify this estimate by investigating the individual's background through the inmate's case-history file, then recommend that the inmate seek counseling from one of the institution's clerics (priest, minister, imam, rabbi). Or the inmate can be referred to the prison's psychological-services department for analysis and treatment.

Mental Disabilities

The problem. An instructor in a women's prison is notified that an inmate assigned to her class has been diagnosed as schizophrenic.

Analysis. Penal institutions often house inmates who suffer from a variety of psychological disabilities. Consequently, prisons and juvenile centers typically provide psychological and psychiatric services. Because mentally disturbed inmates may enroll in education programs, teachers are obliged to find ways to accommodate them.

Solution. To prepare for serving the schizophrenic inmate, the instructor read the woman's case-history file and consulted with her psychiatric-case-worker to determine the extent of the learner's disability and to ask about medications or treatments the woman was receiving that might affect her classroom behavior. The instructor also tested the inmate's language comprehension, computation skills, and general learning style through the use of classroom instructional materials. On the basis of the collected information, the teacher was able to adjust both her expectations for what the student could accomplish and her methods of working with the woman.

Who Deserves the Credit?

The problem. The teacher of a prison GED (high-school-level) test-preparation class became concerned that his students gave him too much credit when they passed the GED test series and thereby earned a high-school diploma. He felt the need to address the issue with the class.

Analysis. Many correctional-institution inmates suffer from poor self-images and lack confidence in what they are capable of achieving. This lack often stems from their early childhood experiences in both home and school. Incarcerated criminals often come from dysfunctional families in which parents are absent much of the time, suffer from psychological problems, are addicted to drugs, are unsupportive, are emotionally and physically abusive, have committed criminal acts, and have spent time in jail or prison. Consequently, children who grow up in such homes are frequently neglected or mistreated, are developmentally arrested, have low self-esteem, and lack constructive morals and values. Those characteristics significantly influence such individuals' ability to succeed in school. They have difficulty believing that they are competent because they have been told otherwise throughout their childhood years.

The types of students who fit the dysfunctional-family profile often do not attend school regularly, may become involved in gang activity, use drugs to escape from a harsh lifestyle, and view going to school as a painful, intimidating experience. They frequently become angry and frustrated and, as a result, act-out in disruptive ways while in a classroom, do not complete their academic assignments, and are seen as "bad apples" by their teachers. All of this contributes to their believing that they lack ability and thus are failures. They often drop out of school before making it to the twelfth grade.

Because the foregoing profile is so common among inmates, it is vital that teachers in penal institutions – in order to address their students' problems appropriately – are aware of the psychological baggage those students are carrying. Generally it is very important that instructors be openly encouraging and supportive of students' accomplishments so the learners develop self-confidence and a positive attitude toward school. One way this can be done is by congratulating them each time they reach a learning goal and by helping them recognize that they are the ones who have been chiefly responsible for their success. Another way is to reward accomplishment with certificates of achievement for completing assignments or mastering subject matter (Figures 4.1, 8.2, and 8.3). A third approach is for the teacher to provide inspirational discussions and audiovisual presentations designed to convince students of their worth and capabilities.

Solution. In order to get his students to recognize that they were the ones primarily responsible for passing the GED test series, the instructor led a class discussion. The first point he made was that he, himself, was not the one who had taken the tests, nor was he even in the room when the tests were administered. He pointed out that, although he provided materials and facilitated the learning process, the students were the ones who had to study and understand the material on their own. Finally, he had the class read an abridged version of *The Wizard of Oz* in order to help the class members realize their own potentials. He did this by drawing an analogy (a) between himself and the Wizard – the Great Oz – and (b) between the students and three of the film's main characters (Scarecrow, Lion, and Tin Man). The instructor emphasized that those three characters actually had the capabilities they were seeking before they ever met the Great Oz. In the end, the Wizard merely provided a bit of counseling and explained that the way the three had been behaving proved that they already had the sought-for traits. The Scarecrow had already shown he was intelligent, the Lion had demonstrated bravery, and the Tin Man had proven that he was not "heartless" but, instead, was already quite emotionally sensitive.

Seeking Legal Aid

The problem. An inmate engaged the computer-laboratory instructor in a conversation about the inmate's attempt to submit a written appeal that challenged legal issues in the court decision that had resulted in his current prison sentence. It was apparent to the instructor that the inmate was seeking sympathy for his plight and wanted advice about how to handle his appeal.

Analysis. Inmates love to talk about their legal affairs because they consider themselves persecuted by an unjust legal system. They want others to agree with their plight and, by agreeing, reinforce their own view that they are innocent victims. Teachers are easy targets for inmates' "venting," as teachers are usually willing to listen to students' concerns. However, it is poor policy for teachers to get dragged into a discussion about inmates' legal affairs. Instructors should not respond in any way that sounds as if they were making a commitment that would entangle them with the inmate's case.

The solution. When it became apparent where the student's conversation was headed, the computer-laboratory instructor listened without comment, then turned the conversation to other matters.

Offensive Odor

The problem. Several students in a computer laboratory complained loudly about the fetid body odor of one of their classmates.

Analysis. Inmates with disgusting body odor are rather common in correctional institutions. And the problem is not always the result of an inmate's lack of attention to personal hygiene, because regular schedules may be interrupted by such events as fights or rumors about drug dealing so that an inmate loses the opportunity to bathe. But for some inmates, offensive body odor is a persistent problem, openly objected to by fellow inmates. Inmates who suffer mental-health problems seem particularly prone to avoiding routine physical-hygiene practices and thus must frequently be reminded to bathe.

Solution. The student who had attracted the ire of his classmates was one who had chronically smelled bad. Thus, the computer-laboratory instructor felt obligated to correct the problem by speaking to the inmate about it, but doing so privately so as not to embarrass the inmate in front of his classmates. The instructor directed the inmate to return to his housing unit to take a shower, and the instructor then phoned the correctional officer at the housing unit to explain why the inmate was returning. The instructor also asked the officer to monitor the inmate's behavior in the future to ensure that he continually followed reasonable hygiene practices.

Hostile Learners

The problem. A recently arrived inmate periodically disturbed a computer-laboratory class by objecting to being forced to enroll in the course, by scowling at the instructor and classmates, by rebelling at assignments, and by generally showing he was unhappy. However, on other occasions he participated constructively in class activities without complaint.

Analysis. Inmates frequently resent being enrolled in an educational program against their wishes, and they reflect this resentment when they arrive in class. Hence, it is often difficult for an instructor to recognize the merits of apparently recalcitrant learners. Thus, it is important to allow sufficient time for such students to get used to the classroom setting and procedures. Initial hostility toward the teacher and the fact of being placed in school often subside when a student recognizes the teacher's good intentions. Additionally, giving those sorts of inmates small tasks to help in running the program will often bring them on board – such tasks as watering the classroom plants, handing out and collecting materials, or filling up the hot-water coffee urn. If they see that the teacher is willing to place some trust in them, they will feel assured that they are welcome members of the class.

Solution. The instructor guessed that the reluctant student was potentially a constructive class member who simply needed to feel that he was appreciated. Therefore, the instructor asked the newcomer to assist in rearranging materials on the classroom supply shelves and to help a classmate use a computer to complete an assignment. Soon the newcomer was no longer displaying resentment toward the class.

Rival Gangs

The problem. The male instructor of an ABE2 (upper-elementary-level) class at a medium-security male prison noticed that there seemed to be tension between two of his students. Both inmates were of Hispanic heritage. Both were in their mid-twenties. Not only did the two make it a point to sit in different sections of the classroom and appear to intentionally avoid each other, but the instructor also noticed that they glared at each other from time to time. The instructor thought there might be trouble here that needed attention. Thus, he detained the pair after the rest of the class had left for the day. When he asked them if they had a problem in their relationship, each denied any antagonism between them. But during the interview, the instructor noticed that the two had rival gang tattoos on their forearms.

Analysis. People who teach in correctional facilities are expected to inform custody officials of any confrontations or problems their students have with one another while in the classroom. In the present case, the instructor's speculation could be either correct or incorrect. But he did the right thing to pursue the matter, since he could be accused of negligence should the two students become involved in a violent confrontation and if they said the instructor had been aware that there was a potential problem. It is not unusual for students to deny that they feel any animosity toward each other, because their unwritten code of conduct precludes one inmate from "snitching" on another. Hence, their denial did not warrant the instructor dropping the matter.

Solution. Once the interview ended and the students had returned to their housing units, the instructor wrote a report of his observations and of his discussion with the two class members. He also phoned the education department's custody officer, the inmates' housing-unit custody administrators, and the academic vice-principal to inform them of the incident. Custody personnel then summoned the two students for counseling. During the process, the antagonists' rival gang status was recorded, the two were advised that their relationship would be closely monitored, and each was warned against any attempted aggression against the other. As a result, the instructor was relieved of any legal liability, and the two adversaries could expect less pressure from their fellow gang members to commit an act of violence.

Chapter 5

ASSIGNING STUDENTS TO PROGRAMS

An important step in providing educational opportunities for inmates is that of assigning them to a program that (a) will contribute to their welfare and (b) fits their current level of knowledge and skill.

The word *welfare* refers to educational opportunities that both promote inmates' constructive use of their time while in prison and prepare them for living a productive, crime-free life after their release. The expression *current level* means that students should be assigned to a program in which they can master the learning material through their applying consistent effort. In other words, they should not be placed in a program that is either too difficult for them or too easy.

The two purposes of this chapter are to (a) describe assignment methods, along with their advantages and disadvantages, and (b) identify problems that improper assignments can cause and suggest ways teachers can cope with such problems.

PROGRAM-ASSIGNMENT METHODS

Three indicators commonly used for estimating the program in which newly arrived offenders should be placed are an offender's (a) past record of schooling, (b) entrance-test scores, and (c) expressed interests.

Past Schooling Record

Offenders' schooling record (the highest grade they completed before being incarcerated) usually serves as only a rough guide to the type and level of class suited to their present academic or vocational skill. Such can be the case of inmates who, in the past, attended schools that practiced *social promotion*, advancing pupils from grade to grade along with their agemates, whether or not they had mastered the knowledge and skills in the classes they attended. Consequently, their report of the highest grade they completed may not be an accurate indicator of their present ability level. It is also possible that over the years since they were last in school, their original skills had deteriorated through the lifestyles they followed, so that their actual ability or grade level upon entering the prison or jail had declined.

Entrance Tests

Tests administered to offenders when they arrive at the prison or the juvenile detention facility usually serve as the most important – and sometimes exclusive – guide for determining which program new arrivals will enter. In prisons and jails, the most widely used instrument for assessing newcomers' academic achievement is the set of *Tests of Adult Basic Education (TABE)*. The tests were created to evaluate the academic skills of adult learners and are widely used in adult learning centers, corrections programs, career centers, and the U.S. military. The TABE are intended to determine levels of proficiency in basic mathematics, English language, spelling, and reading comprehension. TABE results are reported in terms of a test-taker's average-grade-level of skill or knowledge. Thus, inmates who earn scores equivalent to the average public-school primary-grade pupil will be assigned to an ABE1 class (equivalent to grades 1–3). Inmates scoring at grades 4–6 will be assigned to an ABE2 class, and so on. Therefore, the TABE is useful for placing inmates in a class which seems suited to their current achievement level in English language, reading, and math.

The TABE not only provide a means of assigning a student to an appropriate class level but also serve as a method of determining students' learning gains when the tests are repeated. Test results are reported by subject areas and include the examinee's average subject-area grade level. In addition, the statistical report to the teacher shows the number of correct and incorrect responses to test items that measure for specific skills. For instance, the TABE report for mathematics presents data about a test-taker's proficiency in adding, subtracting, multiplying, and dividing whole numbers, fractions, decimals, and percents. Thus, TABE reports aid teachers in identifying subskills in which students are weak.

Students' Interests

Students' expressed interests are most often considered in decisions about whether new arrivals will be placed in an academic or a vocational program. Depending on whether there are openings in programs that inmates would prefer, newcomers can ask to be assigned to classes that match their interests.

ASSIGNMENT PROBLEMS AND SOLUTIONS

The following five problems concern inmates who were placed in classes either below or above their ability level or whose class assignment resulted in a mismatch between a teacher's instructional style and the students' preferences.

Faulty Program Placement – Too Low

The Problem. A 26-year-old offender was transferred from an inmate reception center to the prison in which he would serve his commitment time. His score on the TABE (Tests of Adult Basic Education) that he took at the reception center placed his English-language reading at the level of a third-grade pupil (3.0). At the prison, he was assigned to a primary-school-level class where his performance in the early weeks proved to be much higher than that of his classmates.

Analysis. At the time of their initial incarceration, prisoners are sent to a reception center where they remain for one to several months. During that time their custody level (light security, medium security, heavy security) is determined. They also take a battery of psychological and cognitive-skills tests, including the TABE. On the basis of the assessment, they are sent to a prison suited to their classification profile, a profile that includes their custody level and educational status.

However, cases such as that of our 26-year-old cast doubt on the accuracy of the original TABE score.

The Tests of Adult Basic Education were created to evaluate the academic skills of adult learners and are widely used in adult learning centers, corrections programs, career centers, and the U.S. military. The TABE are intended to determine levels of proficiency in basic mathematics, English language, spelling, and reading comprehension.

Research studies show that it is not unusual for prisoners to perform poorly on the initial TABE testing. Jason Piccone compared the TABE scores of 1,825 newly arrived inmates in the Virginia state prisons with their TABE scores on a second testing at a later date and discovered that the average student scored 18.5 percent higher on the second testing than at intake. In effect, over 76 percent of offenders – whether male or female – performed better on the second testing. The improvement could not have been due to a formal educational program in the prison, because none of the participants in the study had taken classes between the first and second test sessions, although some may have gained some useful knowledge on their own. In an effort to explain the results of the study, Piccone wrote:

> Incarceration is an anxiety- and depression-inducing experience. These states are maximal at prison intake, when the offender is struggling to adjust to dramatic changes in daily life. . . . The increased sensations of anxiety and depression may impair offenders' ability to accurately complete their [intake TABE test] assessments [and because of a poor performance may] be assigned education that is inappropriate for their ability. (Piccone, 2006)

In addition to Piccone's interpretation of score changes, our own experience suggests that some newly arrived offenders are angry at prison officials or the prison system and thus intentionally do poorly on tests. Another cause is that offenders may fail to take entrance tests seriously. They mark the multiple-choice answer sheets in a thoughtless, random fashion, rushing through to get the task out of the way. They fail to realize that the test results can significantly affect the kinds of opportunities they will have and the requirements they will face when they reach their permanent imprisonment destination.

Solutions. One way to determine whether students' class-placement TABE scores are accurate is to interview them to discover the testing circumstances and how they felt at the time they took the TABE. Another method is to have students complete a different diagnostic entrance-exam consisting of mathematics, language skills, and reading comprehension items, then to compare those results with the earlier TABE scores. A third approach involves impressing on students the importance of doing well on the TABE and then to retest them with the TABE.

Faulty Program Placement – Too High

The problem. A young adult female prisoner was enrolled in an ABE2 class after having achieved a 4.5 average grade-level score on the TABE. However, when she subsequently took diagnostic math and language-skills tests in the class, she was unable to complete most of the math section, and she responded incorrectly to a majority of the problems on the language exam.

Analysis. To learn why the inmate had been assigned to the wrong class, the teacher needed to understand the particular nature of the TABE exams.

The TABE do not simply have a single test for each cluster of grades. Instead, the tests are at five levels of difficulty (with two versions at each level). Each level is identified by a code letter. In ascending order from the easiest to the most demanding, the codes letters are *L* (literacy), *E* (easy), *M* (medium), *D* (difficult), and *A* (advanced). The tests are scored in terms of grade-level equivalencies (GLE) that range from 0 (illiterate) to 14.9 (college sophomore). Therefore, an inmate earning a GLE of 4.5 would be expected to perform like an average pupil halfway through fourth grade, and thus the inmate would be enrolled in an ABE2 class. An inmate with a GLE of 11.2 would appear to command the academic skills and knowledge of a high-school eleventh-grader and thus seem suited to a GED course.

Solution. In the present case, the discrepancy between the student's TABE score and later poor performance on diagnostic tests suggested to the teacher that the wrong version of the TABE had been administered when the inmate was first tested for class placement. When the teacher investigated the matter, she discovered that the woman's TABE score had been earned on a *E-level* version of the TABE. The teacher, therefore, asked that the woman be retested with the *M-level* version. This time the grade-level-average turned out to be 2.0 – the equivalent of a second-grader's performance, so the inmate was reassigned to an ABE1 (primary-grade) class.

Instructor/Student Mismatch

The problem. Shortly after a 19-year-old prison inmate advanced from a junior-high-level class to a class that prepared students for a General Educational Development (GED) certificate, he began disrupting the GED class by critical remarks about the instructor. He openly charged the instructor with failing to explain mathematics operations accurately, for mistaking the causes of historical events, and for voicing political opinions. The disgruntled student complained about the teacher to classmates, to the teacher's aide (an inmate), and to the correctional officers in charge of the youth's dormitory. The teacher, highly distressed about the rebellious student, expressed his anguish to fellow teachers and the supervisor of academic instruction.

Analysis. What might be done to solve this problem depends on the interpretation of the underlying cause – or causes – of the conflict. Possibly the inmate is a chronic complainer with a chip on his shoulder. He wouldn't be satisfied with any kind of teacher. And he might resent anyone in a position of power and control. Or perhaps the inmate is correct in his assessment, so that the instructor actually is doing a very poor job of teaching. Or both the inmate and the instructor may be at fault, with the inmate unreasonably critical and openly abrasive while the teacher lacks both a command of the GED subject matter and classroom-management skills.

Solution. The attempt to resolve the teacher/student conflict can begin with discovering which of the potential causes is most likely. The education-department supervisor could interview the instructor of the junior-high-level class from which the inmate came in order to learn if the inmate had been a serious student in that classroom or, in contrast, had been a hypercritical crank. In addition, the supervisor could interview the bothersome inmate to learn the nature of his complaints about the instructor so as to estimate the validity of the complaints. If the GED instructor is indeed inadequate, other instructors likely have heard about it from their students, so those instructors might either verify or discredit the dissatisfied inmate's criticisms. The supervisor could also visit the GED class to observe how it was conducted, but that might not be of much help, because the supervisor's presence in the classroom would likely alter the nature of that class session, thereby making that session atypical.

Let us assume that the supervisor concludes that both the inmate and the instructor deserve some of blame for the conflict. To solve the immediate problem, the inmate can be withdrawn from the class, perhaps assigned to study on his own from workbooks and texts that focus on GED requirements. Or, if he had been a diligent student in the earlier junior-high class, he might be reassigned to that class where the instructor could guide his study for the GED tests.

Whereas removing the fault-finding inmate from the GED class may solve the immediate problem, it fails to solve the more serious problem of the instructor's doing a poor job of teaching and thus retarding the educational progress of more inmates. Four of the supervisor's options for coping with the teacher's incompetence are (a) dismissing the teacher, (b) assigning one of the education program's successful instructors to serve as a mentor to the GED instructor, charged with improving the GED instructor's skills, (c) assigning the GED instructor to visit classes conducted by successful teachers so that the instructor could observe those teachers' methods, and (d) doing nothing about the instructor in order to avoid the troubles the other options could generate. Which of solutions will be most appealing depends on such conditions as (a) the GED instructor's willingness and ability to improve, (b) whether other instructors would agree to assume the role of mentor, (c) how easily the GED instructor could be dismissed without objections from the teachers' union or without the teacher filing a lawsuit against prison authorities, (d) how readily a competent new teacher could be hired, and (e) the supervisor's willingness to deal with the troubles that the different options could involve.

Forgotten Skills and Knowledge

The problem. A recently arrived offender earns an overall TABE entrance-test score of 7.5, suggesting that he qualifies for a junior-high-level class. Thus, he voluntarily enrolls in such a multiple-subjects academic program and is a model student. However, after five months, the prison's education department learns from a former penal institution in which the student had served time that he already had a high school diploma.

Analysis. Correctional institutions often deny high-school graduates the chance to enroll in classes that are at the junior- or senior-high level, because such individuals would be taking a place that is needed by an inmate who had yet to finish high school. But it is also the case that the longer the period between a student's graduating from high school and his entering prison, the more he will have forgotten what he had learned. Thus, numbers of inmates freely choose to attend prison classes as a way of productively spending time behind bars. Some of them, in order to enroll in junior- or senior-high programs, hide from authorities the fact that they are high-school graduates.

Solutions. When prison policies preclude inmates who have a high-school diploma from enrolling in academic programs at the primary though the GED levels, there usually are no restrictions that would prevent inmates from taking vocational courses. Thus, in the present case, the student could be transferred to a vocational program, such as an *Offices Services Class* that provides instruction in English-language grammar and mechanics, word processing, basic mathematics, and calculator functions. The inmate could also use the library with its self-study resources. And at an increasing rate, penal institutions are offering distance-learning delivery systems that include partnerships with colleges and universities which provide opportunities to earn associate-of-arts and bachelor degrees.

Alternative Perceptions of "A Good Teacher"

The problem. During interviews with a researcher, a woman in a halfway house (during her transition from prison to the community) expressed her disappointment with the impersonal attitude of the teacher of the General Educational Development (GED) class in which the woman was currently enrolled. She compared the present teacher unfavorably with a teacher from her elementary-school years, one who had shown sincere interest in the student as an individual and who had served as her esteemed mentor (Mageehon, 2006).

Analysis. The researcher in this case was Alexandria Mageehon who sought the opinions of nine women, ages 22 to 50 (three African-American, three Latina, three Caucasian) who were enrolled in a ten-week course in the halfway house. The interviews focused on the respondents' notions of the characteristics of a "good teacher."

> To [these women], a good teacher was one who got to know his or her students as individuals – both in terms of learning style but also in terms of who they were as people. This notion of a teacher who brings awareness of both self and others to the classroom in a compassionate and engaged way fits with the idea of education that is

empowering. . . . Equally important is that the successful classroom teacher allows students self-determination and responsibility over the education. Combined with a commitment to work with students on their own terms, a teacher can then assist his or her students in negotiating complex problems. (Mageehon, 2006)

The problem for the nine women appeared to be the discrepancy between their ideal of a "good teacher" and the style of the instructor of the class in which they were enrolled. The class centered on students completing worksheets intended to prepare them for the GED test that would earn them a high-school-equivalency certificate. The instructor made no attempt to know class members as individuals.

Solution. Despite the students' expressed disappointment with the instructor's impersonal style, Mageehon's observation of class sessions showed that the women remained in the class and completed the assignments without complaint. Hence, Mageehon concluded that the women felt the class served their primary purpose. As a caution to other researchers, Mageehon concluded that she had originally conducted the study to determine how well the halfway-house class empowered the learners, with empowerment defined as

> the ability to critically inquire and discuss one's own situation within a social context. However, to my participants, empowerment may be a very different thing that involves getting a GED and being able to support one's self. In this sense, my own lenses may have clouded the ways in which the concept of a good teacher was interpreted. In an authentic way, from the participants' viewpoint, the teacher in the halfway house may have been a very "good teacher" as she was providing the tools necessary for the women to pass their GEDs. The idealized notion of who a good teacher is and the practical notion of what it takes for a woman to succeed in attaining this particular goal may simply be in conflict. (Mageehon, 2006)

In sum, at the outset of Mageehon's study, there appeared to be a problem of assigning students to a class that resulted in a mismatch between an instructor's style and students' needs. However, by the end of the study, it seemed that the ostensible problem was of no consequence. The students' most pressing self-perceived needs were apparently being met, despite the lack of a personal-mentor relationship between instructor and students.

Chapter 6

MANAGING THE CLASS

The expression *classroom management,* as used throughout this book, refers to teachers' ability to direct a class so that each student is continually learning at the level and rate of which he or she is capable. Some people equate *classroom management* with *maintaining discipline,* in the sense of preventing students from disrupting the class with arguments, irrelevant comments, silliness, or fights. But the meaning of classroom management that we intend goes far beyond misbehavior that disturbs a class. Thus, any student behavior – either active or passive – that prevents any class member from advancing consistently toward the learning goals represents less than optimum classroom management. Although it is apparent that perfect management is never achieved in daily classroom life, perfection is still a desirable ideal to pursue.

Clearly, there is no single formula for conducting a class successfully, because the task is influenced by multiple conditions that vary from one place and time to another. Those conditions include the number of students in the class and their characteristics, the instructor's traits, the nature of the learning tasks the students face, the available teaching facilities, the school's policies, and more. Consequently, management techniques that work well in one setting may not work well in another.

So, what sort of useful guidance can be offered to prospective correctional-education teachers to help them manage classes successfully? We suggest that such guidance can take the form of (a) a description of several principles of teacher/student interaction that underlie teachers' management techniques and (b) examples of how three experienced correctional-education instructors would cope with typical problems of management under different classroom conditions. In the following pages, the description of principles precedes the solutions to specific classroom-management problems that have confronted the three instructors – Colleen Laney-Kobata, Basil DuBois, and Rob Thomas.

PRINCIPLES OF TEACHER/STUDENT INTERACTION

We believe that the foundation of teachers' classroom-management practices is their set of principles or guidelines about the best way for teachers and students to interact. Those principles may be either conscious and explicitly stated or only subconscious, so that they must be inferred from the way teachers treat students. The following four principles are ones we believe are constructive guides to instructors' interactions with correctional-education students. Each principle is first defined, then its application in correctional-education settings is illustrated with specific classroom applications. The applications are ones suggested by Colleen, Basil, and Rob.

The principles concern mutual respect, prejudice, firmness, and reward-and-punishment.

Mutual Respect

The principle. Instructors should view inmates as worthwhile individuals deserving the same courteous treatment that instructors would want if they were inmates. In turn, students should treat instructors with the civil, polite deference that is due someone who is trying to improve inmates' knowledge and skills.

Inmates can profitably recognize that their instructors are trained professionals whose job is to provide the best possible education for class members. Students should be aware that classroom rules will be enforced and that agreeing to follow the rules is a prerequisite for participation in the class – such rules as "study quietly during independent-learning activities, and stay on task at all times."

Classroom applications. The following are ways the three instructors attempt to promote mutual respect between the teacher and students and among the students.

- *Rob* – Perhaps the most convincing thing I do to foster mutual respect is to demonstrate genuine interest in the success of each student, regardless of his ethnic background, physical appearance, age, or learning ability.

  I tell students that I judge them solely by their classroom demeanor and their approach to the education program. If they want my respect, they must behave respectfully, demonstrate enthusiasm for their studies, and willingly complete assigned academic tasks. I also explain that I have little respect for those who lack a serious commitment toward improving themselves educationally, or who must be prompted regularly to participate in learning activities.

  I insist that any words such as *dumb, stupid,* or *idiot* that are intended to demean a classmate are not to be used in my class. I often remind them that they are all capable, even though some may grasp information more slowly or have had less formal education than others. I emphasize that each student will be given whatever time he needs to master the knowledge and skills of our curriculum.

  And I use the fable of the race between the tortoise and the hare to underscore the importance of staying on task at all times. I make it clear that I have a great deal of respect for those who work on their assignments steadily throughout the school day in an effort to learn as much as they can.

- *Colleen* – I live by the rule that you must treat others the way you want to be treated. Inmates enrolled in my class come as *students* and are treated as such. They know that, as much as possible, the prison stops at my classroom door. Inside the classroom, we treat each other with respect. I create a safe environment for making mistakes – including for mistakes I make. Committing mistakes is how we learn, and we can learn from each other. We may lightly tease each other, but no student is allowed to put down another student.

- *Basil* – Showing empathy for students in a spirit of professionalism sets the right tone for the class. Mutual respect stems from the need for each student to have a safe, orderly learning environment in order to reach his or her educational goals. Teachers have the responsibility to ensure the right of each student to have such an environment.

Prejudice

The principle. Teachers should avoid basing their treatment of students on either negative or positive stereotypes that are held in society about lawbreakers' ethnicity, types of crime, mode of dress, grooming, and manner of speech. The treatment of each student should be based entirely on that specific individual's behavior in the classroom.

As is the case in any classroom, a teacher is bound to like some students more than others based on the way students act toward the teacher and fellow students and on the effort learners display in completing assignments. However, instructors are wise to encourage and support all class members and not show favoritism. Teachers are also wise to mete out discipline impartially, based on specific transgressions instead of allowing subjective impressions of individual learners to influence decisions about student conduct.

We are convinced that if teaching is to be most effective, instructors need to avoid two errors that can lead to the prejudicial treatment of learners.

First is the inmate's appearance error. To some extent, everyone depends on stereotypes, based on impressions from the past, for estimating the nature of a person they newly meet – the person's size, visage (beard, blemishes, cosmetics, eye shape, nose size, and more), clothing, language accent and fluency, manner of greeting, and the like. However, teachers in correctional facilities who let those first impressions affect their interactions with students can be committing a serious mistake because the stereotype may not fit this particular individual. Thus, it is important for instructors to hold their stereotypes in abeyance until they have worked a while with the student.

- *Basil* – To a new teacher, some inmates' appearance may shock at first. However, it's important for the teacher to look beyond the veneer and give each student a fair chance to succeed.

- *Colleen* – It is natural to assume that an inmate who looks disheveled and has poor grooming habits will be a careless student, or that the neatly-pressed, clean-shaven inmate will be an excellent one. Just as in life outside of the prison, you cannot judge your students by their appearance or even their demeanor the first few weeks that they are assigned to your class. Inmates are rarely who they appear to be at first glance. The disheveled and aloof student can be fearful of re-entering an education setting. These students often become enthusiastic learners once the environment has proven to be "safe" to learn in. Likewise, the neatly-pressed and friendly student can be concerned with appearances only and gives you only partial effort in class.

- *Rob* – There have been a number of occasions when I made assumptions about students – either positive or negative – based on their physical appearance, but changed my opinion after getting to know them and observing their approach to learning in the classroom. For example, I have had students who were large and intimidating, but who turned out to be gentle and friendly – excellent, self-motivated learners. I have also had students who were not at all physically imposing but, rather, were the stereotypical scholarly computer nerd, yet were actually enrolled in the class against their will and quite disinterested in improving themselves through education.

Second is the inmate's offense error. In some ways – often in many ways – occupants of prisons, jails, and juvenile centers are not nice people. They were locked up for having stolen, sold drugs, forged, defrauded, raped, set fires, told lies, maimed, and murdered. So there always is the likelihood that an instructor will treat students in a prejudicial manner if the instructor knows the offenses for which students have been incarcerated. So here is the question: Is it better to know an inmate's offense than not to know it?

- *Rob* – I recall a pleasant, hard-working student whom I felt very comfortable working with until a colleague told me that the young man had been imprisoned for child sexual abuse. This information so tainted my feelings that I found myself avoiding him. The information about his offense damaged my ability to be as helpful as I should have been in furthering his education.

- *Colleen* – Inmate-students are not in your classroom for singing too loudly in the church choir. They have all committed a felony that the courts determined worthy of separation from their families, friends, and "outside" life. On more than one occasion I have read the details of a student's offense and been hard-put not to be repulsed by his presence. Unless you have a sound reason (or an instinctual one regarding your safety) to read a student's central file and the details of his offense, it is better to accept and evaluate your inmate-students for who they present themselves to be in your classroom. In general, I prefer not to know the offenses of my students. However, a female teacher in a male prison will sometimes find it important to read a student's record-file and learn the offense for which he was committed. I believe it is always a good idea to listen to one's instincts if something about a student's behavior doesn't "feel right." Keeping the lines of communication open between the teacher and custody staff is vital.

- *Basil* – Inmates are very skilled at the confidence-game. They have lots of free time for scheming about how to manipulate the institution's staff members. Having some knowledge of inmates' background through reviewing their central file can be very useful. For example, reviewing an inmate's disciplinary history will alert a teacher to the type of behavior to be expected from a particular student. Then, being non-prejudicial after knowing the inmate's background is part of what is expected of a truly professional educator.

Firmness

The principle. Instructors should be compassionate, understanding guides for students, but instructors and students are not *equals*. Their roles are different, and it is important that instructors firmly maintain their role. This is particularly true in correctional settings.

Teachers – and particularly ones new to the profession – sometimes wish to establish a very friendly personal relationship with their students, or at least with some students. Such teachers desire to create a "pal" instructor/learner relationship. Teacher and learner will be chums in the pursuit of knowledge and skills. This is the *let's-be-buddies* error. Whereas instructors and inmates should display mutual respect, it's important to recognize that their positions are quite different. They are not equals. The instructor has been charged by society to help socialize or rehabilitate lawbreakers. Although friendliness and humor can play important roles in carrying out that charge, it is important that both instructors and students recognize the nature of their positions and that instructors be firm in maintaining that relationship. Some idealists speak of "the democratic classroom" and encourage teachers to conduct their business as if classrooms were democracies. But that's a misconception. In a democracy, everyone has an equal voice (at least theoretically) in choosing the goals to achieve and the methods for pursuing those goals. Although classrooms can be training grounds for youths who will be members of a democratic society, classrooms are not democracies. The classroom – and most certainly the correctional-education classroom – is the province of the teacher, who is the in-house representative of American society, obligated to help reform the lives of delinquent youths, drug dealers, thieves, robbers, arsonists, forgers, liars, child molesters, rapists, murderers, and more. Prisoners are often skilled in manipulating other people for their own benefit. To cope with such students, correctional-education instructors need to recognize the responsibilities implied in their positions and to firmly carry out society's charge.

- *Colleen* – Firm, fair, and consistent are the watchwords in a correctional setting. Good teaching is similar to good parenting. You need to be aware of the behavior you expect from your students and the behavior you yourself exhibit. An example of this is tardiness. A life skill many inmate-students lack is timeliness. They have trouble holding down jobs due to absences and tardiness. In my classroom I hold the students accountable for returning from breaks on time and they me. When I notice that the break schedule is not being honored, and more and more students are coming later than required, I give a verbal warning to the entire class. Rarely does everyone heed my verbal warnings, and inevitably four or five students will return late from break. In the spirit of firm, fair, and consistent, I write Rule-Violation notices for all late students. Inevitably, there is someone in this group whom I would rather not "write up." However, it must be done, and it must continue until the behavior changes.

- *Basil* – A sense of humor adds a nice touch to the classroom atmosphere so long as it is tasteful and does not demean the students. A teacher's modeling good language usage and professionalism sets a constructive tone that students will respect. Teachers are wise to avoid using prison lingo or vernacular, because inmates will interpret such speech as weakness on the part of the teacher – as an attempt to fit in with the inmates and be accepted by them. In successful parenting, children need parents, not buddies. In successful classroom management, inmates need teachers, not "homies" (hometown pals).

- *Rob* – It's been my experience that inmates generally respond well to a teacher who is friendly yet resolute in enforcing classroom rules. It is vital that the instructor makes it clear that the purpose of maintaining discipline is solely to promote the welfare of the students and not to demonstrate the instructor's personal power and authority over them. It is also useful for instructors to recognize that inmates have their own unwritten code-of-conduct that prevents them from disrespecting each other or complaining to authorities ("snitching") about fellow inmates. Thus, it is important for a teacher to maintain classroom order without creating an adversarial relationship between the teacher and class members or among the students themselves.

Reward and Punishment

The following description of the classroom use of rewards and punishments is described in terms of five principles.

Principle 1. The behavior-modification process. People willingly pursue activities that they find rewarding, in the sense of fulfilling their needs and interests. People avoid activities (a) that they believe do not fulfill their needs or (b) that they interpret as distressing and painful – physically, mentally, or emotionally. Therefore, the more that inmates find appropriate classroom behavior rewarding, the more likely they will adopt such behavior.

Analysis. A host of research evidence as well as teachers' personal experiences attest to the success of the instructional technique known as *behavior modification*. The process of carrying out behavior modification can be summarized in four basic steps:

1. Identify the specific behavior you wish to have the student substitute for the presently unacceptable behavior.
2. Arrange for the student to try this new, desirable behavior
3. Estimate what sorts of consequences the student will find rewarding (reinforcing) and what sorts the student will consider punishing.
4. Manipulate consequences so the desired behavior, when it appears, will yield greater reward and/or less punishment than does the undesirable behavior. In other words, arrange rewards and punishments so that students find adopting the new behavior more profitable than remaining with the old behavior.

Classroom application. The operation of behavior-modification in a junior-high-school-level correctional-education classroom can be illustrated with the following example.

1. *Identifying the desired classroom behavior.* The new behavior to be acquired is that of working diligently on class assignments. The old behavior for which the new behavior is to substitute includes such things as sitting passively in class, talking with classmates about matters not related to the current lesson, day dreaming, reading a comic book, telling jokes, or engaging in horseplay.

2. *Attempting the new behavior.* Students cannot experience the rewards that the recommended new behavior will yield until they try it. One way to motivate the students to attempt the desired behavior is to tell them (1) what rewards to expect for studying diligently and (2) what punishments to expect for failing to do so.

3. *Potential rewards and punishments.* The rewards described for adopting the new behavior include (a) the self-satisfaction of mastering the learning task, (d) a high score on the current assignment, and (c) a checkmark on the student's record verifying mastery of task. The students' past experiences in the class let them know that faithfully studying will also result in the instructor orally commending them and writing on their test or essay such comments as "nice job" and "great progress." Past experiences also inform them that consistently working on assignments can earn them periodic certificates of achievement and high marks on report cards.

   Expected punishments do not need to be described to most students, for those sanctions are by now well known from the teacher's past management techniques. But for inmates new to the class, the instructor may explain that failing to conscientiously study will result in the instructor admonishing slackers and adding critical comments on their next periodic behavior report.

4. *Manipulating rewards and punishments.* Each time a student tries the new behavior, the teacher furnishes a reward. Each time a student reverts to an unacceptable behavior, the teacher withholds rewards and/or applies punishments.

With the foregoing sketch of behavior modification in mind, we now turn to the principles that guide each of the four steps in the behavior-modification process.

Principle 2. The desired behavior. Students need to understand clearly which classroom behaviors are considered desirable and which are considered undesirable. It is unfair to punish students for acts that they did not realize were unacceptable.

Classroom applications. One way to help ensure that students understand which acts are forbidden – and thus punishable – is to furnish them a printed *behavior contract* that they are required to sign, thereby affirming that they fully understand the contract's content.

Prisons and juvenile detention centers may provide such contracts at three levels of the administrative hierarchy – statewide, individual institution, and individual classroom. The first of the following examples, from the California Department of Corrections and Rehabilitation, applies to all of the state system's institutions. In the document, the phrase "earning work-time credit" refers to the Department's policy of reducing the length of an inmate's sentence by one day for each day the inmate engages in a constructive work activity, such as attending class in an education program.

> Conditions of Assignment: Do not participate in off-duty activities during your [education program's] work hours (i.e. play sports or games, make phone calls, go to the library, go to a chapel, go to canteen, eat meals, watch TV, read books or magazines, study non-education-assignment-related materials, work on legal work, sleep, etc.). Inform your supervisor [teacher] of institutional obligations (i.e. medical appointments, family visits, etc.). You are responsible for notifying your supervisor [teacher] immediately should you receive any duty limitations from the medical department. Failure to comply could result in disciplinary action and being unassigned from your school program. Inform your supervisor [teacher] of injuries received during working hours. Return work-assignment cards to their work area supervisor at the termination of the assignment, or upon acceptance of a new work card. Any inmate found in possession of more than one work assignment card, or an inaccurate or false card, is subject to serious disciplinary consequences.
>
> Acceptable Standards: You are expected to perform your assigned work duties to the BEST of your ability at all times. You must maintain a good working relationship with staff and peers. You are expected to report to work on time and may not leave work without permission from the work supervisor [teacher]. You are expected to

maintain and display an acceptable attitude and demeanor at all times. Personal appearance and hygiene are to be neat and clean. You must be dressed in state-issued clothing and wear all applicable safety items. You must perform assigned tasks diligently and conscientiously and must not pretend illness or otherwise evade attendance in your assigned [school] work and program activities.

<u>Failure or Refusal to Meet Expected Standards:</u> If you fail to comply with the requirements of this [schooling] job and/or the *California Code of Regulations Title 15*, progressive discipline will be adhered to. Any absence time from your [schooling] assignment, regardless of duration, will preclude the earning of work-time credit for the day. (California Code, 2007).

The second behavior contract is from the education department of a particular prison in the California system – the California Men's Colony.

<u>Class Expectations and Standards.</u>
1. Each student is expected to report to class on time with school equipment. Reporting late to class will result in the student receiving no credit toward reducing the length of his prison sentence.
2. Each student is expected to work quietly and diligently on class work during class time.
3. Each student is expected to complete all assigned classwork.
4. Each student is expected to follow all classroom rules and teacher directives, and to cooperate with the instructor, teacher's aides, and fellow students.
5. The following are not allowed:
   • Long conversations with others
   • Profanity
   • Horseplay
   • Sleeping
   • Smoking in the education area at any time
   • Eating in class
   • Remaining on restroom breaks for more than five minutes
   • Activities not related to classwork, such as drawing pictures, playing games, reading non-class materials, etc.

This notification is your warning. If you are late or absent you will not receive credit toward reducing the length of your sentence.

I have read and understand all [education department] standards and expectations. Signed, (*inmate's signature*) (Class expectations, 2007)

The third example illustrates a behavior contract at the classroom level that explains more precisely than the first two examples how a particular teacher expects students to act. This contract includes the instructor's commitment to helping inmates achieve their educational goals.

Education Program Contract – ABE3/A – Classroom 377A. In order to maintain a disciplinary-free record and successful 90-day progress reports (that include marks on effort, conduct, cooperation, and initiative or willingness to stay busy without being told), I [the undersigned student] understand and agree to the following classroom regulations.

I agree to behave as a mature adult who can accept constructive criticism and use it for my personal advantage.

I agree to participate in all class activities unless I have made an arrangement with the instructor based upon special circumstances.

I agree to begin working on my learning assignments as soon as I enter the classroom and not spend time on personal matters such as letter writing, art work, and talking about non-educational subjects.

I agree to avoid horseplay while in the classroom.

I understand that the class meets Monday through Friday from 7:45 A.M. to 11:15 A.M. and from 12:45 P.M to 3:45 P.M. I realize that if I am late for class by even five minutes (unless due to circumstances beyond my control), I am subject to losing work-incentive credit [toward reducing the length of my prison sentence], and can receive additional disciplinary consequences.

I understand that becoming educated is, at times, very frustrating and at times somewhat boring, but that it is rewarding in the end.

Your Instructor's Note: If you, as the student, understand and promise to follow the above rules, I, as your instructor, promise to help you reach your educational goals as quickly as you are willing and able to do so. You must understand, however, that this will only happen if we can develop a cooperative working relationship. I will not tolerate any individual who is not serious about becoming educated – who does little more than just show up in order to receive work-incentive credit, or who in any way disrupts the learning environment of the classroom. If your intention is to just show up and not make any effort to study or if you disrupt the class, you are in the wrong program and can expect disciplinary consequences and to be dropped immediately from the class.

I truly believe that I am an understanding person who has the serious student's best interests in mind. I realize that everyone has good and bad days and that the prison setting contains may negative influences which may keep you from being able to concentrate on your education program. But in general, you and I must try to keep a positive frame of mind and to leave our personal problems behind when we enter the classroom. Our personal problems will still be there to be dealt with when school ends for the day.

To put it all in a nutshell, you and I have a professional relationship and a responsibility to work as hard as possible to achieve your educational goals. The harder each of us strives, the more satisfied we will be with what you accomplish and the greater will be our rewards. Remember, the more educated that a person becomes, the more powerful he will be and the less he will have to depend on others to get along in life.

Signed, (*inmate's signature*) (Thomas, 2007)

Principle 3. Trying the desired behavior. It is necessary for students to try the new behavior before they can discover that the new behavior brings greater reward and less pain than did the previous acts that the new behavior is to replace.

Classroom applications. There are several ways teachers can get students to try substituting a new behavior for an inappropriate one. Three of the most practical ways involve (a) describing the desired new actions, the inappropriate old ones, and why it would be wise to exchange the new for the old, (b) modeling the change process, and (c) gradually shaping the new behavior.

Verbal description. Here are two examples:

Mr. W, your best chance of moving up to the GED class within the next couple of months will be to spend more time reading the social-studies book and answering the questions at the end of each chapter rather than using so much class time drawing cartoons.

Mr. X, instead of wandering around the room and bothering other class members, you should be at your desk completing the assigned pages of the math workbook. If you do complete those pages today, you'll earn points toward a math-progress certificate. If you don't complete them, you'll not only miss the points but you'll end up sitting at the desk next to my own desk at the front of the room.

Modeling. Modeling consists of demonstrating the desired behavior. The demonstration can be offered either by the instructor or by a class member. First is an instructor serving as the model.

Here, Mr. J, let me show you how to use the table of contents and the index of a book to quickly find the information you want rather than your just turning the pages and hunting. As I do this, I'll think out loud so you'll see why I search the way I do.

Next, a popular way class members can function as models consists of an inmate observing the way the instructor treats other class members when they follow the rules or fail to do so. In other words, by watching what happens to classmates, inmates learn which rewards and punishments are meted out for different ways of behaving, and they thus discover what consequences to expect from how they themselves act.

Shaping. Frequently an inmate does not change entirely from an unacceptable way of acting to an acceptable way. A student who has been told to stop interrupting others during class discussions may sometimes wait for his turn to speak but other times interrupt. The instructors' goal then becomes that of gradually shaping the desired behavior so that it becomes consistent. This may be accomplished by the instructor (a) complimenting the student each time he or she asks permission to speak before offering an opinion and (b) stopping the student from speaking each time he or she interrupts.

Okay, Mr. R, I appreciate your holding up your hand to speak. Let's hear what you have to say.

Wait a minute, Mr. R, you'll get your turn when I call on you, not before.

Principle 4. Selecting rewards and punishments. Choosing consequences that will constructively influence inmates' behavior is not always an easy task because inmates may not agree with instructors about which consequences are rewards and which are punishments. Hence, choosing rewards is rather like choosing bait to catch fish. Some fish bite on worms, others on spinners, and still others on flies. Thus, it may take a bit of experimenting for instructors to discover which rewards and punishments are effective in altering a particular inmate's behavior. However, in our years of teaching prisoners, we have found that the following kinds of incentives are interpreted by most students as rewarding and thereby encourage beneficial behavior.

- Oral compliments – Telling students they are on the right track and doing a good job can be a strong motivator. Such comments can be applied to any sort of learning task and cost nothing. But compliments should be sincere, since their motivation value is diminished when students recognize that the praise was undeserved.

- Written compliments – Words of approval are jotted in the margin of an essay or at the top of a test paper – *nice job, good idea, well described, you're right on target.*
- Public recognition – A student is openly commended in class by the instructor or the student is featured in an article in the institution's newsletter or newspaper.
- Certificates for *Student of the Week Award, Perfect Math Papers, Outstanding Progress.*
- Symbols – A sticker (*star, red dot, cartoon figure*) on a test paper or essay. A double plus (++) written on a worksheet.
- Supplies – A pencil, inexpensive pen, or notebook for significant progress.

We have also found that such consequences as the following are usually interpreted by students as punishment that discourages unacceptable acts.

- Oral criticism – Such negative comments as "You're wrong" or "You've missed the point entirely" may either stimulate a learner to do better or may simply anger and discourage rather than reform the student. The likelihood that negative comments will improve behavior is greater if the criticism is accompanied by a suggestion of what should be substituted for the objectionable behavior, such as:

Maybe you didn't realize that betting on ball games during class time isn't acceptable. But completing that science assignment is acceptable.

Instead of jamming the used papers under the desk, put them in the recycling bin.

Calling her "idiot" won't be tolerated in this class. You know her name, so please call her by her name.

Some aversive consequences that are successful in discouraging undesirable behavior are of questionable value because they also yield collateral damage. For instance, openly ridiculing students in class may reduce the frequency of their misbehavior but, at the same time, may cause them to hate the instructor and the class so they are no longer interested in learning.

Principle 5. Manipulating consequences. The instructor's purpose in distributing consequences is to have inmates find that obeying the rules is more rewarding than disobeying the rules. Instructors therefore are wise to respond to desirable behavior with obvious approval and to react to undesirable behavior with clear disapproval, or at least with a lack of approval.

Some teachers, like some parents, appear to believe that acceptable behavior is what should normally be expected of their charges and thus requires no commendation. In effect, learners should not expect compliments for acting properly. Hence, unacceptable actions are what need correcting, so improper behavior should be met with a teacher's or parent's reaction in the form of criticism and punishment. But a teacher's or parent's responding only to misbehavior is usually a less effective way to effect behavior change than by both providing liberal compliments for acceptable actions and reserving punishment (or lack of reward) for unacceptable actions.

CONDITIONS AFFECTING PROBLEMS AND SOLUTIONS

As explained earlier, we believe the task of managing a class successfully is influenced by multiple conditions that can vary from one classroom to another. Thus, there is no single method that works well in every setting. We illustrate this conviction in the following pages by describing the solutions offered for typical management problems by our three veteran state-prison instructors. But first we describe conditions in three types of classes that may affect the kinds of management problems that arise and the kinds of solutions that are likely to succeed.

In each class, the students are minimum-or-medium-security-level inmates whose prison sentences are between five and 10 years, yet with a few serving life sentences. The offenders' crimes include drug-trafficking, fraud and embezzlement, burglary and theft, armed robbery, manslaughter, and sexual child-abuse. All major ethnic groups are represented, with the majority of students Hispanic and the rest African-American, White, Native American, Asian, or European.

Conditions – Computer-Skills

Basil – The Computer Assisted Instruction Laboratory is designed to provide inmates individualized remedial, intermediate, and advanced instruction in language, mathematics, reading, writing, and keyboarding. Because the students are obliged to learn chiefly by means of computer programs, their ability to read English is particularly vital for their progress. It is the case that all of the inmates assigned to the laboratory have below-average reading skills in comparison to their overall TABE (Test of Adult Basic Education) scores. Fortunately, much of the instruction provided by the computer is in both visual images and computer-generated spoken directions that are of significant aid to weak readers.

Conditions – English-Language-Development

Colleen – Who the students are in an ELD (ESL) class varies greatly depending on the correctional facility and the education department within that facility. Some settings do not have a specific class for the English language learner; they are simply assigned to the lowest level of Adult Basic Education and the teacher is left to deal with their special needs. In other facilities English-language learners are grouped together in an ELD class that can be a mixture of various levels of language proficiency or divided out into various levels. The ELD student can wear many faces and come from many places. Some students are illiterate in their primary language, making literacy in English more difficult. Some students have a degree of oral language proficiency that is not reflected in their literacy skills, and vice versa. The prison system houses inmates from numerous countries. In California the typical ELD student's first language is Spanish, but students can speak various other languages also. I have taught Armenian, Vietnamese, Korean, Cambodian, Laotian, Italian, and Russian students.

Contrary to popular belief, the ELD instructor does not need to be a speaker of his or her student's first language. In some cases students learn at a faster pace when they cannot rely on translation into their first language. Immersion is a proven method of language acquisition; however, one must be wary of leaving students confused and unable to complete assignments. It is not fair to expect a student to complete an assignment if the student has no understanding of what he or she is being asked to do. A way to deal with this is to have bilingual dictionaries available in the classroom. Hiring a teaching assistant who is fluent in the language that is most prevalent in the classroom is also a good idea. Another strategy is to occasionally group same-language speakers together for peer assistance on assignments. The ELD classroom can benefit from heterogeneous grouping of students. This facilitates peer coaching. Lower-ability students in the group get the additional support they need and higher-ability students experience the role of teacher.

Conditions – Junior-High-Level and GED Classes

Rob – In both the ABE-3 (adult basic education, junior-high level) and the GED (general educational development, senior-high level) classes, the ages of students have extended from 16 years to 84 years.

There are often wide-ranging differences among students in skills and knowledge of English language, reading, and mathematics. It is unclear how many inmates actually suffer learning disorders because they rarely have undergone diagnostic examinations. However, some admit having been in special-education classes when they attended public schools. In addition, their current prison instructors often recognize symptoms of learning disabilities – visual and auditory impairment, attention-deficit disorder, knowledge-retention difficulty, and dyslexia.

In their class behavior, the vast majority of students over the years have been polite, cooperative, enthusiastic, and industrious learners. Many admit that the opportunity to learn, the positive support they get in class, the humor the instructor provides, and their own self-esteem improvement from their academic accomplishments make the class a much more desirable place to be than is their housing unit. Furthermore, I have found that the inmates view the classroom as a neutral ground in which (a) ethnic and gang affiliations are not significant factors and (b) all class members are united in the common goal of being educated. The result is that students of all backgrounds typically work together amicably, and they openly applaud one another's accomplishments. In response to such behavior, I often point out to the class that the friendly relationships that students form in the classroom should be viewed as a lesson about judging one another by the content of individuals' character and not by prejudicial stereotypes.

CLASS-MANAGEMENT PROBLEMS AND SOLUTIONS

The 13 classroom-management cases inspected in the following pages concern inmates' (a) violent behavior, (b) claims of illness, (c) lack of interest in studying, (d) absence from class, (e) stealing items from the classroom, (f) leaving class en masse, (g) awaiting test outcomes, (h) cheating on tests, and (i) over-familiarity. Four additional cases concern teachers' (j) introduction to prison life, (k) ways of conducting security searches, (l) forbidden gifts, and (m) seductive garb.

Violence

The problem. In a men's prison, when students were leaving the classroom at lunchtime, one of them, in a rush to get out the door, banged another inmate hard against the door jam. The one who had been bumped immediately turned to knock his assailant across the room, and a fight broke out between the pair.

Analysis. Violence between students is not a common occurrence in the typical prison classroom. But it may occur, so teachers need to be prepared. The following is the standard procedure followed in at least some California state prisons.

The most expedient method of summoning assistance is through the use of the instructor's Personal Alarm Device (PAD). All prison personnel who work with inmates inside the prison walls are required to wear the device attached to a waist-belt. Once the PAD is activated, it sets off an alarm sound. If the violence occurs in an office, dormitory, or classroom, a blue light flashes on the top of the building.

A second way to sound an alarm is to remove the telephone from its cradle position for an extended number of seconds. That sends a signal to the Central Control Office where personnel announce the emergency over the public-address system and direct responding custody-officers to the trouble spot.

A third method of summoning assistance is by the teacher blowing a whistle that all inner-institution employees must carry on a key ring or attached to an easily accessible article of clothing.

At the time a fight starts between inmates inside a building, the first step is for the staff member – such as a teacher – to give the combatants a direct order to stop fighting. Failure to obey that order is a serious rules violation that can result in disciplinary consequences. While giving the command to stop fighting, the teacher is expected to press the PAD and then leave the building to wait for security personnel (prison guards) to arrive, which normally takes from 30 to 60 seconds. Once the inmates involved in the fight have been taken into custody, the staff member – such as the teacher – is required to write a report documenting how the fight occurred, who appeared to be the initial aggressor, and what actions each inmate took during the fight. The report is then forwarded to the staff member's direct supervisor for review and is next sent to custody administrators who will use it during the prosecution of the offenders when they are brought before an adjudication committee.

Solution. In the present case, the teacher's response once the fight began was to activate her PAD and then to order the pair of combatants to stop fighting. She then stepped out of the classroom and began shouting for assistance. The first to arrive was the education officer (a guard assigned to the classroom complex) followed by two search-and-escort officers. Once the two inmates had been handcuffed and removed from the education complex, the teacher reentered the classroom and restored order. By that time, the academic vice-principal had arrived, and he recommended that the teacher dismiss the class for lunch so that she could recover emotionally and could begin outlining what had taken place. Afterwards, she wrote a formal incident report. As part of a standard procedure, the teacher received post-trauma counseling from a trained custody staff member to ensure the teacher was not suffering any psycho-emotional difficulties stemming from the episode.

A day later, while thinking about the altercation, the teacher remembered the inmates' tattoos and decided to contact the Institution Security Squad Gang Unit to inquire about the possible relevancy of the tattoos. The Gang-Unit coordinator estimated that the tattoos could have a bearing on the investigation of the incident, and he asked the teacher to write a supplementary report that would include the teacher's impressions of what the tattoos might imply about the relationship between the pair of combatants.

Too Ill to Attend Class?

The problem. A student reported to class and immediately told the teacher that he felt too ill to sit in the classroom and do his schoolwork.

He requested permission to return to his housing unit.

Analysis. Both federal and state prison systems issue manuals containing rules designed to regulate prisoners' behavior. For instance, California state prisons follow guidelines delineated in a document entitled *Director's Rules: Title 15.* One directive (*Rule 3041: Performance*) is used more than any other by teachers in coping with infractions by their students. The rule's *Subsection a* requires students to report on time to their place of assignment – whether that place be an institution job or an education program – and not to evade their obligation by feigning illness or using other illegitimate excuses. *Subsection d* of the same rule directly addresses students who are enrolled in school. The regulation states that students are to perform all required assignments and abide by teachers' directives.

Solutions. In order to verify the student's claim of illness, the teacher should contact the institution's medical department and request that the inmate's state of health be evaluated by a medical staff-member. If that evaluation verifies that the inmate is indeed sick, the inmate can be issued a medical-excuse document and not lose any of the early-parole credit that he would have earned through participating in his school assignment that day. The medical personnel must then telephone to the teacher, explaining the results of the examination and treatment. Or, instead of the information coming to the teacher by phone, the student may report to the classroom and show the medical excuse to the teacher prior to returning to his living area. In either case, it is prudent for the teacher to inform the student's housing officer to expect the student to return to the housing unit directly. By doing so, the teacher can release any liability relating to his or her inmate-supervisory responsibilities.

Obstinate Scholar

The problem. A female inmate who has just been enrolled in a primary-school-level class introduces herself to the teacher and declares that she has no interest in attending school.

Analysis. Once a prisoner is placed in an education program, she or he is obligated to accept the assignment. If she refuses to do so, disciplinary action will typically be taken. In the California penal system until 1990, participation in educational programs was voluntary. However, since that time, legislation has required all inmates to attain at least a minimum TABE score of 9.0 (ninth-grade level) in reading comprehension – a level that a large portion of the prison population has not reached. As a result, inmates who enter prison with TABE reading scores below 9.0 are placed on an education-assignment waiting list. As soon as space becomes available in a program suited to an inmate's apparent educational level, the individual is assigned to a classroom and required to stay in school until reaching at least the 9.0 level. An inmate's refusing to attend school is considered a serious rules infraction.

Solution. The teacher's first obligation in response to a newly enrolled student's resistance is to inform the inmate of the consequences she or he faces for declining to participate in a mandatory education assignment. Reluctant inmates in California prisons face such penalties as (a) losing up to 90 days of early-release-time credit, (b) being required to perform extra-duty work such as janitorial or waste-disposal services, (c) being confined to her or his housing unit for a period of time, (d) losing the opportunity to phone friends and family members, and (e) being denied access to the inmate convenience-item store.

If, after being counseled by the teacher about the wisdom of willingly performing class assignments, the inmate is still resistive, the teacher may contact the custody-officer in charge of supervising inmates in the education compound in order to have the inmate removed from the classroom so as to be interrogated by an educational or custody administrator.

In the event that the inmate cannot be convinced to attend school, the teacher is required to write a disciplinary report that explains the sequence of actions taken by both the inmate and the staff members involved in the incident. The report will be delivered to the teacher's supervisor for review, then forwarded to the inmate's housing-unit administrators. Finally, a disciplinary hearing determines the consequences the reluctant scholar must face.

Missing Persons

The Problem. When taking roll at the beginning of class, the instructor of an academic program noted that four students were absent.

Analysis. All employees in prisons, jails, and juvenile facilities are charged with protecting the safety of both the institution and the general public. Therefore, instructors must account for the whereabouts of all of their students during school hours. Should a teacher fail to promptly notify the appropriate authorities of a students' absence, the teacher could be held responsible in the event that a student commits a violent act or escapes from the facility. However, by following the required procedure, the teacher is protected from personal liability for actions of students who are outside the classroom.

Two documents from California state penal-institutions' regulations illustrate a typical system for tracking inmates' movement within a prison. One document is the Daily Movement Sheet (DMS), the other is the Master Ducat List. Both are distributed daily to all employees who supervise prisoners. The Daily Movement Sheet lists changes in inmates' housing units, work or training assignments, custody-level classifications, and arrivals to and departures from the institution. The Master Ducat List provides information about inmates' medical appointments, custody-related interviews, self-help and religious programs, and education-related activities, such as testing and evening literacy-tutoring sessions. A *ducat* is a notice or order issued in the form of a slip of paper directing an inmate to report to a specific location within the institution for such things as medical treatment, consultation with a custody official (like a case-worker), a new job assignment, participation in education testing, or to receive mail or packages sent from outside the prison.

Items on the ducat list are color-coded to indicate the level of importance of each type of ducat. Pink and blue ducats are issued for mandatory appointments, whereas white ones identify activities that are flexible and are not supposed to interfere with job or schooling hours. Almost all medical and custody appointments are considered mandatory, while such things as notification of the arrival of packages (from inmates' families or items that inmates have ordered from venders) are low priority and must be handled during non-work or non-schooling hours.

When students are absent from class, the teacher should consult the Daily Movement Sheet to ensure that none of the missing students have either been given an institution-assignment change or have been moved out of the prison to another location. Sometimes the instructor is already aware of a pending assignment switch (such as from an educational program to a job), but the DMS is often the most expedient source of information about such things as an inmate having been involved in violent or illegal activity during after-school hours and thus placed in disciplinary detention. In other cases, an inmate might have received an emergency transfer to another institution overnight or have suffered a medical complication and been hospitalized.

Most official movements of inmates are identified on the Master Ducat List. Prior to the time that students are to attend a ducat appointment, they are obligated to inform their schooling or job supervisor. However, many appointments take place before the school day starts, or inmates may be sent as emergency cases to the prison's medical facility via a special pass that will not be recorded on the ducat list. In such cases, the teacher can either call the education-complex custody-officer to assist in finding the missing student or else attempt to locate the inmate by making a series of telephone calls to places the missing student might be.

If the absent inmate is not listed on the Master Ducat List, and the instructor chooses to find the student personally, the first action to take is to phone the inmate's housing-unit officer to determine if the student has overslept, is intentionally evading school, or has been transferred to another location. The next logical step is to call medical personnel to find out if the inmate suffered a health emergency. If neither of these recourses is successful, the teacher is obligated to initiate a formal search by contacting the education-department's correctional officer and the inmate's housing-unit authorities.

Solution. In the case of the four missing students in our present problem, the teacher did the following. First, she checked the Daily Movement Sheet, where she found that one of the students had been placed on pre-parole status. Consequently, the man had been unassigned from school two weeks prior to his release from incarceration in order to provide time for prison officials to process essential paperwork.

Next, the teacher consulted the Master Ducat List and discovered that another of the missing class members had an early morning medical appointment, while a third student had been summoned to take the TABE (Test for Adult Basic Education) in the education testing center to update information about his reading, math, and language skills.

In trying to find the fourth student's whereabouts, the teacher phoned to the inmate's housing-unit officer and was told that the inmate was not in the unit. As a result, the teacher called the nearby education-department officer who used the public-address system to locate the student in the housing-unit exercise yard. The fellow confessed that he had cut class in order to improve his physical fitness.

Missing Materials

The problem. The teacher of an ABE1 (primary-grade-level) class walked to the back of the classroom and, when he returned to his desk, he noticed that his favorite pen was missing from where he had just recently placed it.

Analysis. Although theft is not a frequent problem, occasionally items belonging to the classroom, instructor, or students are stolen. Favorite targets of thieves are pens, paper, glue-sticks, rulers, textbooks (especially dictionaries), coffee cups, reading glasses, and such articles of students' clothing as jackets and hats.

There are numbers of things teachers can do to minimize theft in the classroom. When students first enroll, they can be informed of the classroom rules, including the consequences of being caught stealing. The issue can also be addressed in behavior contracts that all students are required to read and sign.

As a safeguard against thievery, instructors can keep particularly attractive supplies under lock-and-key. It is also wise to lock any personal or easily concealable stationery items inside a desk before moving about the classroom. Another useful procedure is to catalogue all textbooks so they can be assigned to specific students. In addition, students can be required to sign a contract in which they agree to pay – out of their institution bank account – for the loss of any borrowed classroom materials. For items not assigned to any particular student (such as dictionaries, thesauruses, and encyclopedias), a quick count of the books can be taken during both the morning and afternoon school sessions before students are released from class.

In the event that a theft does occur and the instructor notices it immediately, one way to respond is to address the class immediately after discovering that the item is missing and to request that it be returned promptly. In the process, the instructor might want to provide a grace period of a few minutes, during which the culprit can return the stolen article without being punished.

If the request to return the item fails, the instructor can first announce that no student can leave the classroom, then telephone for the education unit's correctional officer (the guard assigned to the education complex) and one or two search-and-escort officers. Once they arrive, it is best that they conduct a *clothed-body search* of all the students inside the classroom to prevent the possibility that the item could be disposed of easily if the search were conducted outdoors. As part of the search, the inmates may be required to remove their hats, coats, shoes, and socks. The officers will then perform the *pat-down* of all inmates and check their pockets. Once it is decided that none of the students have the missing item, they will be escorted from the classroom while it is searched.

In most cases, when the theft has been promptly noticed, the missing item is found through such a search process. However, if a few minutes have elapsed after the theft occurred, whatever was stolen may no longer be in the classroom, but might have been taken outside by someone who claimed to need a quick break to use the bathroom or to get some fresh air. Once the item has left the room, it can be hidden, then picked up later or passed to an inmate from another class.

If too much time has elapsed between the theft and the discovery of the item's loss, other measures may be attempted. As an example, unless regular checks are made of classroom materials, the disappearance of a dictionary might not be noticed until well after the book was taken. In such a case, the teacher can telephone to each student's dormitory officer and request a search of the inmate's cell or locker. When this procedure is used, it is a good idea not to alert the students and to have the living areas searched while the inmates are in the classroom so as to prevent a stolen item from being hidden elsewhere or passed to another prisoner. Also, in many prisons whose education compounds are enclosed by walls or fences, officials try to protect against theft of school materials by requiring that when students leave the compound they must pass through a metal detector and be subject to search by custody officers.

Another course of action an instructor can take is to impose sanctions on the entire class for a specified time period or until the missing item is returned. For instance, a teacher can suspend such valued events as the distribution of awards or the showing of instructional videos.

Sometimes, holding a discussion concerning morals and values can be helpful in shaming individuals into giving back something they have stolen. One way this can be done is to compare the act of theft to a show of disrespect for the teacher and members of the class. The analogy can appeal to the inmates' own code of honor which makes disrespecting one another a serious transgression that can result in violent retaliation as punishment. It is also beneficial for the instructor to emphasize that it is not the value of the stolen article that is so important but, rather, taking what does not belong to you is the key issue.

Solution. In the present case, the ABE1 instructor noticed that his pen was missing only a few minutes after the theft had occurred, so he was fairly certain that the pen was still in the classroom, or at least somewhere in the education compound. As a result, he confronted the entire class and chose to give the thief an opportunity to return the pen immediately without being disciplined. However, the instructor also explained that he considered the theft to be an act of personal disrespect, so he threatened to postpone distributing weekly performance awards to class members for at least one month unless the pen was returned. He also used the opportunity to associate the act with the reason that people end up in prison and to discuss how failing to correct the behavior was an indication that the thief had not learned his lesson about breaking laws. After this speech, the instructor directed the class to begin their reading assignment, and he sat down at his desk to grade some students' papers. Within a few minutes, one of the inmate teacher-assistants approached the instructor and handed over the missing pen, but he did not identify who had taken it. That ended the missing-pen incident.

Mass Exodus

The problem. After an English-as-a-Second-Language (ESL) class of 25 men of Latin American descent reconvened following the midday lunch break, a 38-year-old inmate stood up and confronted the 62-year-old, non-Spanish-speaking female instructor who was of Anglo ancestry. The 38-year-old spokesman loudly stated that the class members were tired of being treated like children and not allowed to speak a word of Spanish without threat of punishment. Once the speaker had concluded his pronouncement, all of the students walked out of classroom in protest and stood in the education-department compound's outdoor-break area.

Analysis. Many prison ESL instructors do not speak Spanish fluently, if at all, and they are not of Hispanic heritage. On the other hand, most students in such classes speak Spanish as their primary language since they are immigrants from Mexico and Central and South America. As a result, a communication barrier exists between the instructor and the students. Such students often benefit from hearing English words they are learning spoken both in English and in the words' Spanish equivalents. So there are defensible pedagogical reasons for some Spanish to be used in ESL classrooms.

But what about the inmates' method of advertising their grievances? Regardless of the their justification for walking out of class, inmates are not permitted to behave insubordinately towards prison personnel. Openly inciting others to demonstrate against a staff member, such as an instructor, is considered a serious rules violation. When such incidents occur, the staff member's immediate supervisor is called on to solve the problem through mediation.

Solution. In response to the actions of her students, the ESL teacher first telephoned the education-department's custody officer and then the academic vice-principal to inform them of what had taken place. The officer and vice-principal reacted by going to the education-department's compound where the students had congregated, and they addressed the group. The inmates were warned to return to the classroom or face punishment. They were also informed that walking out of class was inappropriate. Any complaints they wished to express should have been registered on an official inmate-grievance form and sent through the proper administrative channels. The confrontation ended by the students agreeing to go back to the classroom and to behave properly.

The spokesman who had instigated the walkout was detained by the custody officer for further questioning in the vice-principal's office. During the discussion, the inmate stated that the teacher was often unreasonable and arbitrarily harsh in her treatment of students. Additionally, he explained that the students needed to speak to each other in Spanish in order to better understand the content of lessons they were given. The vice-principal then informed the inmate that the matter would be investigated further, but that the rebellious walkout could not be overlooked and the inmate would be cited for a serious rules violation.

At the end of the day, the vice-principal summoned the ESL teacher to his office and discussed the episode. He directed the teacher to permit her students to use Spanish in the classroom when working on assignments. In order to further facilitate communication within the class, the vice-principal asked the instructor to hire a Spanish-speaking teaching assistant.

Awaiting Test Outcomes

The problem. Eight of the 22 members of a class that was intended to prepare students for the General-Educational-Development tests took the test battery, but it would be two weeks before the results would arrive from the test-evaluation center. Meanwhile, most of the test-takers felt fairly confident that they had passed and thus were now not interested in studying further until they were sure of their tests' outcome. Thus, they became a nuisance, disrupting the class by chatting idly, paying little attention to lecture and discussion sessions, and devoting little or no effort to completing assignments.

Analysis. Once students have taken the GED test series, many become uninterested in studying until they find out how well they succeeded. As a result, they lack focus and behave in ways that are detrimental to the classroom learning environment. One option instructors have for responding to the problem is to demand that the learners complete assigned work or face disciplinary consequences. Another option is to allow such students to entertain themselves quietly in the classroom by reading novels or researching topics of interest in the class's encyclopedias. A third choice is to release them to activities outside the class until the test results arrive. A fourth possibility is to have them officially unassigned from the class, then later reassigned to the class if it turns out that they did not pass the entire GED battery.

Solution. In this case, when the eight students returned from taking the test series, the instructor interviewed them to learn their estimates of how well they had done. Four were very confident that they had passed the entire battery, an impression which was supported by the high scores they had earned earlier on practice tests in class. As a result, the four agreed with the teacher that they should be dropped from the program, with the understanding that if they had failed any of the tests they would enroll in a voluntary-participation class designed to assist students who needed to improve in only one or two subject areas. Two other students were fairly sure that they had passed some of the tests, but they were uncertain about the rest, especially the mathematics exam. Therefore, they opted to go to the education department's library where tutors were available to help them in the studies they thought they had failed. The final two students believed they had failed most of the tests and decided to stay in the classroom to resume working in all subject areas.

Cheating on Tests

The problem. The female teacher in charge of an ABE2 (upper-elementary) class was concerned that some of the students were cheating on mathematics tests, so she wanted to develop safeguards against the cheating methods students were using.

Analysis. The possibility that an inmate might try to cheat on a test or in completing written assignments is an issue all teachers face. Common cheat-methods include (a) secreting written notes in clothing, taped on the back of a classmate's desk-chair, or in a waste-paper receptacle; (b) writing information on the desk-top or on such a body part as the arm or hand; (c) copying answers from another student's test, workbook assignment, or workbook answer-key; and (d) bribing or threatening a teacher assistant who grades tests or written assignments.

There are a number of ways instructors can make it more difficult for students to cheat. First, it is important that the teacher stay focused on students during the administration of a test rather than sitting at a desk to work on other matters. It is also wise for the instructor to walk around the classroom, observing students' eye and hand movements and looking for cheat-notes and students' attempts to copy from a classmate's paper. In addition, for students who have been suspected of copying others' work, the teacher can analyze their exams and written assignments to identify similarities in the content and style of classmates' tests and writings.

Another method of discouraging cheating on exams is to prepare two or more versions of the same test and then inform the test-takers that more than one form of the test was being distributed. Additionally, a student who may have cheated on a test can be individually retested under the instructor's direct supervision. Furthermore, if it appears that a student has been copying answers from the answer key for a workbook, the key can be confiscated and the assignment scored by the teacher or teacher's aide while the student is in the classroom.

As an alternative approach, the instructor can remove unit tests and answer-keys from students' self-paced-learning workbooks, such as tests for mathematics and language-skills instruction. The tests can then be administered to students while they are supervised in the classroom. This strategy can be used to help verify whether students are actually studying the content of workbook lessons and to more accurately identify true learning gains.

It is also important to recognize that what constitutes cheating can differ from one subgroup of society to another. In other words, ideas about "cheating" have cultural overtones. Students don't always interpret their "helping" a friend as "cheating." The teacher could address this issue by discussing the difference between (a) a "street culture" whose rules they may have adopted prior to coming to prison and (b) the classroom culture in which they are expected to reveal their own skills and knowledge on tests and assignments. In effect, the instructor makes clear to students when it is acceptable to help one another and when it is not. And when inmate-teacher-aides have surreptitiously falsified students' test records or provided inmates answers to assignments, such assistants can be warned to expect disciplinary consequences, such as being fired from the job.

Solution. In order to make it harder for students to cheat on a fractions-computation test, the teacher distributed one version of the test to the students seated in even-numbered rows and a second version to those seated in odd-numbered rows. She also walked around the classroom during the test. As a final measure, she announced her suspicion that cheating might be taking place, and she reminded the students that they were only hurting themselves if they did not make an honest effort to complete assignments and take tests the legitimate way.

Over-Familiarity

The problem. The female instructor of an Adult-Basic-Education class in a male prison received an anonymous note making comments about the teacher's attractiveness, and the note included requests for sexual favors.

Analysis. Instructors working in a prison can expect to deal with situations of this nature at some point during their careers. There are strict rules governing the interactions between staff and inmates. This suggestive-note situation is considered a serious rules violation and should not be taken lightly. If the inmate is identifiable, disciplinary consequences can include removing him from the program, credit loss, and time in an administrative-segregation housing unit. In the case of an anonymous note, not much can be done. However, the event should serve to remind the instructor to be aware of his/her surroundings and to be careful to establish clear boundaries when interacting with inmates. The instructor may also want to be cautious of inmates who want to talk before class or stay in the area after the class is dismissed. In all cases, the instructor's supervising administrator and custody officers should be made aware of the event.

Solution. In this case of an anonymous note, the teacher informed her supervisor and the custody office. She recognized that she should be more aware of the actions of students assigned to her class and of other inmates in the education complex, paying close attention to those who tended to linger or desire her attention.

New Teacher's Orientation

The problem. A newly hired instructor in a state prison is unaware of the policies and procedures she must follow and of how to properly interact with the inmates whom she will be teaching.

Analysis. Every employee in a correctional institution is, above all else, charged with protecting the security of the prison, its personnel, and the public at large. In order to fulfill this responsibility, employees who work directly with inmates must be aware of inmates' behavior tendencies and of rules bearing on inmate/staff interactions. Therefore, penal institutions typically require their staff members to participate in formal training sessions periodically throughout their careers.

The most extensive training is provided immediately after an employee has been hired. The newcomer must attend a series of classes that impart essential information. The sessions are normally conducted in classroom settings by custody officers and ancillary staff members. Among the topics presented are: general safety and security procedures; ways to react to inmate escape attempts and confrontations with staff members; inmate gang activity; inmates' psychological profiles; first-aid instruction; and appropriate relationships between inmates and staff as well as among staff members. In addition to the training sessions, new employees normally tour the institution's facilities, including administrative offices, medical department, custody-operations offices, education services, industries, and inmate-housing areas.

Upon completing the institution's employee-training program, a new instructor may be asked to spend time visiting classrooms, (a) observing teachers' methods of instruction and classroom management and (b) discussing policies and procedures with veteran teachers and administrators. Following this period of orientation, the novice instructor will be assigned a classroom and begin teaching.

Solution. The newly hired prison teacher began a two-week training process on the first day that she reported for work. During the first week, she completed the series of classes for new employees, then spent the second week visiting classrooms and receiving information that was directly related to the education program and her daily activities as an instructor.

Security Search

The problem. A new teacher in a prison was informed that he must conduct a security search of his classroom at the end of each day. However, since he had never performed a search, he was unsure about how to go about it.

Analysis. Prison inmates often hide contraband items – drugs, homemade tattooing devices, weapons – where the items cannot be directly linked to specific inmates if the items are discovered. The school classroom is a logical choice for concealing goods, especially if students believe the teacher is not security-minded. But, by teachers conducting regular inspections of their classroom, the problem of concealing contraband there can be minimized.

Typical hiding places in a classroom include desks, shelves, cabinets, false compartments in books, waste containers, electrical wall-sockets, overhead light fixtures, and areas inside the walls, ceiling, or floor. Inmates also secrete materials outside the classroom in flowerbeds, beneath the building, or in crevices or behind loose boards in the building.

Among the tools that can be used during searches are a hand-mirror (especially one attached to a three-foot handle), a probing instrument (such as a screwdriver), and a pair of latex gloves to protect hands from injury. A mirror can be used to more easily inspect the undersides of desktops and areas too low or too high to be readily viewed. The probing instrument can serve for prying open loose wall fixtures or places where the classroom structure may have been altered to create a hiding place. The latex gloves protect the searcher from scratches and harmful microorganisms.

It is prudent to search a classroom when students are not there. It is also wise to conduct the inspection methodically by choosing a starting place and systematically advancing from there to a selected end point. For example, all desks in one row can be searched prior to checking those in a second row. Wall shelves can be inspected one at a time.

Preventive measures can be utilized to discourage students from hiding illegal items in the classroom. First, the teacher can inform the students that the classroom is searched regularly. Second, classroom materials can be stored consistently in designated places, so the teacher at the close of the school day can readily see whether items that were there at the beginning of the day are in their proper place. Third, it is a good idea to keep all file and storage cabinets locked, opening them only when specific contents are needed. Finally, an instructor can ask personnel from the prison's Security-and-Investigation Unit to perform periodic searches of the classroom and surrounding area, using such tools as metal detectors.

Solution. To instruct the new teacher in proper search procedures, the academic vice-principal enrolled him in an in-service training class taught by a custody official. The vice-principal also discussed and demonstrated search methods in the teacher's classroom. The teacher then began applying what he had learned when completing mandatory daily searches that he reported in search-logs submitted to the vice-principal at the end of each month.

Forbidden Gifts

The problem. As a way of thanking the teacher for helping him succeed in an ABE1 (primary-grade-level) class, a male student presented the female instructor with a wind-chime that he had constructed out of scrap metal procured from another inmate who was enrolled in a vocational sheet-metal program.

Analysis. Any attempt by an inmate and an employee in a penal institution to exchange gifts and gratuities constitutes and act of over-familiarization and is thereby illegal. Whether a student's gift is a piece of fruit, a flower, a greeting card, or a hand-crafted item, the student risks punishment – having the period of incarceration lengthened, losing early-release-time credit, being placed in a disciplinary housing unit, or being transferred to another penal setting. In addition, classroom instructors caught in transactions with their students can be dismissed from their jobs or can face legal action in a civil court if such contraband as drugs was involved.

Most attempts by students to give presents to their instructors are well-meaning. However, in some cases the motive may be to persuade an instructor to engage in a personal relationship or to import illicit materials into the prison – an act referred to as *becoming a mule*. New employees are perceived by inmates as especially vulnerable to manipulation. Students often test a new teacher by politely requesting that the teacher provide them with postage stamps or any number of inexpensive items. In the deal-making process, the inmate may try to play on the teacher's emotions by claiming to be indigent and to receive no assistance from family members or, perhaps, by claiming to be forced to choose between going to school and getting a job within the penal institution in order to earn enough money "to make ends meet."

An instructor who does comply with a student's request may find himself or herself falling into the first stages of a trap in which the inmate's demands become progressively more substantial. At first, the student may appear friendly and seek sympathy, but over time may threaten to report the instructor's misconduct unless the instructor continues to provide what is requested. Ultimately, the inmate may seek sexual favors, money, or the service of the teacher as the link between the prisoner and people outside the prison who will furnish drugs and other materials to be transported into the institution by the teacher.

The best method for instructors to avoid undue-familiarity problems is to explain very clearly to students the institution's policy about giving and receiving gifts. This can be done through discussing the matter with the class, including the rule in the classroom behavior contract that all students must sign, and documenting and reporting any attempted transaction to both the education administration and custody officials. Due to the sensitivity of the issue, it is also wise for a teacher to consult the institution's regulations regarding gifts and to acquire approval from a supervisor prior to spending personal money to purchase learning materials such as pens, pencils, and paper that are to be distributed to students.

Solution. In response to the student's attempt to present her with the wind-chime, the teacher remarked that the gesture was most thoughtful, but she politely declined to accept the gift. She also counseled the inmate regarding the rules against the giving of gifts between staff members and inmates. She then wrote a report of the incident that she submitted to the education department's vice-principal. The inmate was later summoned to the department office to be counseled by both the vice-principal and the department's custody officer to ensure that the inmate was fully aware of the consequences of offering gifts in the future.

Seductive Garb

The problem. An attractive female teacher in a juvenile male correctional facility arrived at work one day wearing a semi-see-through, low-cut blouse, a short skirt, and high heels.

Analysis. Convicted criminals who are incarcerated are deprived of any contact with members of the opposite sex, other than those who work at the correctional facility and family members who occasionally visit. As a result, prisoners often become sexually frustrated, and it is important that employees are aware of the effect they have on inmates, including anything they might do that could be interpreted as provocative. Specifically, those who work in institutions are expected to be conscious of what they say, how they act, and what they wear. Accordingly, many penal institutions have a written dress code in which facility workers are warned against wearing closefitting attire, low-cut shirts and blouses, and transparent or semi-transparent garments.

Solution. As the instructor in this case was signing-in at the beginning of the workday, the academic vice-principal noticed how the woman was dressed and summoned her into his office. He produced a memorandum delineating the institution dress code and explained why the instructor's garb was inappropriate. The instructor was sent home to change into suitable clothing.

Chapter 7

SPECIFYING LEARNING GOALS

The teaching process can usefully be compared to taking a trip, as guided by three questions:

- Where should we go?
- How can we best get there?
- How can we determine how close we have come to the intended destination?

For teachers, the first of these questions concerns the learning goals students are expected to pursue (the present chapter). The second question involves the methods and materials for pursuing those goals (Chapters 8 and 9). The third concerns ways to assess how well students have learned (Chapter 10).

Chapter 7 is divided into two sections – (a) the nature of objectives and (b) problems and proposed solutions.

THE NATURE OF OBJECTIVES

Throughout this book the terms goals, aims, and objectives are used as synonyms. Four important characteristics of objectives are their sources, whether they are explicit or implicit, their levels of specificity, and their focus.

Sources of Objectives

Proposals about what students should learn can come from a variety of sources – federal and state legislatures, the U.S. Department of

Education, state departments of education, professional associations, textbook authors, local school boards, school-district curriculum committees, individual schools' faculties, and individual classroom teachers. The following examples illustrate the sorts of correctional-education objectives that may come from different sources and represent different levels of specificity.

The Source	An Objective
State legislature	Study American history
State Department of Education	Study U.S. Government structure
School District Curriculum Committee	Study U.S. Constitution
Classroom teacher	Analyze the Bill of Rights

Explicit and Implicit Objectives

Explicit objectives are the ones specified in a school's course of study. Implicit objectives are not stated but, instead, are ones that teachers infer from two sources.

First, the objectives issued in a curriculum guidebook or textbook can be at different levels of specificity. When a more general objective has not been decomposed into its constituent specific aims, it becomes the instructor's task to imagine what those specific aims would be, then compose lessons directed at those outcomes. Such would be a teacher's job when devising lessons aimed at the following more general goals.

As a result of their lessons, the students:

- Use proper verb forms in their speaking and writing.
- Add and subtract accurately.
- Cite reasons for the outbreak of World War II.
- Adopt constructive health practices.

A second source of implied objectives is the culture in which the education system operates. These aims are the rules of conduct generally accepted in the particular society. Such objectives can be either behaviors that students are expected to adopt in the classroom (the *do's*) or behaviors they are to avoid (the *don'ts*). Teachers are expected to abide by the same rules. By way of illustration, consider examples of implicit positive actions. Do:

- Apply your best effort to your studies.
- Speak politely to the teacher and classmates.
- Raise your hand to receive your turn to speak during class

discussions.
- Compliment classmate on their successes.

Next are examples of implicit actions to avoid. Don't:

- Copy classmates' work and pretend it's your own work.
- Cheat on tests.
- Fight with classmates, either physically or verbally.
- Utter curses, such as *God damnit-to-hell* or *Jesus Christ Almighty.*
- Use coarse language, such as *shit, f--k,* or *pissed off.*
- Use denigrating ethnic epithets, such as *nigger, sheeny, wop, dago, spic.*
- Ridicule classmates or the teacher.
- Spit on the floor.
- Mark on a desk or on walls with pen, pencil, paintbrush, or knife.
- Steal or damage other people's property, including classroom supplies and equipment.

In summary, a significant portion of teachers' time usually is spent implementing implicit objectives – ones not included in the printed course of study. Such objectives can differ somewhat from one classroom to another, as different teachers can hold different implied standards. Furthermore, inmates may be unaware of classroom rules of behavior because their own social backgrounds differ from the teacher's, as in cases of prohibited cursing, coarse language, and ethnic epithets. Therefore, conflicts can arise in correctional-education classrooms over which implicit objectives are proper ones to include.

The Specificity of Objectives

As noted above, learning goals appear at different levels of specificity. This can be illustrated with the very general objective "The learner solves mathematics problems accurately." This is a typical level of a goal identified by legislatures for their state's schools. The state's department of education may carry that aim to a more specific level by identifying the intended kinds of mathematical problems, such as (a) arithmetic, (b) algebra, (c) geometry, and (d) statistical analysis. School districts' curriculum committees then cast those kinds into more specific mathematical functions. For instance, skills under the category *arithmetic* become those of adding, subtracting, multiplying, and dividing whole numbers, fractions, and mixed numbers. Next, textbook authors dissect such functions into constituent skills, so the category "adding whole numbers" includes one-column problems, two-column (double-digit) problems without carrying, two-column problems with carrying, and more.

So it is that school systems and textbook authors furnish teachers objectives at different levels of specificity. Teachers are then obliged to devise lessons aimed at the most specific level, with the lessons focusing on the very detailed skills and knowledge that learners are expected to master. In effect, classroom teachers are the people who ultimately decide the exact objectives that students pursue.

The Focus of Objectives

Probably the most common foci of statements of goals are the topic, the question, the teacher, and the student. The way these four differ is illustrated in the following samples of a social-studies goal that might be labeled "the skill of identifying people's prejudices about ethnic groups."

- *Topic*: "Identification of prejudice in people's statements about ethnic groups."
- *Question*: "How do people reveal their prejudices in what they say about ethnic groups?"
- *Teacher*: "To teach the ways people reveal their prejudices in what they say about ethnic groups."
- *Student* or *learner*: "The student identifies ways people's prejudices are shown in what they say about ethnic groups."

Teachers often apparently believe the way objectives are phrased doesn't matter – that instruction will yield the same results with any of the four foci. But our own experience suggests otherwise. Because the aim of education is to improve the learner's knowledge and skills, the most suitable target of objectives is the learner – how learners act in order to show how well they have reached the goal. For instance, if the goal of a class session is stated as the instructor's intent "To teach how to divide fractions," then, following the session, the instructor can attest that the goal was reached because he or she had, indeed, demonstrated how to divide fractions. However, if the goal is "Following this lesson, the students accurately divide fractions," then the instructor does not assume the objective was achieved until the students have demonstrated in their workbooks or on a test how accurately they divide fractions.

In summary, we endorse the practice of stating teaching goals in terms of observable student behaviors because we believe such a form helps ensure that teachers focus on improvements in students' knowledge and skills rather than on how the instructor presented information to the class.

A particular advantage of the student-behavior form of objectives is the guidance it offers about ways to evaluate how well students have achieved the objectives. Consider, for example, the assessment methods implied in the statements of objectives in Table 7.1.

LEARNING-GOALS PROBLEMS AND SOLUTIONS

The eight problems in the following section concern (a) changing inmates' attitudes, (b) objectives and learning speeds, (c) starting from the learner's present position, (d) competing against oneself, (e) converting general objectives into specific lesson objectives, (f) coping with objectives overload, (g) avoiding prohibited aims, and (h) selecting spelling words.

Attitude Change

The Problem. An offender, sent to prison for safecracking, enrolled in a correctional-education class where he learned to divide fractions, to spell lists of words, and write in complete sentences, but he did not change his attitude about breaking the law. When released on parole, he would be better-educated, but still might return to his criminal life style of opening other people's safes.

Analysis. Some critics have faulted correctional-education programs whose goals focus exclusively on skills and factual information to the neglect of inmates' ways of understanding and interacting with other individuals and society in general. In their book *Time to Think: A Cognitive Model of Crime and Delinquency Prevention and Offender Rehabilitation* (1985), Ross and Fabiano analyzed research reports of the connection between the nature of correctional programs and recidivism. Among the 50 programs studied, 34 were labeled *non-cognitive*, in the sense of focusing entirely on academic or vocational skills and facts. The remaining 16 were called *cognitive*, in that they included attitude-change objectives. When the two program types were com-

Table 7.1

Evaluation Methods for Student-Focused Objectives

Objectives	*Evaluation Methods*
As a result of their studies, the students:	
English Language	
Spell words correctly.	Written test, essay
Punctuate sentences correctly.	Written test, essay
Pronounce words correctly.	Observe student's oral responses
Mathematics	
Convert fractions to decimals accurately.	Written test
Identify geometric figures.	Written test
Add quantities mentally.	Oral quiz
Science	
Explain the meanings of *atom, molecule, cell.*	Written or oral test
Convert Fahrenheit figures to Centigrade.	Written test
Social Studies	
Identify the meanings of *latitude, longitude, equator,* and *time zone.*	Written test
Do a fair share of the work on small-group projects.	Observe group, report from group leader
Offer reasonable estimates of causes of the American Civil War.	Written test, oral quiz

pared in terms of how successfully they reduced recidivism, 15 (94%) of the *cognitive* programs were judged effective and 1 (6%) deemed ineffective. In contrast, 10 (29%) of the *non-cognitive* were judged effective and 24 (71%) ineffective (Zaro, 2007, p. 29).

Solutions. Efforts to correct this program weakness involve (a) adopting specific objectives aimed at improving students' attitudes about how to conduct their lives successfully without breaking the law and (b) then developing lessons designed to promote attitude change. The following are examples of potential objectives.

As a result of the class's learning activities, inmates:

- More often accept responsibility for the results of their actions than they had in the past.
- Express anger in ways that are less destructive (for self and others) than in the past.
- React to frustration in more controlled, thoughtful ways than in the past.

- Express greater empathy and sympathy for the plight of others than they had in the past.

To illustrate the use of such objectives, Zaro (2007) has described lessons in which an instructor directs class members to write responses to a series of questions that the instructor poses — questions requiring students to analyze their attitudes about responsibility, anger management, impulse control, and empathy under various life situations. The intent is to have inmates carefully consider how they have thought and acted in such situations in the past and how they might act more constructively under similar conditions in the future.

If the officially assigned learning objectives for a class fail to include attitude-improvement goals, instructors may wish to add such objectives to those of the established curriculum.

Objectives and Learning Speeds

The problem. The women in a prison food-preparation course were assigned to read a 28-page textbook chapter titled *Nutritious Meals*. The objectives of the assignment were reflected in the following directions given to the class at the outset of the activity.

> After reading the chapter, you should:
> 1. Write the meaning of each of these words or phrases: *calories, empty calories, proteins, fats, carbohydrates, vitamins, minerals, percent of daily value.*
> 2. Write a menu for one breakfast, one lunch, and one dinner.
> 3. For each food that you included on the menu, explain why that food would contribute to good health.

From past experience, the instructor could predict that some students would finish the assignment far sooner than others. She thus faced the problem of what to do with the faster readers once they had completed their assignment.

Analysis. In every classroom some students master the learning objectives faster than others do. Therefore, if all students are to use their time profitably, teachers need instructional methods that enable the faster learners to work on new learning goals while their classmates are still working on earlier ones. To care for the slowest learners, remedial measures may be needed to prevent them from falling far behind the bulk of their classmates.

There are two main ways to care for the faster learners — *acceleration* and *enrichment*. The acceleration method moves the faster learners to the next set of objectives that the bulk of the class will soon be pursuing. For example, if students are learning to add two-column figures without carrying, the learners who quickly master the skill can move immediately ahead to work on two-column addition that involves carrying. But the trouble with acceleration is that the faster learners keep get farther and farther ahead of their classmates, a condition that teachers find difficult to handle since pupils – now strung out along the sequence of arithmetic objectives – need the teacher to explain how to approach each new objective in the sequence. In effect, acceleration makes it difficult for the instructor ever to teach the class as a group. Instead, the teacher must tutor pupils individually or in small groups.

In contrast to acceleration, the enrichment approach enables students who master the current objectives sooner than their classmates to pursue supplementary objectives that the average-speed or slower learners are not expected to pursue. For example, while most members of an arithmetic class are still working on two-column addition without carrying, the ones who already mastered that skill can be given simple math puzzles to figure out. Or, for a class in reading, the faster learners can be assigned supplementary books to expand their range of interests and vocabularies while their classmates are still working in the basic reading textbook. Thus, the more adept readers will use their time profitably until all class members – or at least the great majority – are ready for the next section of the basic textbook. At that point, the entire class can start the next section together.

Enrichment activities can be closely related to the original class assignment or can involve an entirely different field of interest. For instance, students who quickly finish reading about ways to invest money can then be assigned a workbook exercise in how to prepare a personal budget. Or, instead of the budget task, they can study material unrelated to finance, such as a booklet about how to draw pen-and-ink sketches or a book chapter about how to predict changes in weather.

Solution. For the food-preparation class, the instructor had clipped pictures of meals from magazines and had arranged the pictures in pairs. A student who finished the basic reading assignment early was given one pair of pictures and asked to describe in writing which of the two meals was the more nutritious and why. If the student completed that task before the rest of the class had finished the original reading assignment, the instructor gave the student a second pair of meals to evaluate, and so on. Thus, each member of the class was able to spend her time productively until the slowest workers had completed the initial reading task.

Starting from the Learner's Present Position

The problem. The instructor of a GED (senior-high-level) class chose to use the first period of the day to teach a health lesson, the second period to teach English-language usage, and the third period to teach math. The question he faced was whether he should teach the class as a single group (whole-class instruction) or use small groups or individualized instruction.

The objectives for the three lessons were as follows.

As a result of the health lesson, students will
- Define AIDS and HIV, their symptoms, and how they are contracted.
- Describe the history and incidence of AIDS in Africa, important social consequences of AIDS in Africa, and the success of efforts to control the disease.

As a result of the English-language lesson, students will
- Identify and correct faulty capitalization and punctuation in business letters.

As a result of the math lesson, students will
- Improve in mathematical computation involving whole numbers, decimals, fractions, integers, and percents.
- Improve their skills of estimating, measuring, analyzing data, statistical analysis, and pre-algebra problem solving.

Analysis. A widely accepted principle of instruction (though often neglected in practice) is this: The learning objectives a student is currently expected to pursue are ones (a) for which the student has proper foundational knowledge and skills and (b) which the student has not already mastered.

The (*a*) part of the principle derives from the fact that in most subject-matter areas, the learning process is sequential. Whether students can learn something new depends on how well they have mastered previous knowledge and skills on which the new learning is based. Learning to add fractions depends on already knowing how to add whole numbers. Learning to compose a letter on a computer depends on already knowing the meaning of such terms as *format, font, edit, document, spell checker,* and *save.* Understanding reasons for the War of 1812 depends on already knowing causes and outcomes of the American Revolution. Understanding why the flashlight battery "went dead" is founded on already knowing the meanings of *electrons, terminals,* and *resistance.*

The (*b*) part of the principle is concerned with economizing students' time and effort. If learners have already mastered an objective, they should not be forced to waste time studying it over and over again. Instead, their time should be used to extend their education by pursuing additional knowledge and skills.

In order to apply such an instructional principle, a teacher needs to know (*a*) what previous knowledge and skills are needed for students to succeed with the objectives of an upcoming lesson and (b) how well class members command that knowledge and skill. In schoolrooms outside of correctional institutions, teachers usually offer lessons for which earlier lessons provided the foundation needed for students to understand the later lessons. Consequently, teachers can – with some measure of confidence – assume in December that most, if not all, of the class members will have learned in October and November the foundations of what is to be studied in December. But, as explained throughout this book, such an assumption is unreasonable in correctional settings where new students can arrive at any time during the school year.

Now consider the connection between students' knowledge/skill background and such instructional approaches as whole-class, small-group, and individualized methods.

Whole-class instruction (lecture, demonstration, discussion) works best when the class's members are much alike in their command of background knowledge and are equally ignorant in terms of the objectives at which the new lesson is aimed. In other words, all class members are properly ready for attacking the new objectives. The advantages of whole-class teaching is that such an approach (a) makes economical use of the instructor's time and energy, (b) limits lesson planning to one lesson rather than several plans for multiple groups, and (c) simplifies classroom management, since directing a one-ring circus is usually an easier task than directing a three- or four-ring circus.

Small-group instruction (dividing the class into groups – perhaps three or four) works best when groups of students differ in their readiness for pursuing particular objectives. Grouping learners in terms of their knowledge and skill backgrounds helps prevent (a) overwhelming those students who lack a proper foundation and (b) boring those who have already mastered the objectives of the upcoming lesson. However, dividing up the class requires that each group has a separate lesson plan and suitable instructor or leader.

The great advantage of individualized instruction (every student working independently or perhaps a pair of students working together) is that the objectives to be pursued can be suited to each individual's present knowledge and skill level. However, individualized instruction does not work well if many students need an instructor's help with their learning tasks. Under such a condition, learners can waste a good deal of time and suffer frustration if they must wait a long time for help.

If instructors are to make a wise decision about how to organize the class for a lesson (whole-class, small-group, or individualized), they need a way to estimate students' present command of (a) preparatory knowledge and skills and (b) the objectives of the upcoming lesson. Typically that estimate is based on students' past performance tests, written assignments, and oral responses in class discussions and question/answer sessions.

However, in correctional settings, instructors often lack such evidence because the membership of their classes can change so often. In effect, instructors have had little or no experience working with students who recently enrolled. In such cases, the instructor can profit from reviewing the scores that newly arrived inmates earned on the tests that determined the grade-level class to which they were assigned. As noted in Chapter 5, the test battery most often used nationwide for grade placement is the *Test of Adult Basic Education* (TABE), which not only reports a total score for each test in the series (reading, math computation, applied math, English language usage, vocabulary, language mechanics, and spelling) but also reports the percentage of items a student has answered correctly within each subpart of a test. For example, the six subparts of the language-usage test are (a) general usage, (b) sentence formation, (c) paragraph development, (d) capitalization, (e) punctuation, and (f) writing conventions. Thus, an instructor can estimate from the subpart scores the extent to which a student has mastered the objectives comprising each subpart.

Solution. In the GED class, the instructor decided to teach the health lesson (AIDS and Africa) by the whole-class method, to teach the English-language lesson (capitalization, punctuation) in small groups, and to teach the math lesson through individualization. He arrived at this decision through the following line of reasoning.

The health lesson. From students' earlier casual comments in class, the instructor judged that many of them knew something about AIDS but that their information was not very accurate. He imagined that no class member knew much about AIDS in Africa. Therefore, he concluded that the students were about equal in both (a) the background knowledge needed to pursue the health lesson's objectives and (b) lack of accurate knowledge about the objectives of the lesson. Hence, teaching the entire class as a whole by means of an illustrated lecture/discussion seemed appropriate.

The English-language lesson. Sixteen of the 27 students had been in the class several months, so they had studied capitalization and punctuation before. With few exceptions, they were now well schooled in identifying and correcting capitalization and punctuation errors. The other 11 students were more recent arrivals. Three of the 11 had scored above 50% but below 80% in capitalization and punctuation on the TABE. The remaining eight had scored well below 50%.

The instructor decided to divide the class into three groups. He would teach the 16 who were already adept at capitalizing and punctuation. The materials for the lesson were five business letters that involved subtle, debatable capitalization and punctuation issues, and particularly the use of commas. Group members were challenged to propose, and support with a line of argument, how those issues should be settled.

The second group consisted of three students who, under the guidance of an inmate teaching assistant, would be assigned to identify and correct errors in three business letters.

The third group of eight inmates would study basic capitalization and punctuation rules under the tutelage of a second teaching assistant. Armed with a page of rules, the students' were to go through a business letter, line by line, and judge the accuracy of capitals and punctuation by citing the appropriate rule for each instance they identified.

The math lesson. We may recall that the objectives were as follows:

As a result of the math lesson, students will:

- Improve in mathematical computation involving whole numbers, decimals, fractions, integers, and percents.
- Improve their skills of estimating, measuring, analyzing data, statistical analysis, and pre-algebra problem solving.

The aims of the lesson were cast in such an all-encompassing manner because the instructor realized that there was a vast difference among class members in their mathematical skills. Some students were still having trouble multiplying and dividing decimals. Others could calculate with decimals but struggled with fractions. Still others calculated accurately but were not adept at estimating results and measuring. And some could calculate, estimate, and measure but were puzzled by statistics. These differences among class members were identified by the instructor from the students' past performance on class tests and assignments and from recent arrivals' scores in the 15 math subparts of the TABE.

Thus, the math lesson was individualized to suit each student's current level of competence. Every student was provided a workbook that contained an explanation and practice exercises focusing on the math function for which he seemed ready. The instructor had prepared an assignment note for each class member, identifying the pages in the particular workbook which the student would study. During the class period, the teacher and teaching assistants moved about the class to offer aid to individuals. A confused student could also ask a classmate for help.

Competing Against Oneself

The problem. A 24-year-old member of a prison ABE3 (junior-high) class complained to the instructor, "Why did Jones get that Student-of-the-Week award when I'm a lot better at math and reading than he is?" In effect, this disgruntled inmate was objecting to the instructor's policy of rewarding a classmate who had achieved fewer learning objectives than had the complainer.

Analysis. Symbols of achievement in school — marks, commendations, awards, diplomas — are indicators of how well a student has competed against a standard. The two most common standards are (a) an ideal amount of work produced and the quality of work accomplished — such as the percentage of test questions answered correctly — and (b) other students' performances — such as where each student's essay or test score ranks in comparison to classmates' essays or test scores. A third standard, less popular than the first two, is a student's own past performance record, such as how the number of this month's correct test answers compare with the number of last month's.

The most widely recognized function of schools is that of equipping learners with knowledge and skills that will enhance the quality of their lives and contribute to the welfare of the society within which they live. But schools also perform a selection function – filtering out students according to their accomplishment. In other words, schools eliminate some students from competing adequately for economic and social rewards. Learners who fail to complete elementary school lose the chance to pursue a great range of attractive occupations and be in a position to make important social contacts. Ones who earn a college degree enhance their occupational and social opportunities well beyond those available to high-school graduates. This selection-and-elimination function has very important consequences for correctional education because jails, prisons, and juvenile facilities are full of losers – offenders who failed in school before they broke the law and were incarcerated. They had flunked out or dropped out before finishing high school. Or some – particularly immigrants – had no opportunity to attend school.

Obviously, all students cannot be expected to progress at the same rate and reach the same height of competence because genetic and environmental differences among them affect what they can learn, how they learn it, and at what speed they can progress. Thus, each student in a correctional-education class can fairly be expected to have mastered more knowledge and skills by the end of a given month than he or she commanded the preceding month. In effect, students can properly compete against their own past performance rather than against other students' performances.

Solution. In answer to the complainant's question, the teacher explained that the Student-of-the-Week award was not given automatically to the class member who had the most knowledge or was able to accomplish tasks the fastest. Instead, the award was intended to recognize students who had put forth the greatest effort and made the most progress in terms of their own particular ability. The instructor then conceded that the complainant was indeed a very bright and capable learner when he applied himself, but he had been spending too much time talking with classmates about matters unrelated to his academic assignments and he had often wandered in and out of the classroom, thus failing to take full advantage of his learning opportunity.

Converting General Objectives

The problem. The statewide curriculum-planning board sent a revised set of learning objectives to teachers of ELD (English-Language-Development or English-as-a-Second-Language) classes. The following example illustrates the form of the objectives.

> ELD/ELS students, in both speaking and writing, will learn to use standard English (a) verb tenses, (b) agreement between subject and predicate, and (c) contractions.

The problem for the ELD teacher was that of converting those general objectives into specific ones for the purpose of planning lessons. For instance, she had to decide which verb tenses should be taught, which sorts of agreement between subject and predicate should be emphasized, and which contractions qualify as "standard English."

Analysis. When faced with this situation, the teacher is left to find a standard in his or her field upon which to base his or her decisions. In the English Language Development field there are numerous "experts" to turn to. A good resource is the TESOL website. From this website a teacher can find reference books, workbooks, and teacher-developed materials. Another sequencing guide would be the textbook issued to the class. Also, many dictionaries include reference pages with grammatical information or refer students to workbooks that complement the dictionary.

Solution. Due to the lack of specificity in the objectives she had received, the teacher gathered materials that she judged were at the appropriate level to meet her particular students' needs. She decided that there was no one sequence of verb tenses, subject/verb agreement, or contractions that had to be followed for her students to acquire the English language.

Objectives Overload

The problem. The teacher of in an ABE2 (upper-elementary-level) program finds it extremely difficult to teach the entire series of mathematics- and language-competencies included in the mandated curriculum that his students must learn to pass the course.

Analysis. There are a number of factors that make the task of teaching toward all of the objectives in the prescribed curriculum of a typical academic program a daunting challenge. The most obvious problems relate to (a) when various students are enrolled and how long they remain in the class, (b) the differences in inmates' levels of knowledge, (c) the breadth of subject matter they are expected to master, and (d) what they will likely need to learn in order to function successfully in mainstream society after their release from custody.

Teachers are often obliged to judge which parts of the curriculum are essential for students' lives and which are less important. One way to make this judgment is to estimate the kinds of skills and information the average inmate will need in his or her life in relation to the skills and knowledge in the penal institution's education offerings. Based on this estimate, teachers can have students first concentrate on the components of the curriculum that seem most vital for an inmate's future before progressing to less essential and more advanced subject matter.

In addition to thus prioritizing the curriculum's components, instructors can profitably combine individualized and group instruction. For example, it is difficult to maintain continuity in a series of lessons when using whole-class lecture-style teaching to deliver lessons that extend over several weeks and which build progressively from one day to the next. The longer the instructional time-period and the more consecutively the subject-matter is developed, the greater will be the turnover in class enrollment and fewer students will remain to master all of the objectives. This is especially apparent in teaching mathematics, which is best learned systematically, beginning with whole-number computation and advancing sequentially through fractions, decimals, and percents prior to the study of algebra and geometry. On the other hand, a language unit, such as one on capitalization, can be successfully mastered during a lecture-style lessons presented to all students in the class, regardless of how long they have been enrolled.

Solution. The teacher of the ABE2 class, in considering how to prioritize the objectives students should pursue in mathematics and language, arrived at the following plan.

He decided that students should learn how to perform lower-level math fundamentals prior to attempting more advanced lessons. This decision was based on the instructor's experience teaching mathematics. For example, he had found that even though all students were able to memorize geometry terminology, they could not perform computations in geometry problems without already having mastered four basic skills (add, subtract, multiply, divide) involving whole numbers, fractions, and decimals. As a case in point, students needed a sound command of fractions in order to calculate the perimeter and area of a rectangle whose dimensions were expressed as fractions. Thus, the teacher provided the less knowledgeable students individualized instruction in the necessary fundamentals so they could then participate in the lectures and demonstrations that were designed for the bulk of the class. To care for the needs of the advanced students who had already mastered the skills on which the lectures focused, the instructor furnished textbooks and workbooks by which individuals could study more complex math skills on their own, given help by the instructor when needed.

When teaching language mechanics, the instructor focused on concepts and skills he considered most essential in inmates' lives. Thus, in teaching punctuation, he emphasized the use of question marks, exclamation points, commas, apostrophes, quotation marks, and colons. He gave less attention to semi-colons, hyphens, dashes, parentheses, and brackets. He also recognized that most students could learn language usage piecemeal from group instruction regardless of their English-usage background knowledge. Therefore, language usage was more often taught in a full-class lecture/demonstration fashion than were mathematics skills.

Prohibited Aims

The problem. The prison's academic vice-principal received a written inmate-grievance form on behalf of the majority of the students (plus a teacher's aide) enrolled in an upper-elementary-grade class. The complaint charged the woman instructor with failing to adhere to the required curriculum and with often preaching to the class about her personal Christian beliefs.

Analysis. This is a case of an instructor adding a forbidden objective to the course of study – the objective of promoting the doctrine of a particular religious sect.

The First Amendment of the United States Constitutions requires that "Congress shall make no law respecting an establishment of religion." Ever since that provision was added to the Constitution in 1791, jurists have generally interpreted it to mean that religion should be strictly separated from federal and local governments, a policy known as "the separation of church and state." As a result, it is permissible for teachers in public institutions to discuss generalities about different religions in an informative, comparative way. However, advocating a specific religious policy in a public education facility is prohibited. Instead, teachers are expected to offer lessons that correlate directly with the adopted curriculum.

Solution. The vice-principal, upon reading the inmates' grievances, asked the teacher to meet with him to discuss the matter. During the conference, the teacher admitted that she did sometimes discuss her religious opinions with the students in her class and that a number of them disapproved of the practice. She agreed to keep his beliefs private in the future.

In addition to reprimanding the instructor, the vice-principal visited her class several times over the next two weeks. As a result, he concluded that the teacher was disorganized, did not appear to be focusing enough on the subject matter, and was not employing sound instructional strategies. To address these problems, the vice-principal closed down the class for six weeks and had the instructor spend that time in the classrooms of four of the school's most respected veteran instructors. At the end of six weeks, the teacher was allowed to reconvene her class, and she began to use several instructional approaches and lessons plans she had acquired from the four mentor instructors.

Exactly Which Words?

The problem. The language component of an ABE2 (upper-elementary) curriculum required that the instructor teach the meanings of vocabulary words and how to spell them, but no specific list of words was provided. As a result, the teacher had to decide both the words students should learn and the methods of study.

Analysis. There are several ways to identify words students should learn. One way is to use professionally produced lists, such as the Dolch sight words that are available on the World Wide Web (at http://gemini.esbrevard.k12.fl.us/sheppard/reading/dolch.html or at http://www.quiz-tree.com/Sight-Words_main.html).

A second approach consists of compiling words that students misspell in writing assignments and workbook lessons. A third method involves collecting word lists from other teachers. A fourth source is the Internet, from which words can be retrieved by entering such terms as *word lists, vocabulary words,* and *misspelled words* into a search engine – *Google, Ask, AltaVista,* or others. A fifth involves collecting words from within other subjects studied by the class, such as a literature textbook or a life-skills unit.

In thinking about what words to use, instructors may estimate the needs of the particular students they teach – the students' current range of English-language knowledge. This can help determine whether vocabulary should be taught from a single list of words that all students in the class must study, or whether more than one list should be used. In some cases, a list can be divided into beginning, intermediate, and advanced levels and assigned to students on the basis of their current vocabulary knowledge. Still another tactic is to completely individualize vocabulary lessons, with each student studying a separate list.

Once vocabulary lists have been established, the teacher decides what instructional procedures to use. One choice is to adopt a traditional approach, having class members write dictionary definitions for the words they are learning and then practice writing the words in sentences prior to taking a spelling test. Word games are another useful instructional strategy. For instance, the class can be divided into teams, with students earning points for their team by correctly spelling and/or defining terms. If more than one spelling list is used in such a game, individual students can be asked to spell words from whichever list they have been studying. Or students can be shown several spellings of a word and be asked to choose the correct version in order to score a point. Yet another useful strategy is to have students work crossword puzzles involving the words they are learning, with the puzzles developed by use of computer software programs.

Solution. To develop lists of vocabulary words for his students to study, the ABE2 instructor consulted colleagues on the teaching staff to learn which words they used. One of them suggested a list entitled *2000 Commonly Misspelled Words,* from which the instructor formed 20 lists of 20 words each for lower-ability learners and another set for more advanced students. When the state correctional department later provided a list of words that ABE2 students were expected to know, the instructor added four more sets of 20 words to those he had been using.

After developing the spelling lists, the teacher required the students to learn to spell the words on a particular list and, for each word, to write its definition and use it in a sentence. Thus, the teacher was able to incorporate dictionary usage, language mechanics, and sentence development in spelling lessons. He gave whole-class lessons about how to use a dictionary, and he encouraged students to apply what they were learning about capitalization, grammar, punctuation, and sentence structure during whole-class and small-group lessons and through self-instructional workbooks. By being required to identify subjects and predicates in each sentence they wrote, students practiced deciding if their sentences were complete and whether sentence structures were simple, complex, or compound.

On the fourth day of each five-day school week, the instructor gave a whole-class practice quiz, using two lists of spelling words. He first read a word from the easier list, than a word from the more difficult one. Students were allowed to consult their spelling lists as the teacher enunciated each word, not only in their usual pronunciation but also as the letters would sound according to phonetic rules. This technique was intended to help students develop a mnemonic scheme that helped them remember how a word was written when it did not sound the way it was spelled. On the fifth day, students were given a final test over the words, with the instructor offering the words in random order to make it more difficult to cheat (such as having the words on a hidden piece of paper), and he pronounced the words only as they customarily sounded in daily usage.

As an incentive and a reward for hard work, the teacher issued a certificate of achievement for students who spelled all words correctly on five consecutive tests.

Chapter 8

SELECTING TEACHING METHODS

Teaching methods are the techniques instructors use to carry students to the learning objectives. If objectives concern the question "Where are we going?" then methods concern "How can we best get there?"

The first part of this chapter offers perspectives toward teaching methods in the form of nine teaching/learning procedures. The second part describes problems that can arise with methods and proposes solutions for the problems.

PERSPECTIVES – NINE TEACHING METHODS

The chapter's nine forms of instruction bear the following labels: (a) lecturing, (b) diagnostic teaching, (c) diminishing help, (d) class discussion, (e) small-group work, (f) tutoring, (g) reading assignments, (h) classroom games, and (i) individual projects.

The description of each method follows a five-step sequence: (1) the method's principal features, (2) a typical way of conducting the method, (3) conditions affecting the use of the method, (4) advantages of the method, and (5) the method's limitations.

Lecturing – with Active Participation

From the ancient past into the present, lecturing has been the most common mode of group instruction. A teacher, as the intended font of knowledge, shares that knowledge by talking to a collection of listeners who are expected to understand and remember what has been said.

An important distinction can be drawn between *passive participation* and *active participation* in a lecture. Passive participation involves members of an audience witnessing a lecture without having to make any observable response. As a result, the lecturer has no idea of whether the members are listening rather than dozing or are pondering matters unrelated to the lecture. And if the members are indeed listening, do they accurately understand what the lecturer means?

In contrast, active participation involves members of the audience carrying out observable acts that show they are truly listening and that reveal how well they have grasped the speaker's meanings. Because active participation is more likely to achieve a lecture's purpose than is passive participation, we suggest that all instructors' lectures should require active participation. Two ways teachers can promote active engagement consist of offering preparatory questions and pretesting.

Preparatory questions. At the outset of the lecture, the teacher provides students with questions whose answers will be found in the lecture. The questions are intended to establish the mind-set students bring to the talk, helping them focus on those aspects of the presentation that the teacher considers most important.

The questions are best cast in written form rather than described only orally. Thus, students will have an accurate version of what they are expected to learn. For instance, the instructor can dictate the questions for class members to copy into their notebooks, or the questions can be written on the chalkboard or given to students on printed sheets.

Pretesting. Prior to a lecture, the teacher can have students write answers to questions about key elements of the lecture content. Students are then told that the lecture will contain the correct answers to the test, so that during or after the talk students can change their initial answers in whatever way they see fit. In a variation of this approach, the lecture can be followed by a class discussion during which participants offer their answers and learn different ways class members responded to the test items.

Lecture procedure. Here is an example of a lesson plan for an active-participation lecture.

Topic: Map Reading

Learning objectives. As a result of this lecture, students can:
* Define the terms *map legend, peninsula, bay, cove, channel, estuary, map scale, longitude, latitude.*
* Locate the following features on a map: *legend, compass, scale, roads, waterways, railroads, airports, towns, mountains, bays, estuaries, coves, peninsulas, channels, elevation indicators, longitudes, latitudes.*

Equipment/materials. Instructor: Overhead projector, two map transparencies. One transparency displays an instructor-made map of a fictitious seaside territory (See Map 8.1). The other transparency shows the same territory with each map-feature labeled.
Students: Notebook, pencil, printed Map 8.1.

Participants. Instructor, two teaching assistants, students.

The instructional process. A teaching assistant distributes copies of the first map to the students while the instructor explains to the class the purpose of the lesson, which is to have students master the objectives that are printed on the back of the map.

The instructor uses an overhead projector to display the first map on a screen at the front of the classroom. The lecture consists of the instructor using a pencil to point out each of the map's features in turn as the students follow the instructor's explanation by writing the name of each feature on their copies of the map – such features as *peninsula, scale, railroad,* etc. During the lecture, the teaching assistants move about the room to aid students who have trouble labeling the map features.

After explaining the map items, the instructor answers questions that the students ask about the features. When all of the map elements have been explained, the instructor replaces the overhead projector's first transparency with the second one, which includes labels of all of the map features. The students can then compare their own versions with the second map and can alter any of their labels that need correcting.

Evaluation of students' achievement. The instructor assesses students' mastery of the map-reading objectives by (a) inspecting the students' labeled maps and (b) the following day giving a test that requires students to recognize the proper definitions of such terms as *legend, peninsula,* and *estuary* and to accurately label map features. The map used for the test is of a different territory than the one used during the original lesson so the instructor can determine if the students actually understood the concepts taught rather than simply memorizing the layout of the first map.

Influential conditions. Two conditions that affect the success of a lecture are the listeners' present knowledge and the instructor's ability to hold the audience's attention.

Present knowledge. Lecturing is most efficient when all members of the audience have a similar level of knowledge about the lecture's topic. Hence, lectures are a waste of time for students who already knew everything the instructor talks about. Lectures are also a waste of time for students who don't understand vocabulary and historical allusions that the lecturer mentions but does not explain.

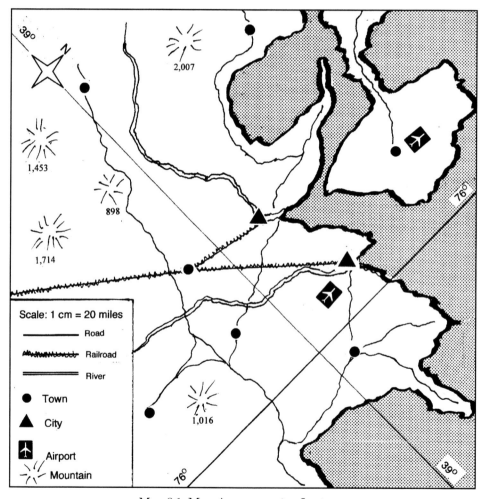

Map 8.1. Map Accompanying Lecture.

Holding the audience's attention. The chance that listeners will closely attend to a speaker's presentation is greater when (a) the students understand ahead of time what they will be expected to recall from the lecture, (b) they have an activity to perform during the lecture, such as taking notes, (c) the lecturer is animated and varies the volume and pacing of his speech rather than speaking in a monotone, (d) the lecturer speaks directly to the audience rather than reading from a script, and (e) the lecture is illustrated with pictures or charts.

The chance that the audience's attention will wander away from the lecture is greater when (a) students have no idea about what they will be responsible for deriving from the lecture, (b) the instructor speaks in a monotone or reads from a script, or (c) the lecture lasts a long time.

Lecture advantages. Unlike tutoring, lecturing can serve multiple learners all at the same time. Unlike reading assignments, lectures can allow students to ask follow-up questions to clarify matters not adequately grasped during the lecture. Unlike motion pictures and television broadcasts, lectures enable teachers to fashion their own interpretations of historical incidents and current events and to match their presentation to the interests and skills of the audience.

The active-participation-lecture model is suitable as well for lessons in which the main body of information is presented via a film or video rather than by the teacher or a guest speaker.

Lecture limitations. Unless the instructor provides ways for students to participate actively, the instructor does not know if class members have understood – or even listened to – the presentation. Lecturing does not adjust to individual differences in students' ability to grasp what the teacher lectures about.

Diagnostic Teaching

The method known as *diagnostic teaching* follows the medical model of a physician first examining a patient, then applying a treatment that has been indicated by the results of the examination. In other words, a diagnostic approach reverses the traditional pattern of teaching that begins with the instructor presenting material – by lecture, reading assignment, workbook, TV program – and then testing students to discover what they have learned.

Diagnostic teaching is particularly well-suited to correctional settings in which students enter a class at any time of the year and come from diverse educational backgrounds, so that instructors are not aware of what newcomers already know when they arrive in class. Information about students' present knowledge is especially important in subject fields that must build new learnings on top of prior knowledge, as in mathematics, science, and English language.

Diagnostic procedure. The method begins with the instructor evaluating the students' present command of the skill or knowledge on which the upcoming lesson will focus. The evaluation may consist of a written test (math problems, spelling, solar system, causes of the American Civil War) or demonstration (repair a radiator, sew a seam, type on a computer).

On the basis of the evaluation, the instructor devises ways to teach each student whatever part of the knowledge or skill the student failed to perform adequately on the evaluation. This means that a separate plan is prepared for each student or for each subgroup in the class. Any given student's plan can involve a special activity, such as completing a section of a workbook, receiving small-group instruction, reading a passage of a book or magazine, being tutored by a classmate, watching a video, completing a computer program, or doing a homework assignment.

Influential conditions. A diagnostic approach works best when (a) students vary markedly in their knowledge and skill levels, (b) the instructor has multiple facilities for teaching students individually or in small groups — such facilities as inmate teaching assistants, a variety of textbooks and workbooks, teacher-prepared self-study units, and computer software.

Diagnostic-teaching advantages. The most obvious strength of diagnostic teaching is its ability to identify at the outset of a lesson what each student needs to learn, thereby avoiding the problem of students' having to repeat what they already know. Thus, diagnostic teaching conserves the more knowledgeable students' time by freeing them to enrich their education by studying new material while their less-advanced classmates are pursuing the current lesson's goals.

Diagnostic-teaching limitations. The larger the class and the more diverse the students' mastery of the upcoming lesson, the more difficult it is for the instructor to offer each student the service he or she needs. There is obviously a limit on how much a teacher can customize instruction to suit every learner.

Diminishing Aid

An instructional approach labeled *diminishing aid* is especially useful in helping students master complex skills. A skill such as writing an essay, solving a complicated math problem, repairing a motorcycle engine, or creating a decorative quilt can be analyzed into its constituent steps. The teaching process begins with the instructor demonstrating how to solve each step, thereby acquainting the learner with the sequence of steps. Next, the instructor works through a second example, but omits filling in one step. The learner's task is to complete that missing step. Then the instructor goes through the process once more, this time leaving out two steps, which the learner must complete. And thus the process is repeated over and over, with the teacher leaving blank an additional step each time until finally the student, unassisted, is completing all the steps on his or her own. In effect, aid from the teacher diminishes with each iteration of the skill.

The diminishing-aid procedure. The following example illustrates the application of the diminishing-aid approach in teaching students how to write the type of essay required in the tests for a General Educational Development (GED) certificate.

To begin, the instructor divides the essay-writing process into eight steps that are introduced to students in the following fashion:

> Although you will not have time to go through all of the steps during the actual GED test, you will develop a good understanding of the structure and elements of a typical GED-style essay by practicing the steps listed below.

1. Select a topic on which to write.
2. Write a topic sentence to explain the main idea of the essay to the reader.
3. Identify 3-to-5 specific ideas as reasons that support your opinion about the topic you are writing about. Once you have identified the reasons, number them in the order that you intend to offer them in your essay.
4. Write the essay's introductory paragraph.
5. Write details that help explain each of the reasons you are using to support the main idea of the essay.
6. Write the paragraphs that will make up the body of the essay.
7. Write a concluding paragraph that reminds the reader of the main idea of the essay and of the support for that idea.
8. Write the final version of the essay.

The instructor gives class members a three-page description of how the eight steps can be carried out for the topic "How Consumers Are Influenced by Advertising." As the students follow the instructor's explanation of each step, they ask questions about matters they don't completely understand.

During a subsequent class session, the instructor distributes a two-page description of the eight steps for a new topic: "The invention of the telephone changed the way people communicate with each other. Discuss the positive effects of the telephone." The instructor has filled in all of the steps except the last – writing the final version of the essay. The students' assignment is to write the essay based on the contents of the preceding seven steps.

For the next writing session, class members receive a guide-sheet for the topic "Why might a married couple decide not to have children?" The instructor has completed the first six steps of the writing process, but has left the last two blank. The students are to complete those two.

And so the process continues, with each successive guide-sheet focusing on a new topic and leaving an additional step blank, to be filled in by the students. During the final writing session, the students are to perform the eight steps on their own, with no aid from the instructor.

To encourage class members to monitor their essay writing, the instructor furnishes each a 14-item evaluation form that focuses not only on the eight steps but also on important rules of writing that students often violate. Here are three of the items to which a student would respond with YES or NO.

- You began each paragraph with a topic sentence.
- You wrote complete sentences that contained both a subject and predicate.
- You used proper agreement between subject and verb in each sentence.

Thus, the diminishing-aid method not only teaches a complex skill by focusing students' attention on a particular subskill during each repetition of the process, but the method also requires students to assess how carefully they have attended to subskills that contribute to effective essay writing.

(See Appendix A for an example of a guide-sheet and a completed essay on the topic *How Consumers Are Influenced by Advertising*.)

Influential conditions. This method is well suited for teaching a complex skill whose mastery depends on students repeating the skill numerous times under slightly different circumstances, such as with different topics and emphases on different constituent subskills.

Advantages. One strength of the diminishing-aid method is that the student, at the beginning, is obliged to recognize all steps in the process and to see where they fit, but is not overwhelmed by having to cope with all of the steps at once. The steps are mastered gradually. Another advantage is the extensive practice afforded by the learner's repeating the process multiple times, thereby seating the procedure more permanently in memory.

Limitations. The diminishing-aid approach is a time-consuming method, for it requires multiple repetitions of the skill being taught.

Class Discussion

The expression *class discussion,* as intended here, refers to a session in which the instructor introduces a topic or problem, then invites class members to expand on the topic or to propose solutions to the problem.

A distinction can be drawn between *class discussion* and *group oral quiz.* A lesson is an oral quiz and not a class discussion if it consists of the teacher posing questions of fact and asking students to answer with the correct facts. Here are examples of factual questions: In American history, when was the Civil War fought? In math, what is the meaning of *mixed number?* In science, what is *the water cycle?* In literature, who wrote *Huckleberry Finn?*

On the other hand, a class discussion concerns questions for which there are alternative answers, with each solution buttressed by evidence and a line of reasoning. So the intent of discussions is to reveal alternative choices, the arguments in their support, and ways of judging which choices are best. For instance, three educational aims that discussions can serve are those of:

1. *Revealing diverse individuals' viewpoints.* The aim is to expand students' understanding of other people's background experiences, needs, interests, and attitudes, by discussing such topics as:

   Should street gangs be outlawed? Why or why not?
   Does it make any sense for adults to read comic books?
   What are the advantages and disadvantages of using tobacco?

2. *Preparing inmates for the future.* The purpose is to help inmates plan ahead by considering such issues as:

When a woman is released from prison, what kinds of problems can she expect to face, and how can she cope constructively with those problems?
What vocations are good ones for offenders to enter when they leave jail, prison, or a juvenile detention center, and why?

3. *Exposing students' knowledge gaps.* As a device for stimulating students' interest in an upcoming lesson, the instructor can direct a discussion that reveals additional knowledge students need for coping with the issues that the lesson involves.

In what kinds of jobs outside the prison do people need to speak and read English?
What do you think is the meaning of each of these expressions – *Declaration of Independence, the right to bear arms, freedom of speech,* and *freedom of association?*

Discussion procedure. The following example illustrates one plan for leading a class discussion – a plan that includes (a) reasons for choosing the topic, (b) the goal to be achieved, (c) rules governing students' participation, and (d) a sequence of questions the instructor will pose in directing the discussion.

The setting. The discussion is conducted among teenage girls in a juvenile commitment facility.

The discussion topic. "Life as a Teenage Mother" The topic was chosen because (a) the decisions reached by the inmates about becoming teenage mothers vitally influence their lives and the lives of children they might have, (b) the issues involved are interesting to teenage girls, so probably they would enthusiastically participate in the discussion, and (c) the inmates are likely to have strong opinions about the issues.

Goal to achieve. As a result of the discussion, the girls arrive at a better informed, more reasoned judgment about teenage motherhood than they would have without the discussion.

Rules of participation. Everyone is encouraged to take part. Participants are to take turns in offering opinions and are not to interrupt each other. No one should ridicule the ideas of other group members.

Questions guiding the discussion. Under what conditions are teenage girls likely to become pregnant? Why might a girl want to become pregnant? Why might a girl not want to become pregnant? If a girl gets pregnant, what different things might she do about it – what are her choices? Which of these things do you think would be best, and why? How do girls decide what to do about their pregnancy? What about the boy who is the father? What should he do, and why? If the girl goes ahead and has the baby, how will this change her life? What kind of life will it be for the baby as the baby grows up? If the girl did not have the baby, how might her life have been different? Do you have any advice to give girls about becoming pregnant? What would that advice be?

Influential conditions. Discussions are most successful when:

- The issue at hand is not simply a well-established fact, such as the distance between Earth and Sun or the names of the justices of the U.S. Supreme Court.
- Class members already have some experience with the issue at hand so they are likely to have opinions about it. Examples of issues not suitable for typical inmate classes are such questions as: Which theory of matter in the universe is more convincing – wave or particle? What were the principal causes of the 1919–1921 Irish war of independence?
- There is more than one rational answer to the issue posed by the instructor, as in such questions as: Should the legal drinking age in this state be age 21 – why or why not? Who should be allowed to carry a hunting knife in public, and why?

Discussion advantages. When the issue debated in a discussion bears on matters of personal concern for class members, the instructor has no difficulty holding students' attention. In effect, motivating students is not a problem. Furthermore, class members gain experience in presenting their beliefs and in responding in a rational manner to viewpoints that differ from their own. Students who recognize the validity of classmates' arguments may well revise their own beliefs as a result of the discussion.

Discussion limitations. Discussions that pit strong, unyielding convictions of one individual against others' beliefs may result in greater animosity between those class members than was true before that class session. Participants whose arguments are made to look ridiculous during a discussion may suffer embarrassment and anger that inhibits their subsequent learning progress.

Small-Group Work

The expression *small-group work*, as used here, means that several class members (as few as two or as many as seven or eight) work together. The following are variations of such a method.

- Two women inmates in an elementary-school-level class drill each other on spelling words. First, one woman asks her partner to write a list of words that the woman dictates. Then the process is reversed, with the partner dictating the words and the woman writing them.
- A junior-high-level class of 25 male students is divided into five groups of five members each to create questions that would test students' recall of the contents of a movie the class has recently seen?
- An ESL (English as a second language) class of 24 men is divided into four groups to practice saying words that many students have difficulty pronouncing correctly. The instructor directs one group, a teaching assistant directs a second group, and the two remaining groups are led by a pair of students whose pronunciation is rather accurate. The class has been organized into small groups so more students will have a chance to speak individually than would be the case if the activity were carried out with the class as a whole.

Small-group procedures. The efficiency of small-group work can be improved by the instructor preparing for seven aspects of the group-activity process – (a) a feasible task, (b) group composition, (c) leadership, (d) task definition, (e) launching the group, (f) monitoring progress, and (g) the final product.

A feasible task. A suitable task is one that:

- Students have the knowledge and skill to accomplish.
- Students take seriously and is interesting so they will work diligently to complete it.
- Can be finished in a relatively brief time – within a class period or over several days – because the membership of a typical class changes so often that members of a group will be lost.

Group composition. There are several ways to compose groups, depending on the aims the instructor intends the group-work to serve. For example, if one aim is to improve ethnic relationships in the class by having individuals from different ethnic backgrounds work together toward a common goal, then each group should contain members from different ethnic backgrounds. Or an aim can be to accustom offenders of different age decades to working together, so each group should have both younger and older inmates. Or if one purpose is to have less capable students learn from the example set by more capable ones, then each group should have members representing different levels of competence or experience.

Leadership. Sometimes it is sufficient for leadership to arise spontaneously within a group, either by an ambitious individual volunteering or by the group voting for a leader. However, in other instances the instructor can profitably select each group's leader on the basis of the instructor's estimate of who would likely perform well in that position.

It is important at the outset of the group work for the instructor to describe the responsibilities of the leader and group members. This description can be either oral, in writing, or both oral and written.

Task definition. At the outset, the instructor defines the groups' task by describing the product the group work is expected to create and the criteria to be used in judging the final product. Here are three examples of instructions.

> What we are trying to do is come up with ideas about incentives – like rewards or opportunities – that could be offered to get more inmates to enroll in an education program, either an academic class like the one you are in or a vocational class – auto shop, carpentry, or such. Each group will have twenty minutes to come up with ideas. So, in your group, you pick somebody as the recorder to write down the suggestions. Each suggestion needs to include why that particular incentive would appeal to inmates.

> As you know, when you take the GED exam, you have to write an essay. Your group's task is to suggest topics for GED essays. We'll use the best of your ideas as the topics for practice essays. A topic can be either a statement like "Finding a Good Job" or a question such as "How can I help my children do well in school?" List each topic on a separate slip of paper. You will have fifteen minutes to come up with ideas. As the end of the fifteen minutes, arrange the slips of paper in alphabetical order and hand them to me.

> So now we've seen the video about American Indians' objections to sports teams' nicknames and symbols that Indians feel are insulting. Each of your groups is to suggest nicknames, symbols, or mascots

that you think would be great but would not insult anyone. You need to include the reasons you think your choices would be popular with fans.

Monitoring progress. The efficiency of group work suffers whenever members (a) don't stick to the topic, but are distracted by other interests, (b) engage in unproductive arguments, (c) become angry with each other, or (d) fail to know what steps to take next in order to make progress toward the goal. Therefore, it is usually desirable for the instructor or teaching assistants to visit one group after another in order to monitor their progress and offer aid when they deviate from the topic or fail to prepare their final report.

The final product. The culmination of group work usually takes the form of the groups meeting as a whole class to report their results and to evaluate how well they performed their task. Typically, the leaders of the various groups take turns in explaining the results of their deliberations, and the class instructor or class members express their reactions to each report.

Influential conditions. The effectiveness of group work is fostered when the leader (a) keeps members on the topic, (b) encourages all members to contribute their ideas, and (c) periodically summarizes the group's progress.

Advantages of small-group work. Small groups can help accommodate individual differences among students by assigning students with similar skills and knowledge to the same group. Furthermore, the opportunity for each student to contribute to discussions is greater in small groups than in whole-class sessions.

Limitations of small-group work. Groups can fail – or at least prove to be inefficient learning devices – if the leader does not keep the members moving toward the goal, members argue incessantly or insult each other, or the task to be performed is beyond the competence of the group members.

Tutoring

Tutoring usually consists of one person instructing one student – or sometimes two or three students. Frequently, the purpose of tutoring is to help a student master a skill or grasp a concept that the student has had difficulty learning during group instruction or from a textbook or workbook. In other words, tutoring is a form of special help.

In correctional settings, the tutor may be the class instructor, but more often the tutor is a member of the class (*peer tutor*), a volunteer from the outside community, or an inmate teaching assistant. For instance, an experienced, competent student in a juvenile-center high-school math class may be assigned to explain the Pythagorean theorem to a newly arrived class member. A volunteer from the community outside the jail may, under the direction of a jail's English-as-a-second-language instructor, drill two Spanish-speaking women on the meaning and pronunciation of a list of English vocabulary words. A teaching assistant in a prison auto-mechanics course may help an inmate understand an instructional manual's diagrams of an auto's electrical circuitry.

Tutoring procedure. It is usually desirable for instructors to prepare students, teaching assistants, and volunteers for their tutoring task. One approach involves a demonstration. That is, the instructor tutors a class member while the assistant or volunteer observes. During or following the demonstration, the instructor describes each step of the process and the reasoning behind the step. The instructor can also offer suggestions to inexperienced tutors – such suggestions as:

- Be patient with your student when he or she makes mistakes or is slow to understand. Don't act disgusted or irritated at the student's errors.
- Encourage the student at each successful step in the learning process with such comments as "Good" or "Well done" or "That's right" or "Nice job."
- If your student doesn't immediately understand what you are explaining, try explaining in a different way with different examples.
- Give the student plenty of practice using a skill or a piece of knowledge before you move ahead to something new to learn.
- As the student attempts to solve a problem, ask him or her to "think out loud" by saying what is going on in his or her mind while grappling with a problem or trying to recall information. Thus, the tutor may discover which part of the student's thought process can profit from improvement.

Influential conditions. Tutoring is more effective when the tutor is tolerant of the learner's errors and offers frequent encouraging responses to the student's progress.

Tutoring advantages. The most obvious benefit of tutoring is its ability to fit instruction to the needs of the individual learner – to the particular inmate's present skills, learning style, learning speed, and confusions. Tutoring also provides the tutor an ongoing assessment of the student's progress, continually exposing the learner's errors of understanding so they can be immediately addressed. In addition, tutoring keeps learners continually on task, since they cannot let their attention drift off the topic as they might do when a teacher is delivering a lecture or leading a discussion with the entire class.

Tutoring limitations. The main shortcoming of tutoring is its cost in terms of personnel. Even when a tutor works with two or three learners at a time rather than just one, the method requires a great deal more staff time than does lecturing, small-group work, class discussion, or reading assignments. A further limiting factor can be the inadequate skills that peers, teaching assistants, and volunteers bring to the tutoring, inadequacies that can frustrate the learners and cause them to acquire flawed skills and knowledge.

Reading Assignments

In all schools – including correctional-education programs – assigning students to read textbooks and periodicals is one of the most popular teaching methods. In recent times, reading assignments have included web pages on the Internet. There appear to be two main ways teachers give reading assignments. The first involves simply telling students which sections to read in a book (such as, "pages 26 through 44") or which website to study (such as, "Franklin Roosevelt's biography on the site http://www.whitehouse.gov/history/presidents/fr32.html"). The second consists of posing questions or tasks that guide students' attention as they read. We believe the second of these approaches is by far the better because it alerts learners to which kind of knowledge – out of numerous potential kinds – the instructor expects students to extract from the assigned passages.

Assignment procedure. One effective procedure involves providing students guide questions and informing them of the form in which they are to respond.

Guide questions. Questions can be ones that require (a) the recall of facts, (b) the sequence of events, (c) the interpretation of meanings, (d) the evaluation of information, (e) the application of information to life, or (f) some combination of all of these aims. The following are examples of questions for students who are assigned to read the chapter on AIDS in a health-education textbook.

Facts. "What is the connection between HIV and AIDS?"
"How can a person get AIDS?"
"What part of the world has the greatest number of people with AIDS?"

Sequence. "Where was AIDS first discovered; then how and where did it spread?"

Interpretation. "What is meant by the phrase *social consequences of AIDS*?
"What is the difference between *preventing AIDS* and *treating AIDS*?"

Evaluation. "What methods have been used to decide how many people have AIDS? Which of these methods do you think is best, and why?"
"Should the government pay the medical bills of people with AIDS? Why or why not?"

Application. "What could you do to help prevent more people from getting AIDS?"
"What might you do to help people who already have AIDS?"

Forms of response. Three ways an instructor can learn how well students answered the guide questions are by written reports, oral reports, and written tests.

Apparently the most frequent method is to require each student to furnish written answers to the questions. An advantage of the written-report approach is that the teacher receives every student's response to every question. However, a problem with this approach is that the teacher doesn't know if some students simply copied classmates' answers. (It should be no surprise that incarcerated felons are willing to cheat.)

In the second method – oral report – the instructor conducts a class discussion during which different students answer the questions. This approach works best when the instructor selects which students are to answer which questions rather than only calling on volunteers who have raised their hands. It is also useful for the teacher to ask a question before selecting the person to answer it. This tactic helps ensure that each class member pays attention to every question, because none of them know if they will be the one asked to answer. Thus, the rule of thumb is "Ask the question first, then choose the student who is to respond." A disadvantage of the oral report is that the teacher does not learn the responses of all students to all questions. An advantage of the approach is that it offers the opportunity for class members to hear others' answers and to debate issues that arise.

Rather than requiring written reports from each student, the teacher can announce at the time the reading passage is assigned that a test will be given over the questions after the class members have studied the passage. Giving a test rather than requiring written reports reduces the likelihood that students will copy classmates' answers. Two disadvantages of testing are that students may lack the time needed to phrase their answers carefully during the test or they may be emotionally distraught by tests and, therefore, unable to furnish accurate evidence of how well they understood the reading assignment.

Influential conditions. The most obvious condition influencing the success of reading assignments is the match between the student's reading skills and the difficulty level of the reading matter. If the difficulty level is well beyond the student's skills, the assignment will clearly fail to achieve its purpose. A further factor is the set of reading aids at the student's command. Those aids are the meaning-clarification sources to which the learner can turn to clarify puzzling words and phrases met in a reading passage. Sources include dictionaries, thesauruses, atlases, book indexes, and the Internet. The better acquainted inmates are with using such resources, the more readily they succeed with reading lessons.

Advantages of reading assignments. Such assignments give inmates practice reading, allow each inmate to learn at his or her own pace, and relieve the teacher of having to lecture.

Limitations of reading assignments. The method does not work well if the difficulty of the reading material is well beyond a student's comprehension ability.

Classroom Games

Two traditional classroom games can be successfully adapted for use in correctional programs. The first is the spelling bee or spelldown. The second is a card game. Both serve as evaluation devices that incorporate a learning component.

Spelling Bee. In what is perhaps the most common form of the spelldown bee, students stand in line around the classroom as the teacher pronounces a word for the first student to spell. If the student spells the word correctly, she or he remains standing. But if the student misspells the word, she or he must sit down. This process is repeated for each person in the line. When the last in line has had a turn, the process starts over again at the beginning of the line until, finally, only one class member is left standing. All the rest had misspelled a word and thus were eliminated.

However popular this version of the spelldown may be, it's really a bad way to teach or test spelling. The poor spellers – the ones who need the most practice – are quickly eliminated, left to sit at their desks where they may pay little or no attention to remaining words in the teacher's list. In contrast, the good spellers get lots of practice and also enjoy publicly defeating their classmates. But changes can be made in this traditional form of the game to correct its disadvantages. The following is one such variation.

Procedure. The dual purpose of the game is to (a) engage all class members' attention throughout the entire class period and (b) teach students to correctly spell words that they have not yet mastered. To invest the game with a competitive spirit, the class is divided into two teams – one consisting of the students sitting on the left side of the classroom and the other of the students on the right side. By having students compete as teams rather than as individuals, less competent spellers may have the satisfaction of being on a winning team. To ensure that each student pays attention to every word, the instructor pronounces a word without indicating which class member will be asked to spell it. Thus, everyone must listen to each word. In addition, the instructor pauses briefly after pronouncing the word so as to give everyone a chance to spell the word in her or his mind. Then the instructor calls a student's name. If the word is spelled correctly, the speller's team earns one point. If spelled incorrectly, the teacher calls on a member of the other team to spell the word. After the word has been correctly spelled, the instructor assigns each class member to write the correct spelling on a sheet of paper. Thus, every student practices writing every word in its proper form. It is also the case that once students have been chosen to spell a word, they cannot relax and pay no attention to subsequent words, because the instructor can call on each class member multiple times and in no particular order. In summary, this variation of the bee draws on the motivational value of team competition, ensures that everyone pays attention throughout the lesson, and adds the learning feature of having everyone write each word in its correct form.

The same approach can be adapted for aspects of the curriculum other than spelling, such as addition and multiplication combinations, grammar and syntax, and historical or science facts. The method appears to appeal to inmates of any age and educational level.

Card game. A flashcard is about the size of a playing card with a problem or question written on the front and the solution or answer on the back. Flashcards have long been popular devices for helping learners memorize facts. The facts can be of various kinds – mathematical, language, historical, scientific, artistic, vocational, and more. The following examples illustrate what can appear on the front and back of a card for various combinations of problems and solutions.

	Front	*Back*
Multiplication fact	6x8=	6x8=48
Addition fact	12+12=	12+12=24
Fraction/percent	3/4	75%
Geometric figure	(cube figure)	cube
English vocabulary for speakers of Spanish	casa	house
Spelling word	adress	address
Word definition	seat belt	car occupant's protective belt
History date	1492	Columbus arrived in America
Event/person	Emancipation Proclamation	Abraham Lincoln
Science vocabulary	Mars	planet in the solar system
Country/continent	Namibia	Africa
River/country	Amazon	Brazil
Book/Author	Don Quixote	Cervantes

Procedure. To prepare for a flashcard game, a player creates a series of cards bearing on the same topic, such as addition facts, word definitions, or events/persons. The game involves either one person playing alone or two persons working together.

In the one-person version, the student progresses through the set of cards by (a) looking at the item on the front of a card, (b) predicting the answer on the back of the card, and (c) looking at the back to discover if the prediction has been correct. If incorrect, the player tries to memorize the correct answer, then moves on to the next card. This process is repeated for every card in the set. The player's score is the number of correct answers in the entire series of cards. The process of going through the series is then repeated, with the player attempting to improve his or her score. Thus, the game consists of a student competing against himself or herself – going through the set numerous times until achieving a perfect score.

In a two-person version of the game, Student A displays the cards one-by-one to Student B who attempts to predict the answer on the back of each card.

Influential conditions. Games of the spelling-bee type are usually more successful when (a) the range of talent is about the same on each team, (b) every student is liable to be called on to answer at any time, and (c) the questions to be answered are factual and not simply a matter of opinion.

Flashcard games are most appropriate when (a) the problems are matters of fact, not opinion, and (b) both the problems and their solutions are very brief.

Advantages of games. For many students, the competitive aspect of games is a strong motivator, serving to hold players' attention and urge them to try hard to succeed. And the task of memorizing facts is less arduous when cast in the form of a game.

Flashcards are especially useful in correctional settings where students enter and leave a class at irregular times throughout the school year. Inmates who enter without having mastered facts that their classmates already know are able to overcome this disadvantage by catching up with the others through individual flashcard drill.

Limitations of games. Whereas spelldowns and flashcards can help students memorize facts, they are not appropriate for teaching reasoning skills, steps in a process, or the interpretation or evaluation of events.

Individual Projects

The expression *individual projects* refers to learning tasks that a student pursues on his or her own initiative, with guidance provided by the instructor, a teaching assistant, a classmate, or a volunteer from the community outside the correctional facility. Here are some sample projects.

- A 15-year-old girl in a juvenile-detention facility chose to write a paper about girls' and women's hair styles, basing the content on books and periodicals in the detention-center's library and on Internet sites that had not been blocked by the center's administrators.
- In a prison's food-preparation class, a 40-year-old inmate elected to prepare Thai cuisine as a special task, creating the various dishes from descriptions in three cookbooks under the class instructor's direction.
- Each student in a prison woodworking class was obliged to build an item of furniture of his choice. Typical items were a rocking chair, a lounge chair, a side table, a chest of drawers, a bookcase, and an entertainment center (to accommodate a television receiver, radio, CD player, books, and magazines).
- A woman in a GED class wrote an article for a church magazine about turning from a life of prostitution and drug dealing to a reformed life as a Christian minister.
- A 58-year-old man in a prison's ABE3 (junior-high level) course collected information from the Internet to write a biography of Malcolm X.
- A 15-year-old boy in an alternative school used the school's video camera to make a movie about how to repair bicycles.

Procedure. A typical project involves the teacher directing the student through four stages.

Topic selection and rationale. Either the student chooses a topic or the teacher suggests one. The student is then obligated to tell what will be learned or who will benefit from the project.

Plan. The student submits an action plan to the teacher that tells (a) what the final product will be, (b) what equipment or supplies will be required, (c) where to search for the information needed to complete the project, (d) the sequence of steps for carrying out the project, and (e) a projected time that each step will likely require.

Monitoring. The instructor sets a schedule of times when the student periodically describes the extent of progress and problems encountered.

Final report. Upon completing the project, the student submits the results to the instructor.

Influential conditions. The feasibility of individual ventures depends on whether (a) the student has the initiative, determination, and needed skills or can acquire the skills during the conduct of the project, (b) the required funds, supplies, and equipment are available, and (c) there is enough time to complete the project.

Advantages of projects. Two strengths of individual special projects are their ability to serve individual students' interests and to give students experience working out problems by themselves.

Limitations of projects. Special projects fail when students lack (a) the skills or facilities needed to carry out the tasks and (b) the diligence and patience necessary to complete the job.

With the foregoing overview of teaching methods in mind, we turn next to a range of methodological problems in correctional settings and to ways of solving them.

TEACHING-METHOD PROBLEMS AND SOLUTIONS

The dozen issues addressed in the following section focus on (a) accommodating shortages in students' background knowledge, (b) coping with instructors' foreign-language limitations, (c) stimulating reluctant learners, (d) expanding educational opportunities to more inmates, (e) motivating students, (f) utilizing teaching assistants, (g) playing instructional games, (h) teaching half a class, (i) merging teaching methods, (j) monitoring individualized assignments, (k) dramatic performances, and (l) dealing with chatters.

Completely Baffled

The problem. During a group mathematics lesson on adding fractions that had unlike denominators, a student was called on to explain how to begin solving the problem on the chalkboard. He responded by admitting that he had no idea about how to perform the computation.

Analysis. Because of the open-entry and open-exit nature of correctional institutions' education programs, any number of students in a class may have enrolled only recently and thus have missed the prior instruction needed to understand the class's present lesson. This dilemma is particularly challenging when the lesson is in such a sub-ject as mathematics where the contents of the curriculum must be learned in a progressive sequence that begins with basic fundamentals on which higher-level functions rely.

Solutions. If students are to profit from more advanced math lessons, they must first master the necessary background skills. To accomplish this, inmates who enter the class without the skills needed for the current lesson can either be (a) tutored by a teaching assistant while the instructor directs the more advanced lesson to the rest of the class or (b) assigned a self-instructional workbook to study until they have mastered the information needed to catch up with their class-mates.

Language Difficulty

The problem. An instructor who speaks only a little Spanish was given the task of teaching and ESL (English as a second language) course in which the majority of students spoke Spanish and were just beginning to learn English.

Analysis. Many instructors who teach ESL courses in correctional settings do not speak the native tongue of most students in ESL pro-grams. As a result, Spanish-speaking inmate-aides are often needed as translators and can help with whole-class, small-group, or individual-ized English-language lessons.

Solutions. When teaching whole-group oral-vocabulary lessons, the teacher could pronounce words in English followed by the teaching assistant reciting the words in Spanish to enhance understanding. Lessons in math, oral reading, social studies, and science could assume a similar presentation pattern. The same approach could be used for creating written or visual-media presentations in which the instructor produces the materials in English with the aide providing a Spanish translation. The teaching assistant could also deliver some lessons of his or her own, with the teacher monitoring the process.

Reluctant Learner

The problem. A 49-year-old white male claimed to be attending school only because it was part of his mandated prison work/training program. He kept a low profile in class by sitting quietly at his desk, completing most of the minimum number of required assignments. He appeared unconcerned about passing written tests, and he typically failed to give acceptable responses when called on to answer questions during whole-class activities. Although he was well behaved, the instructor felt the student was not working up to his ability level.

Analysis. Many middle-aged inmates in prisons are under-educated. The reasons prisoners offer for their negative attitudes toward schooling often relate to their perception that they are too old for a basic academic education to do them any practical good, that they already have a trade or business to which they will return in mainstream society when paroled, or that they disliked school during childhood or adolescence because their lack of success left them with a sense of frustration and failure. In such instances, inmates are often unwilling to put forth the effort needed to avoid disciplinary consequences. However, numbers of inmates with bad attitudes toward education who are enrolled in classes eventually become interested and productive learners. It's a challenge for instructors to try effecting such a change.

Solution. The instructor addressed the 49-year-old inmate's apparent lack of effort by: (a) insisting that the student attempt to answer questions during class discussions instead of automatically saying, "I don't know"; (b) asking the inmate questions that the instructor believed the man could answer, then offering positive feedback when the answer was correct; (c) in personal-counseling encounters, assuring the student that he was capable of succeeding if he stayed focused and gave his best effort; and (d) advising the student to complete the minimum amount of work expected of him – and if he failed to do so, he would face disciplinary consequences.

Treatments (a) and (b) were first applied during a language game in which a sentence was written on the chalkboard and students were asked to identify mistakes in punctuation, capitalization, and grammar in order to earn game points. Initially, the 49-year-old denied being able to recognize any errors in the sentence. However, he gradually began participating by pointing out fairly obvious mistakes in capitalization and spelling, and the instructor praised him in front of his classmates, which seemed to please the reluctant learner. As time progressed, the inmate continued responding appropriately during whole-class language and mathematics lessons, even when the questions became more difficult. After his success during group exercises and supportive counseling by the instructor, the student began completing

156 Effective Teaching in Correctional Settings

all assigned work in a timely manner and making an honest effort on tests. The ultimate evidence of his change in attitude came when the student proudly showed the instructor his perfect score on a test in which he was required to correctly punctuate 20 sentences representing diverse forms of direct quotations.

Expanding Educational Services

The problem. An instructor was given the task of developing a program in which he was expected to teach both a junior-high-level class and a GED test-preparation course. The students were to attend class for half of their six-and-one-half-hour school day and spend the remaining time completing independent-study assignments. Therefore, the teacher needed to design the program in a way that would provide meaningful learning experiences both inside the classroom and outside during independent-study time, all the while ensuring that students worked diligently throughout the entire school day.

Analysis. Traditionally, instructors in prisons and youth detention centers have taught students in self-contained classrooms between six and eight hours a day, four to five days a week. Students normally perform all assigned work inside the classroom and are not necessarily required to do homework. Recently, however, such prison systems as California's have explored other education-delivery methods, including distance-learning models and partnerships with public schools' extended-education programs, especially at the college level. The intention of these approaches is to expand schooling services to a larger segment of the inmate population. One proposal for accomplishing this goal without the need to hire more faculty members has involved creating split-day classes in which students are in a classroom part of the day and then study independently the remaining part, thereby earning credit for a full day's schooling. Under such a plan, an instructor can direct one group of learners in the classroom during the morning and another group during the afternoon.

Solutions. In traditional classes, students' time is normally divided between whole-class instruction and individualized tasks. Under a split-day plan, instructors must decide which kinds of assignments students should pursue in the classroom and which kinds during independent study outside. The following is the way that problem was solved by an instructor who had junior-high-level students in class during the morning and GED students during the afternoon.

In-class activities. Both whole-class instruction (lectures, discussions, films, group games) and individualized activities (workbooks, writing projects) were included during class periods, but more time was dedicated to whole-class activities. Mathematics and language skills were taught through lectures, supplemented by chalkboard, overhead-projector, and computer power-point presentations, reinforced by independent-study assignments. Learning gains were assessed through teacher-developed and commercial tests while students were in class so that the teacher was able to monitor the assessment process.

Out-of-class activities. Obviously the teacher could directly supervise students when they were in the classroom but he could not when they worked independently outside. Therefore, he adopted an independent-learning-activity tracking system that consisted of furnishing each student a printed schedule listing work-completion quotas (pages finished in a workbook, writing assignments completed, problems solved) and had students submit their out-of-class work on a set time schedule when their work was evaluated. Of course, the possibility existed that students might duplicate one another's homework or copy answers from answer-keys in self-instructional workbooks in order to meet the required work-production quota. One way that the instructor safeguarded against such cheating was to compare one students' submitted work with another's to identify any copying that had taken place. Another way was to remove answer keys from workbooks so students were prevented from copying answers from the keys.

In order to ensure that students would spend their time productively in an environment conducive to study, the instructor arranged with the librarian in charge of the education department's library to provide a designated area inside the library where students would spend mandatory two-hour time periods working on independent learning assignments with the assistance of inmate-tutors. The librarian also agreed to sign the participating ABE3 and GED students in and out of the library when they studied there. Figure 8.1 shows the form the librarian received each week from the instructor for recording student attendance.

To acquaint the librarian with the skills students were to pursue that week, each student's assigned topic was listed in column two.

MANDATORY INDEPENDENT-STUDY LIBRARY-ATTENDANCE RECORD
GED CLASS

Week of 7/9/07 through 7/13/07		MONDAY		TUESDAY		WEDNESDAY		THURSDAY		FRIDAY	
STUDENT NAME	Subject needed to study:	TIME IN:	TIME OUT:	TIME IN:	TIME OUT:	TIME IN:	TIME OUT:	TIME IN:	TIME OUT:	TIME IN:	TIME OUT:
STUDENT 1	COMMA USAGE										
STUDENT 2	ADD/SUBT FRACTIONS										
STUDENT 3	CAPITALIZATION										
STUDENT 4	INTRO TO FRACTIONS										
STUDENT 5	MULT/DIV FRACTIONS										
STUDENT 6	CAPITALIZATION										
STUDENT 7	ADD/SUBT FRACTIONS										
STUDENT 8	ADD/SUBT DECIMALS										
STUDENT 9	MULT/DIV FRACTIONS										
STUDENT 10	INTRO TO FRACTIONS										
STUDENT 11	COMMA USAGE										
STUDENT 12	INTRO TO FRACTIONS										
STUDENT 13	ADD/SUBT FRACTIONS										
STUDENT 14	SUBJ/PREDICATE										
STUDENT 15	COMMA USAGE										

Figure 8.1. Student-Attendance Form.

Halfhearted Motivation

The problem. In a men's prison, the instructor of an ABE3 (junior-high-level) class was disappointed with the lackadaisical effort that numbers of class members put into their studies. He was convinced that they could progress more rapidly if they tried harder and more consistently.

Analysis. Perhaps all educators agree that the most desirable source of students' motivation to study diligently is their intense desire to master the particular skills and knowledge that a class offers. Such interest in pursuing subject matter for its own sake is sometimes referred to as *intrinsic motivation.* However, it is also apparent that students will exert great effort in school for incentives other than the intrinsic value of what they are asked to learn. Such incentives – which have no inherent connection with the subject matter being studied – are often referred to as *extrinsic motivators.* For example, many learners study hard to earn high semester marks, advance to the next higher grade, and receive a diploma. But those attractions are rather far in the future. So what many learners need are more immediate rewards to fuel their efforts day by day and week by week. Consequently, teachers face the challenge of finding the kinds of short-term extrinsic motivators that appeal to their kinds of learners.

Our own experience suggests that extrinsic incentives are most practical when they (a) strongly appeal to the particular learners, (b) are inexpensive, and (c) can be applied to any sort of skill or kind of knowledge that students are asked to acquire. The most obvious rewards that fit these requirements are oral or written compliments. Thus, teachers are wise to liberally dispense such comments as "Fine job" or "You're on the right track" or "You deserve to be proud of yourself" or "Just see the progress you're making." However, there are also other forms of incentives that meet those requirements. One such is the certificate of achievement.

Solution. The ABE3 instructor decided to prepare a printed certificate that students could earn by completing an English-language workbook. One colleague who heard of this plan scoffed at the idea of grown men – ones who had been convicted of serious crimes – being interested in studying to receive such a sheet of paper. But the scoffer was wrong. The certificates – each presented to its recipient with considerable fanfare in front of the class – were a great success, eagerly sought by inmates who often mailed the documents home to their families (See Figures 8.2 and 8.3).

Encouraged by the success of the first certificates as motivators, the instructor expanded the types of achievement that could earn such documents – high grades on a series of math tests, perfect scores on four sets of spelling words, excellent overall performance so as to become the exemplary student of the week, and more.

The instructor speculated that part of the reason for the documents' power to stimulate hard work was that many of the inmates had been failures in schools earlier in their lives. That failure was why they now were in a junior-high-level class. Hence, the certificates were symbols of their newly discovered academic prowess.

Utilizing Teaching Assistants

The problem. A basic-education ABE2 class was composed of inmates whose average entrance-test TABE scores ranged from grade three to grade five. However, the instructor inspected students' performance on the separate tests (math computation, language mechanics, reading comprehension) that contributed to the TABE average and discovered some scores as low as first grade and others as high as ninth grade.

```
┌─────────────────────────────────────────────────┐
│                                                   │
│      Certificate of Achievement                   │
│                 John Doe                          │
│                                                   │
│  Is hereby recognized and commended for having    │
│                   achieved                        │
│                     TWO                           │
│    Benchmarks on the CASAS Mathematics            │
│         Lifeskills Testing System                 │
│                                                   │
│                                                   │
│   10 July 2007        Signed: _____     │
│                                                   │
└─────────────────────────────────────────────────┘
```

Figure 8.2. Student-Achievement Certificate.

Analysis. Classes in correctional settings typically include students with a wide range of academic skills. Unlike public schools in which students with similar academic abilities remain together throughout the school year, the enrollment in a correctional institution may change completely several times in the same nine-month period. Therefore, if instruction is to be adjusted to individuals' needs, a great deal of it needs to be individualized.

Solutions. In order to meet the wide-ranging needs of students, teachers can work one-on-one with learners, conduct small-group lessons, and personally evaluate students' work. For the sake of efficiency, teaching assistants can be used to perform such tasks as grading worksheets and tests, tutoring students, tracking and filing class members' written work, conducting program-orientation interviews with newly-enrolled students, and transferring the teacher's hand-written lessons and tests into printed form via a computer.

Game Time

The problem. The instructor of a prison junior-high-level class (ABE3) faced the challenge of finding an enjoyable way to teach English-language skills.

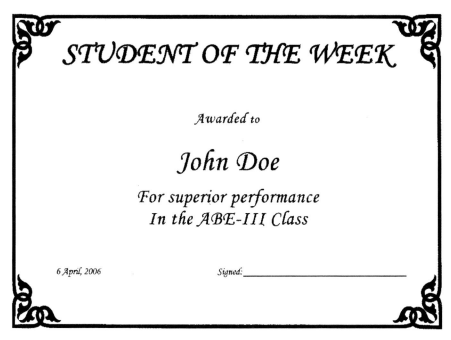

Figure 8.3. Student-of-the-Week Certificate.

Analysis. Students in correctional-education classes are expected to spend as much as seven hours a day, five days a week, sitting in a classroom and learning. One way to enliven the experience is through the use of instructional games. As noted earlier, the traditional spelling-bee form is one example, as are such board games as Scrabble and Monopoly, which can be used for vocabulary and computational-skills development. Some computer software is designed in a competitive form so that when students answer questions or solve problems correctly, they earn points or achieve a particular level of expertise.

Solution. As a means of providing a comprehensive English-language learning experience that engaged students in friendly competition, the instructor developed a game that imitated the traditional spelling-bee format. To begin the game, the class was divided into two teams based on the alphabetical order of the class roster. One team consisted of students whose last names began with the letters A through M and the other team N through Z. Next, the instructor wrote the following sentence on the chalkboard.

> Them student's hadn't did there Homework, during the passed Weak but the Teacher given they an Test over the problem's they was suppose too be studying any way.

The sentence obviously contains numbers of errors in grammar, punctuation, and capitalization. The competition started when the instructor – alternating from one team to the other – selected a student to identify an error in the sentence in order to score a point. The kinds of mistakes in the sentence varied from fairly easily identified ones to others that required deeper understanding of language usage. Thus, all contestants had a chance to succeed, regardless of their levels of knowledge. In order to earn a point, a contestant not only had to correct an error but also had to explain the rule or reason for the correction. In the event that the student who changed an element of the sentence could not explain the reason for the change, other students were invited to provide the proper rationale. The game ended when a final contestant stated that the sentence was now completely correct.

Here are three examples of how participants revised flaws in the sentence.

> Student A earned a point by saying there should be an apostrophe between the letters *n* and *t* in the word *hadnt*, because the word was a contraction of had and not.
> Student B suggested that the word *Teacher* should not be capitalized because *teacher* was not a proper noun.
> Student C earned a point for identifying the need for a comma between *Weak* and *but*. However, he could not remember the rule governing that change. As a result, the teacher asked for a volunteer to give the rule. The volunteer explained that whenever two independent clauses are joined to form a compound sentence, a comma should be placed before the coordinating conjunction, in this case the word *but*.

Barely Half a Class

The problem. When the instructor of an Adult Basic Education class arrived at work one day, he was informed that the inmates in one of the prison's three housing units would be confined to quarters for an undetermined amount of time due to a fight in the unit. As a consequence, 11 of the 27 class members would be unable to attend school that day.

Analysis. When a fight erupts in a prison, an investigation must be conducted. During the investigation an entire housing unit of as many as 1,000 individuals can be locked down while the inmates undergo physical inspection and interviews to determine the source and extent of the disorder. If it turns out that the fight was between only two combatants over a personal disagreement, the lockdown is generally brief. However, if numbers of inmates were implicated and the cause of the trouble appears to be ethnic-related or gang-related, then residents of the housing unit may be restricted to their cells or dormitories for several days or weeks.

All inmate work assignments and training programs are affected by housing-unit disturbances. Thus, teachers in education programs must modify methods of instruction when significant numbers of students are unable to attend class. One possible solution is to have the students who are in class concentrate on individualized learning activities in commercially produced text materials or teacher-developed lessons. Another option is to utilize educational games that can be played by either a few or many students. A further alternative is to conduct whole-group reviews of subject matter covered earlier as a way of providing students additional practice and a chance to clarify areas of confusion.

Solution. In the present case, because more than one-third of the inmates were missing from class, the teacher decided that the remaining students should spend the three-hour morning period working in self-instructional mathematics, English-language, and reading workbooks while the teacher and his aides assisted individual learners. Then, immediately after lunch, he assigned the students to spend one hour working on a vocabulary-development activity that consisted of their writing definitions and sentences for the words they were studying for the weekly spelling test, again aided individually by the instructor and his assistants. During the second hour of the afternoon session, the class played a geometry game in which the students were divided into two teams and points were awarded for team members who correctly identified geometric figures that the teacher projected onto a screen via a computer's digital projector.

Merging Pretest, Lecture, and Study-Guide

The problem. The instructor of a prison ABE2 (upper-elementary) class wanted to combine a pretest and lecture-with-participation when teaching a unit on rules for capitalization.

Analysis. One method of engaging students in active learning involves combining a pretest with a lecture and a reading assignment.

With this approach, students first take a paper-and-pencil diagnostic test designed to assess what they already know about the subject being taught. The teacher collects the tests and places a mark on each error but without identifying the correct answers. Study guides are then distributed to class members. The guides explain vocabulary definitions for the subject matter of the pretest, explanations of concepts, and methods of finding solutions to the test problems. Students are invited to silently read the guide as the teacher reads it aloud and expands on its content. Students can ask the teacher to explain items they find unclear. Next, the marked diagnostic pretests are returned to the students, who use the study guide to analyze and correct their mistakes under the teacher's direction. Once the tests have been reviewed, further explanation is offered as needed and the students are given the chance to practice applying concepts that they originally had misunderstood. When the majority of the class members agree that they have a good understanding of the lesson content, a second version of the test is administered to reveal learning gains resulting from the lesson.

Solution. The ABE2 teacher used the *pretest/study-guide/lecture/posttest* approach for the capitalization lesson. The study-guide consisted of 15 rules and corresponding examples for capitalizing words. After collecting the diagnostic tests, the teacher distributed copies of the study guide and directed the students to follow along as she read through it and responded to class members' questions. When the scored tests were returned to the students, their errors were corrected through a general class discussion. In the process, the teacher called on individuals to identify words that should be capitalized and asked everyone to write above the word the number of the applicable rule (from the list of 15). Following the lesson, the teacher gave the students two days to study capitalization independently before she retested them. The results of the follow-up test showed dramatic improvement in the students' capitalization skills.

Preparing for a High-School-Equivalent Diploma

The problem. The teacher of a GED (General Educational Development) test-preparation program wanted to create a whole-class learning exercise that would help his students pass the test's science section.

Analysis. Three of the GED exam sections – language-arts reading, social studies, and science – depend heavily on reading comprehension. Each consists of passages and diagrams students must read and analyze in order to answer multiple-choice questions. Thus, instructors can profitably teach students how to identify key information from written material as well as how to interpret graphs, tables, and illustrations.

Solution. The teacher was accustomed to giving suggestions to individual students concerning how to select essential information in lessons from their science test-preparation workbook. Therefore, he decided to print a *learning guide*, listing clues he usually gave individuals. He distributed copies of the guide for students to use during a whole-class-instruction session. Among the suggestions in the guide were:

- Inspect the questions at the end of the reading passage before reading the passage so you will know what to look for when studying the passage.
- Among the multiple choices in a question, first eliminate those choices that appear least likely to be correct.
- Skip difficult items and return to them only after answering the easier ones.
- When interpreting graphs, pay careful attention to how the vertical and horizontal dimensions are labeled.
- On maps, give particular attention to *scale*, *direction*, and *symbol* indicators.

During the class session, the instructor directed students to focus on selected lessons in their science workbook as he explained and demonstrated how the study tips could be used. He then asked individual students to try using the hints aloud while the rest of the class observed.

Thereafter, the instructor incorporated the learning-guide procedure to the tests in the social-studies and language-arts-reading workbooks as well.

Monitoring Individualized Assignments

The problem. In an ABE2 (upper-elementary) class, all students diligently finished assignments that were part of whole-class lessons directed by the teacher. However, when students were obliged to complete individualized assignments in workbooks and on teacher-produced worksheets, many failed to complete the work – often struggling vainly with the content, skipping pages, and idly wasting time.

Analysis. As already noted, the open-entry and open-exit nature of correctional-education classes means that much of the instruction must be individualized because students can arrive and leave any time in the school year. But completing individualized assignments in workbooks and on worksheets requires both initiative and diligence – *initiative* in figuring out word meanings and how to solve problems, *diligence* in pursuing tasks that may be puzzling and boring.

Two ways that instructors can cope with the transitory nature of class membership are to (a) teach as many learning objectives by whole-class methods as is feasible and (b) establish a system of monitoring students' individual work.

Solution. First, the instructor examined the ABE2 curriculum and identified the objectives that could feasibly be taught to the entire class, or at least to a large segment of the class.

Second, he controlled the time that each student would work on an individualized assignment by preparing a chart indicating (a) the day that a student would be given a particular individualized assignment (listing the page number of the assigned workbook), (b) the day the assignment was to be completed, and (c) when the instructor would evaluate the completed assignment. Finally, the instructor stamped the completed assignment date on each workbook page to make it easy for the student to keep track of the rate at which he was finishing his tasks.

Dramatic Performances

The problem. The students in a male prison's theater-and-arts program must decide on a theme for a drama that they will write, produce, and present to groups of other inmates. The 40-year-old female instructor of the course makes only one stipulation – the play should contain a moral lesson applicable to people who are incarcerated.

Analysis. Many prisons offer theater and arts programs in which inmates participate and thereby develop a variety of skills. The subjects taught in such courses include art, creative writing, music, and drama.

Drama classes, in particular, are intended to promote inmates'

English-language writing and speaking skills, creativity, critical-thinking, introspection, personal growth, cooperative problem-solving, and positive behavior. The drama instructor teaches class members how to generate themes for plays, write dialogue, create stage scenery, develop acting skills, and appreciate life-lessons that are conveyed through the works of some of the world's most famous playwrights. Students also experience emotional growth during the process of considering the nature of the characters in the plays they produce and during their efforts to convincingly portray the characters.

In addition to learning about the theater and the arts, many participants receive welcome public recognition for what society deems legitimate effort to do a demanding task, with those inmates achieving positive gains in thinking and behavior as a result. Furthermore, the inmates who perform in plays often achieve celebrity status among members of the prison population who view the performances.

Solution. After the students discussed the question of a suitable theme, they chose to base the play loosely on the story of Rip Van Winkle, who fell asleep for 20 years and wakened to find the world considerably changed. The play's storyline focuses on the difficulties that the main character, Rip Rippington (nicknamed *Rip-off*), experiences while attempting to reintegrate into civil society after completing a 20-year prison sentence. While in prison, Rip made no effort to become educated or engage in any rehabilitation program. Instead, he simply served his time and, upon release from imprisonment, returned to his old criminal ways upon reentering mainstream society. As the drama evolves, the paroled convict strikes up a relationship with a young man who Rip does not realize is his own son whom he had never met. The father involves the youth in a crime, resulting in both father and son being brought to trial. In the end – after Rip engages in considerable soul-searching – he recognizes the folly of his ways, confesses to the crime in order to clear his son's name, and commits himself to making positive changes in his life.

The Chatters

The problem. Two students in an ABE1 class were holding a private conversation during a lecture the instructor was giving to the entire class.

Analysis. There are several methods a teacher can use to keep students focused on the topic of discussion during whole-class learning activities. One tactic is to advise students that anyone caught not paying attention will face disciplinary consequences. Another technique consists of posing a question to the class about the lecture topic and then calling for an answer from a student who appears not to be paying attention. A third method is to announce to the class that each member will be expected to write down specific important points that the instructor emphasizes during the lesson, with the written answers to be handed to the instructor at the close of the lesson. Yet another approach involves drawing the attention of the entire class to the behavior of the students who are failing to follow the lecture.

Solution. In this case, when the teacher noticed the pair of class members engaged in a conversation during the lecture, he stopped talking and stared at the chatters. This caused the rest of the class to look at the pair, who immediately ceased their dialogue. At that point, the teacher invited the two students to continue talking with each other while the rest of the class waited until they had completed their private discourse. The instructor then explained that he had stopped lecturing because he wouldn't dream of interrupting people while they were talking; it would be extremely rude. From that moment forward, the pair contritely focused on the rest of the lecture.

Chapter 9

CHOOSING AND CREATING
TEACHING MATERIALS

Teaching materials are the supplies and equipment needed in different teaching methods. Materials can be viewed from two perspectives – form and content.

The expression *form* or *medium* (hardware) refers to the physical appearance of a teaching material – the characteristics that make a material a pen, pencil, textbook, notebook, workbook, magazine, encyclopedia, dictionary, chalkboard, picture, map, chart, film, video, calculator, computer, floppy disk, compact disc, camera, audiorecorder, videorecorder, overhead projector, television receiver, or radio.

The expression *content* or *substance* (software) refers to what the medium intends to communicate. In effect, content is the message that the form is intended to convey, such as a story, math procedure, historical event, reasons to avoid illicit drugs, how to use the Internet, the policies advocated by different political candidates, and far more.

The discussion of materials in this chapter begins with (a) an overview of types media often used in correctional-education programs, along with advantages and limitations of each type, and then continues with (b) problems encountered in using teaching materials and ways teachers can cope with those problems.

FORMS OF MEDIA

For convenience of discussion, commonly used media are reviewed under five categories – (a) reading materials, (b) projectors, (c) audio and video recorders, (d) computers, (e) displays, (f) instructor-produced materials, and (g) student-created media.

Reading Materials

Important reading sources in correctional education include textbooks, workbooks, dictionaries, encyclopedias, atlases, magazines, and teacher-prepared materials.

Over the decades, the advantages of books as teaching tools have made them the schools' most popular instructional material. Books condense large amounts of information within a small space. Books can be carried about and can be read at any time in all sorts of settings. In contrast to a teacher's lecture or a movie, books and magazines permit students to review material they did not fully grasp on the first occasion. Books can also provide instruction and entertainment without the aid of a teacher or tutor so that students can become independent, self-taught learners.

However, the usefulness of reading materials is limited by several conditions. One condition is time. A typical textbook can require three or four years to produce, so its contents many be out-of-date by the time students read it. Another condition is cost. The price of textbooks has risen sharply in recent times, so a textbook's substantial expense can oblige schools to use the same one for years. A third condition is students' reading ability. In order to profit from a textbook, encyclopedia, or novel, learners must have reached the level of reading skill that the particular book requires.

The task of choosing suitable reading materials for juvenile-detention and alternative-school students is simpler than that of selecting appropriate books and periodicals for jail and prison inmates. Juvenile facilities typically use the same books as do the public-school districts in which the facilities are located. However, that same practice is ill suited to the needs of adult learners. A thirty-year-old prison inmate whose English-language reading skill is at the primary-grade level is not apt to take willingly to books designed for six-year-old public-school pupils. Stories about Dick, Jane, and their dog Spot are hardly the sort of thing that appeals to adult felons. Thus, adult correctional institutions need reading materials whose vocabulary and syntax are simple enough for a learner's stage of skill but whose subject matter is suitable for adults. As a guide to kinds of reading matter that meet this requirement, Appendix B later in this book includes the names of texts and workbooks used in a typical state prison.

Projectors

Machines useful for projecting images onto a screen in front of a class include overhead, motion-picture, slide, and digital projectors.

An overhead projector enables an instructor, while writing on a transparent plastic sheet on the projector's faceplate, to have the writing cast large on a screen in front of the classroom. Or the projected transparency can be an already-prepared chart, table, or diagram. Using the projector saves the instructor the need to write on the classroom chalkboard while trying to explain a math problem, a common grammatical error, a historical time line, a map, or a science chart.

Traditional motion-picture projectors are rapidly being replaced by computer-operated projectors that can display motion pictures on a classroom screen. The film on which movies have always been printed is replaced by compact discs (12 centimeters in diameter) known as DVDs (*digital versatile discs* or *digital video discs*) that store large amounts of information (4.7 gigabytes on a single-layer disc, 8.5 gigabytes on a dual-layer disc), including movies.

In the past, slide projectors provided teachers a convenient tool for displaying photographic slides on a screen. The scenes were typically ones photographed by teachers or students of historical events, geographical sites, geological formations, inventions, art works, and more. Like movie projectors, slide projectors are currently being replaced by computer-linked projectors. Photographs taken with a digital camera are easily stored in a computer and projected onto a screen in the classroom. Computer software, such as the Microsoft company's *PowerPoint*, equips teachers with the ability to create instructional slide programs of professional quality.

Audio and Video Recorders

Audiorecorders enable instructors or students to capture speech and music to be played back later. Videorecorders permit instructors and students to copy both visual images and their accompanying sounds for viewing at a later time. The recorded material can be captured either on magnetic tape (tape recorders) or as images on digital *cards* whose contents are transferred to a computer on which the pictures can be viewed or projected onto a screen.

Computers

Electronic computers in correctional education can assume several forms – desktop, laptop (notebook), and hand-held. Before the 1980s, there was no such thing as a personal computer that would fit atop a school desk. Since that time, personal computers have become standard equipment in correctional-education programs. Not only are special classes in using computers offered in prisons, juvenile centers, and alternative schools, but computers are also available in regular academic and vocational classrooms. The two most useful computer skills inmates acquire are those of word processing and searching the Internet. Training in the operation of computers not only improves inmates' efficiency in their classroom studies but equips them with an ability that can prove valuable when they are hunting for a job after their release from imprisonment.

Displays

Media that qualify as displays include posters, pictures, charts, wall maps, models, exhibits, dioramas, historical artifacts, and the like. The following are examples of displays in correctional-education classes.

Animal-grooming class: A poster of hairstyles for different dog breeds.

Meat-cutting course: A chart showing where on a cow various cuts of beef are located.

Meteorology course: Maps with symbols of various weather conditions.

ESL (English-as-a-second-language) class: Photos of familiar objects accompanied by their English-language names.

ABE1 (primary-level) class: A chart of common sight words.

ABE2 (upper-elementary-level) class: A graph comparing amounts of calories in typical servings of popular foods.

ABE3 (junior-high-level) class: A chart of geometric forms and their names.

GED class, earth-science unit: A collection of stones illustrating kinds of igneous, sedimentary, and metamorphic rocks.

GED class, social-studies unit. A time-line of events in American history.

Instructor-Produced Materials

Teachers often create their own instructional materials – reading passages, worksheets, charts, posters, maps, exhibits, collections, photographs, audiotapes, *PowerPoint* slide shows, videos, and more. The chief advantage of instructor-produced materials is that they can be designed to suit particular learning objectives, important characteristics of the students, and the instructor's talents and teaching style. Consider the following types of media created by teachers to fit particular instructional conditions.

Reading material: A study guide for a GED biology unit on evolution.
    A list of frequently misspelled words in an ABE2 (upper-elementary-grade) class.
    Sample business letters in a vocational office-practices course.
    A description of proper health and safety practices for students in a vocational health-care-assistants program.
    Worksheets focusing on key math concepts in order to strengthen students' command of math skills that need more reinforcement and practice.

Projectors: The instructor of a vocational building-maintenance course uses a digital camera to photograph good and poor janitorial practices, then organizes the photos as a PowerPoint slide-show presentation.
    In her ABE1 (primary-grade) class, the teacher uses an overhead projector to display a sequence of words on a screen in front of the class as students take turns pronouncing the words.

Audiotapes, videotapes: An ESL teacher records on audiotape a passage that she reads aloud from the students' textbook. Students listen to the recording, then read into the tape recorder the same passage. Later, each student – along with the teacher – compares the two readings so as to identify ways his enunciation and pronunciation might be improved.
    The instructor uses a video camera to record a student-enacted drama so that participants might judge how their acting could be enhanced when they present the play before an audience.

Computers: From the Internet, the teacher of an ABE3 (junior-high) class downloads two outline maps – one of the United States and the other of South America. Printed copies of the maps are distributed to students who are assigned to label the states on the U.S. map and label the countries on the South American map.

In a computer laboratory, the instructor creates PowerPoint presentations of basic grammar and writing skills.

Displays: A GED instructor prepares a chart showing the stages through which a proposed bill must pass in the state legislature before the proposal can become a law.

The chief disadvantage of teacher-developed materials is that creating such media requires time, expense, and specific skills.

Student-Created Media

Inmates who contribute their own creations gain experience and satisfaction from sharing their work with classmates. Their classmates also profit from studying such contributions.

Reading material: Students' short stories, essays, poems can be posted on a bulletin board or printed and shared with classmates.

Computers: Members of an ABE2 (upper-elementary) course use a computer to produce a biweekly newsletter of class events, editorials, letters-to-the-editor, and drawings.

Displays: An inmate with an artistic flair draws a cartoon depicting a current political debate. The teacher adds the cartoon to an exhibit of newspaper political cartoons on the classroom wall.

INSTRUCTIONAL-MATERIALS' PROBLEMS AND SOLUTIONS

The three cases in the following section focus on (a) how to cope with a shortage of funds for materials, (b) matching textbooks to students' levels of skill, and (c) explaining why child-centered books are used.

Budget Crisis

The problem. At the beginning of the fiscal year, a teacher is informed that she will be given half the normal amount of money to purchase learning materials for the upcoming academic year.

Analysis. There are several reasons why the money allotted for materials may fluctuate from year to year. One cause is an economic downturn that result in tax revenues being lower than normal. Another is that education administrators may reprioritize financial resources within their department in order to replace equipment or to purchase machinery used in vocational programs. A third possibility is that wardens, when they have discretion over apportioning funds for the prison as a whole, may decide to utilize money designated for education for other purposes, such as capital replacement or officer overtime wages.

Solutions. As noted earlier, the transient nature of correctional-institution populations results in students entering and leaving education programs at any time of the year. Thus, instruction must, to a great extent, be individualized. This means that consumable, self-instruction workbooks are commonly used in classrooms to teach language, mathematics, and reading skills. However, due to the rapid class enrollment turnover (as much as a third of the students may leave and be replaced within a given month), and in times of low budget allocation, it may not be possible to purchase sufficient workbooks to provide a new book for every student throughout an entire academic year.

Teachers can meet this challenge in different ways. One way is to issue students folders containing lined paper (newsprint is the cheapest) and have students copy workbook exercises and write responses in the folders instead of in the workbooks. To keep materials properly organized, a student can have a different folder for each subject area or text material. The same approach can be used with non-consumable textbooks used in the class.

Instructors can also compensate for a shortage of published textbooks by creating learning materials for students. For example, a teacher can use a computer's digital projector, overhead projector, chalkboard, or whiteboard to display information for students to copy. Instructors can also develop consumable study-guides, practice exercises, and tests addressing the class's curriculum.

Matching Textbooks to Students' Skills

The problem. The teacher of an ABE3 class (junior-high-school level) was assigned a pre-algebra textbook that was part of an effort to standardize instruction throughout the state's prison system. When she inspected the text's content, she recognized that the text was too advanced for nearly all of the students in her program.

Analysis. In the past, instructors in the state prison system had been permitted to select the learning materials – including textbooks – used in their classes. However, a recent change in philosophy led to prison officials adopting the state public schools standard academic curriculum. To effect the transition to a standardized curriculum, committees of veteran teachers from prison-education programs throughout the state were directed to select textbooks for use in different grade-level classes in all state-government-operated prisons. The main objective was to ensure that inmates enrolled in prison education programs were afforded an education comparable to what they would have received in the public system. A secondary goal was to establish a uniform education program through which inmates enrolled in one institution could make a smooth transition when they were transferred from one prison to another and there reenrolled in the same grade-level class.

The concept of aligning prison curricula and learning materials with those of mainstream public education is well intended. However, there are some drawbacks. First, with few exceptions, the students enrolled in public-school classes remain together over the course of an entire nine-month scholastic year; whereas – as noted earlier in this book – the typical prison class operates year-round with an open entrance and exit enrollment policy in which the class roster is in constant flux. A second factor is that students in a public-school junior- or senior-high math or English or science class perform at about the same basic grade level. In contrast, prison inmates are assigned to a multiple-subject-matter class in which math, language, science, and social studies are all taught. Students are assigned to their class on the basis of the average grade-level score they earned on TABE tests in the various subject fields. Consequently, there are often wide ranging differences among a class's students in terms of their knowledge and skills in the several subject areas. As an example, Student A was enrolled in the class with a 6.5 (sixth grade plus) TABE average, based on a 3.0 (third grade) that he scored in math, a 9.0 (ninth grade) score in reading, and a 7.5 (seventh grade plus) in English language. In contrast, Student B entered the class with the same overall 6.5 grade-level average, but it was composed of a 10.5 in math, 4.0 in reading, and 5.0 in language.

Solution. After realizing that the pre-algebra textbook was too advanced for most of her students, the teacher of the ABE3 class decided to assign the book to only her most advanced mathematicians. She then requisitioned a sufficient number of math texts used in lower-grade-level programs and supplemented them with workbooks she had customarily used in order to meet the needs of the other learners in her class. At the same time, she selected basic concepts and vocabulary terms from the pre-algebra book and began teaching them through whole-class learning activities in order to introduce the students to what they would be studying in greater detail once they began using the adopted pre-algebra text.

Offended Learner

The problem. A 39-year-old student in an ABE2 (upper-elementary) class briefly inspected the contents of a reading textbook he had been assigned, and he asked the teacher which grade level the book was intended for. When the teacher said that the book was typically used in public-schools' fourth-grade classes, the student winced and shook his head in disgust. He obviously felt offended.

Analysis. In some correctional institutions, a central authority chooses the textbooks and workbooks for classes. Frequently those books are ones used in public schools. Thus, the vocabulary, sentence structures, and formats (type size, pictures, topics) will be designed for pupils at the various grade levels – primary, upper elementary, junior high, and senior high. So inmates enrolled in ABE1 (primary) and ABE2 (upper elementary) classes can understandably be embarrassed by the content of reading, language, math, social-studies, and science texts intended for children ages 6 to 11.

In other correctional settings, classroom teachers are either responsible for selecting textbooks or are free to supplement the central authorities' choices with ones of the teachers' choosing. In these cases, instructors can pick books that have easy vocabulary and syntax but adult oriented subject matter and format (type size, pictures). The books listed in Appendix B include a sampling of materials of that sort.

Solution. The instructor responded to the student's distress at the textbook's format and subject matter by explaining that the vocabulary and sentence structure of the book were well suited to the student's present reading skill and that the student would soon be advancing to more mature subject matter. The instructor explained further that inmates often had forgotten basic elements of reading and math that they had studied in the distant past, so it was well for them to recapture those elements before moving ahead to more difficult material. He also pointed out that the most skillfully designed textbooks with easy vocabulary and sentence structures were written for children, because the major market for such materials were the primary and upper-elementary grades.

Chapter 10

ASSESSING STUDENT PROGRESS

In earlier chapters we compared the teaching-and-learning process to taking a trip. Specifying the learning objectives students should pursue provides the answer for "Where are we going?" Proposing instructional methods and materials answers "How can we best get there?" Finally, identifying how to assess student progress answers "How close have we come to where we intended to go."

The first half of Chapter 10 compares assessment techniques in terms of their characteristics and uses. The second half of the chapter describes common assessment problems and proposed solutions.

A COMPARISON OF ASSESSMENT TECHNIQUES

Authors who write about ways of estimating students' progress sometimes distinguish among such terms as *assessing, evaluating, appraising, judging,* and *measuring.* However, in this chapter we treat all five terms as synonyms that refer to ways of estimating how well students have achieved the learning objectives.

Teachers evaluate students for a variety of reasons, including to:

- Diagnose the strengths and weaknesses in learners' performance so the weaknesses can be remedied.
- Assign students a mark or grade reflecting how well they have met an achievement standard. The mark can represent performance on one occasion (test, oral presentation, written essay, classroom behavior) or an entire semester (summary of all past performances).

179

- Determine if students deserve a reward (oral compliment, certificate, diploma, a more advanced set of lessons, or advance to a higher class).

The first of the above functions is sometimes referred to as *formative evaluation* – periodic appraisal of how students are progressing so that problems they experience can be corrected promptly. The second and third functions are often labeled *summative evaluation* – assessment at the end of a period of study that can lead to such actions as the awarding of a mark or a diploma or promotion to a higher level of schooling. Summative appraisals are often in the form of a report card or letter of recommendation.

Three ways that teachers judge students' progress are by giving tests, observing students' behavior, and appraising the quality of students work products. The following discussion reviews those ways in terms of their defining characteristics, their advantages, and their disadvantages in correctional education.

ACHIEVEMENT TESTS

Three kinds of tests used in schools are designed to assess students' (a) general aptitude or intelligence, (b) personality structure, and (c) achievement. The purpose of aptitude/intelligence tests is to estimate how individuals "think" so as to predict how well they might succeed at some task, as in university studies or in a job. The purpose of personality tests is to reveal people's emotional stability or ways of viewing life. The intention of achievement tests is to discover how well people have learned skills and knowledge. Achievement tests are the only ones discussed in this chapter, since they focus on what learners are expected to acquire from correctional education.

Three types of achievement tests used in correctional settings are (a) standardized, (b) textbook-related, and (c) teacher-prepared.

Standardized tests. Such tests are created by experts, then administered to large numbers of students whose scores are summarized statistically. The summaries tell the average scores earned by students at different grade levels or age levels. As explained in Chapter 5, the most widely used standardized test battery in correctional institutions is the Test of Adult Basic Education (TABE), which has separate sections for English language, reading, and mathematics. The TABE reports a test-taker's scores in terms of his or her average-grade-level of skill or knowledge. Thus, newly arrived inmates who earn scores equivalent to those of the average public-school primary-grade pupil will be assigned to an ABE1 class (equivalent of grades 1–3). Inmates scoring at grades 4–6 are assigned to an ABE2 class, and those scoring at grades 7–9 are assigned to an ABE3 class. Thus, the TABE is useful for placing inmates in classes that seem suited to their current achievement level in English language, reading, and math.

The most popular standardized-test battery for summarizing students' academic achievement in correctional facilities is the General Education Development (GED) test series that qualifies students for a certificate that is the equivalent of a high-school diploma. The GED tests are prepared and scored by the American Council on Education. The battery consists of six tests: (a) language-arts analysis, (b) language-arts essay writing, (c) English-language reading, (d) social studies, (e) science, and (f) mathematics. The components of the tests and the percentage that each component contributes to the final test score are as follows (American Council on Education, 2007):

Language-arts analysis. Fifty multiple-choice items assess students' ability to revise and edit documents. The four content areas measured by the items are:

- Organization (15%). Restructure ideas in the passage.
- Sentence structure (30%). Correct syntax errors.
- Usage (30%). Correct mistakes in subject-verb agreement, verb tense, and pronoun reference.
- Mechanics (25%). Correct capitalization, punctuation, and spelling errors.

Essay composition. Students write an essay on a general topic. The analysis and composition are combined to produce a single score.

English-language reading. Forty multiple-choice items measure test-takers' ability to interpret reading passages from literary classics (75%) and nonfiction sources (25%).

Social studies. Fifty multiple-choice questions concern

- History (United States, 25%; World, 15%)
- Geography (15%)
- Civics and government (25%)
- Economics (20%)

Science. Fifty multiple-choice items focus on

- Physical science (physics and chemistry) (35%)
- Life science (45%)
- Earth and space science (20%)

Mathematics. The 50 mathematics questions concern

- Number operations and number sense (20%–30%)
- Measurement and geometry (20%–30%)
- Data analysis, statistics, and probability (20%–30%)
- Algebra, functions, and patterns (20%–30%)

Three advantages of standardized tests are that (a) they relieve instructors of the burden of creating tests, (b) the test items have been carefully constructed and tried out with a wide range of students, and (c) they enable instructors to compare their own students with the scores achieved by students in other institutions.

However helpful standardized tests may be for placement purposes, they are only useful for judging students' recent progress if what the instructor has taught precisely matches the content of the test items. If some test items evaluate for knowledge that was not taught, then it is unfair to expect students to have mastered that knowledge. Furthermore, standardized tests frequently fail to include items that measure students' command of important skills that the instructor did teach. Hence, standardized tests are of limited value for measuring what inmates have learned in their current class.

Textbook-related tests. Publishers of textbooks and workbooks sometimes include tests that instructors can use to evaluate how well students have understood the books' content. Instructors who expect their students to reach the books' objectives find such tests useful. But, as with standardized tests, text-related tests are valid measures only to the extent that their content precisely matches what the instructor has actually taught.

Teacher-prepared tests. The chief advantage of teacher-created tests is that, when well done, they measure for precisely what was taught. Their main disadvantages are that (a) preparing test items is a time-consuming task and (b) an instructor may not be well-schooled in test construction, so the tests fail to accurately assess students' skills and knowledge.

As an effort toward helping instructors improve their test-making, the following paragraphs offer a bit of guidance in the selection and construction of test items.

Creating Items for Teacher-Made-Tests

Four of the most popular kinds of test items are the true-false, multiple-choice, completion, and essay types.

True-false items. An alternative-response item consists of a statement which students are to judge as *true* or *false, right* or *wrong, correct* or *incorrect.* True-false tests are often popular with teachers because they are simple to create and score. The easiest way to generate a true-false item is to copy a sentence from a textbook and use that sentence as an item to be judged *true* or *correct.* Then, to construct a *false* item, the teacher merely alters a true sentence by inserting such a word as *not* or *never* or else by changing the time, place, or person mentioned in the item.

Despite true-false items' popularity, they suffer from such serious shortcomings that they are best rejected in favor of more trustworthy types – multiple-choice, completion, or essay. The chance of a student getting an alternative-choice answer right without knowing anything about the subject-matter being tested is the number of possible correct answers divided by the number of possible choices. So the chance of getting a correct answer to a true-false item by blind guess is 1 divided by 2 or 50%.

And there are additional disadvantages of alternative-response questions. When a student decides that an item is *false,* the teacher doesn't know which part of the item the test-taker believed was untrue. For example, a student may earn credit for marking this sentence false: "*The Star Spangled Banner* was written by Francis Scott Keys during the War of 1812." The student thought the false part was the date 1812, on the mistaken impression that the national anthem was written during the Spanish American War of 1898. However, in the teacher's mind the false part was the poet's last name, which should have been *Key,* not *Keys.* Furthermore, a clever student would be judged wrong for marking the following sentence false when the teacher intended it to be true: "Christopher Columbus discovered America in 1492." Imagine that the clever student judged both the name of the man and of the discovered land to be false by reasoning that the Spanish version of the explorer's name was Cristóbal Colón, and in 1492 there was no geographical area labeled "America."

Thus, despite the fact that alternative-response items are easy to construct and score, a "correct" answer does not necessarily signify that a student successfully reached the learning objective. Furthermore, such items measure only whether students can *recognize* the correctness of a fact, not whether they can *recall* the fact independently or apply it in lifelike situations.

Multiple-choice items. A multiple-choice item consists of two parts. The first is an incomplete statement or a question, sometimes called the *stem* of the item. The second consists of several alternative ways of completing the statement or answering the question. The test-taker is to identify which of the alternatives is the best choice.

Multiple-choice items can perform far more functions than true-false types and are thus the most useful kinds of objectively-scored tests available to teachers. Consider the following array of functions for which multiple-choice items are suited.

1. Recognize the *definition* of something:

____The event in which American colonists dressed as Indians and threw crates from a British ship into the harbor water is known as the:

    A. Boston Massacre   C. Harbor Prank
    B. Boston Tea Party   D. Halloween Party

2. Recognize the *purpose* of something:

____The job of the United States Congress is to
    A. Collect taxes   C. Make new laws
    B. Punish lawbreakers   D. Choose state governors

3. Recognize the *cause* of something:

____Much of the water pollution near large cities is caused by
    A. rotting fish   C. too much sewage
    B. heavy rainfall   D. too much salt water

4. Recognize the *effect* of something:

____What did Europe gain from the discovery of America?
    A. Horses and cows   C. Cloves and nutmeg
    B. Turkeys and corn   D. Tin and rubber

5. Identify *people, places,* and *dates*:

____A European country without a seacoast is
    A. Denmark   C. Norway
    B. Germany   D. Switzerland

6. Identify *similarities* and *differences*:

____If you had $500 and wanted to save it, which of the following would get you the highest interest?
    A. A bank checking account C. A bank savings account
    B. A certificate of deposit D. Municipal bonds

In summary, multiple-choice items successfully test students' ability to *recognize* or *identify* meanings. However, they do not measure learners' ability to *freely recall* the answers to questions. In multiple-choice questions, the alternatives from which students are to select the correct response are already provided. Hence, students need not create the answers from their own minds but merely to recognize the correct choice.

Completion items. A *fill-in* or *completion* item consists of a sentence in which a word or phrase is deleted. Or else a question is posed, and the answer is to be a word or phrase; such an item is often referred to as a *short-answer* type. For fill-in or short-answer items, the test-takers' task is to complete the sentence's missing words or to write a brief answer to the question. Here are three examples:

1. The present-day U. S. President is a member of the _____ political party.
2. The bottom number in a fraction like 3/4 is called the _____.
3. Which part of this sentence is the *subject* of the sentence – "The Giants won the ball game last Friday"? _____

Completion and short-answer items are most appropriate for testing students' recall of facts. Such items are more demanding than multiple-choice questions because they require test-takers to generate correct answers rather than simply select an answer from several displayed options.

When composing fill-in items, teachers are wise to delete only one element of the sentence so as to give students a fair chance to produce a reasonable answer. Consider the difficulty students face with such a butchered sentence as the following:

"Residents of _____ regions can expect more _____ and _____ than normal when rainfall exceeds _____ during _____ and _____."

Essay items. Whereas multiple-choice and completion questions are well adapted to measuring learners' command of facts and definitions, essays are better suited to testing students' ability to organize facts into a well-reasoned argument. Essays are also appropriate for evaluating the desirability of a policy or behavior and for appraising a plan of action, such as a proposed method of solving air pollution, reducing drug abuse, or preparing prisoners for parole.

The way an essay question is presented to test-takers can determine whether the students' task will be simple or complex. Note how the following four essay items differ in complexity.

1. Explain the differences among (a) being a United States citizen, (b) having a green card, and (c) being an illegal alien. (Prison upper-elementary-level class)

2. Tell what scientists mean by the phrase "the water cycle". (Jail junior-high-level class)

3. Imagine that a woman brings her car for you to repair. She complains that the car is difficult to start in the morning, and sometimes the car stalls and the engine dies. Tell the steps you would follow to discover the cause of her problem. (Men's prison auto-repair class)

4. Write an essay about "Irresponsible and Responsible Mothers." First, tell what an irresponsible mother would do about her child's health, schooling, and friendships. Then tell what a responsible mother would do about her child's health, schooling, and friendships. (Teenage girls' detention center)

A disadvantage of assessing inmates' learning progress by requiring that they write essays is the essay's heavy dependence on inmates' English-language writing skills. Students who can answer complex questions orally may not be able to do so in writing. This is particularly true of inmates whose native language is not English. Therefore, in lieu of requiring that a student write an essay, an instructor may interview the student in order to evaluate the adequacy of his or her thought processes.

(The diminishing-aid teaching method described in Chapter 8 and extended in Appendix A illustrates one way to train inmates in essay writing.)

An additional disadvantage of essay items is that many instructors lack training in how to score essay responses. Even instructors who are given a rubric to guide their scoring process often are unsure of how to use the guide sheet.

Observing Students' Behavior

Students' achievement of some important aims of correctional education cannot be assessed by written tests. Such is the case with inmates' speaking skills, working effectively in a group, repairing a car in a vocational-training auto shop, sticking at a task until its completion, and more.

The most frequent way teachers record observations of student behavior is by simply remembering what occurred. The next most popular way is to write a brief note – an anecdotal record. Clearly, the written note provides a more trustworthy record than does "just remembering," because memories easily fade and become distorted.

A written record can (a) describe a specific incident, (b) summarize a series of incidents, or (c) summarize a series of incidents, then offer examples of the kinds of events represented in the summary.

Specific incidents

"When Jane Doe explained her project to the class, she frequently inserted 'you know' and 'I mean' into the narrative."

"Ralph Roe offered to help a classmate with the math computer program."

"Johnson spilled red paint all over the end table that Jones was building."

Summary

"Jane Doe always sprinkles her speech with non-functional insertions."

"Ralph Roe is a loner. He rarely offers to help classmates or to accept help from others."

"Johnson is always irritating other inmates."

Summary plus examples

"Jane Doe fills her speech with non-functional words, such as *I mean, you know, it's like, well,* and *so it's.*"

"Ralph Roe is a loner who rarely interacts with classmates. On only one occasion did I see him offer to help another student use a math computer program."

"Smith continually irritates classmates by doing such things as spilling paint over another student's end table, failing to put tools back in the rack, and laughing when someone gets hurt."

Anecdotal records can consist solely of statements of fact or they can include interpretation, evaluation, or a proposal for action.

Factual statements

"During the movie, Ms. Brown fell asleep again. This is the fourth time she has fallen asleep in class. Each time, it's been in the late afternoon."

"While taking the science test, Carl periodically consulted a cheat-sheet he had hidden under his shirt."

Facts plus interpretation

"John K. finished less than a quarter of the essay even though he'd had plenty of time. When I pressed him to offer reasons for America losing the Vietnamese War, he answered with very sensible arguments, so it seems that his poor performance resulted from a lack of effort and not a lack of ability or knowledge."

"D. V. badgers any class member who's not a skin-head White. I imagine he feels that Whites' traditionally favored position in society is threatened by Blacks, Hispanics, and Asians."

Facts plus evaluation

"Four times today Soto interrupted the class with what he seemed to think were comical remarks about other class members, but he wasn't funny, just insulting."

"I was pleased to see Mrs. Clay volunteer answers to math questions today. She seems to be coming out of her shell."

Facts plus a proposal for action

"While taking the science test, Carl periodically consulted a cheat-sheet he had hidden under his shirt. Since this is the fourth time he's tried that trick, I suggest that he be dropped from the class."

"During the movie, Ms. Brown fell asleep again. This is the fourth time she has fallen asleep in class. Each time, it's been in the late afternoon. I think the supervisor of her dormitory should investigate to discover if Ms. Brown is getting enough sleep or perhaps is on drugs."

A further way to record evaluations of observed behavior is to mark a checklist or rating scale. Rating devices are better than written notes at focusing the instructor's attention on a set of standards or aims that are being assessed. And it is usually easier to mark a rating scale than to write comments about behavior.

Figure 10.1 illustrates a rating scale for recording an instructor's or teaching assistant's evaluation of how well an inmate performs in delivering an oral report or speech.

Judging Students' Work Products

Examples of work products are students' written compositions, workbook exercises, paper-pencil tests, drawings, diagrams, and projects in vocational classes (shoe repairing, eyeglass assembly, dressmaking, cabinet making, plumbing, and more).

Directions: On each scale below, check the point on the line that best describes
the student's speech. Use the space below each line to write comments that
help describe how the student spoke.

Student ~~R. Jones~~

1. Enunciation   ✓

| All words easily understood. | Some words unclear. | Most words Incoherent. |

2. Stammering or stuttering ✓

| Smooth flow of speech. No hesitating. | Some hesitation or repetition of syllables. | Many repetitions. Often hesitates. |

3. Pronunciation   ✓

| All words properly pronounced. | Several words mispronounced | Many words mispronounced. |

"winner" for "winter"
"wanna" for "want to"

4. Grammar ✓

| No errors. *He don't* | Several errors. | Many errors. |

5. Logical thought sequence ✓

| Moves logically from one idea to another. | Sometimes wanders off topic. | Sequence of ideas very erratic. |

6. Mannerisms, gestures ✓

| Gestures emphasize speech well. No distracting mannerisms. | Occasional hand, face, or body movements distract from the speech. | Many distracting hand, face, body movements. |

Scratches nose.

Figure 10.1. Speech Rating Scale.

Like the instructor's task of writing notes about inmates' observed
behavior, notes about their work products can focus on facts, interpretation, evaluation, and proposed action. Instructors' judgments of
student work products can also be cast as marks and comments on a

checklist or rating device. Such instruments are useful for informing students of the strengths and limitations of work products that they have been assigned. Consider, for example, the "one-week's-menus checklist" in Figure 10.2.

Student's name ___R. Carter___   Date ___9-16-08___

Note to Students: You are to write seven days' menus (three meals a day). In addition to describing the contents of each meal, you are to add information about the nutritional elements of that meal. The following checklist will be used for evaluating how well you did the job.

Note to Evaluator: Write an appropriate number on the line beside each item to show how well the menu assignment has been done. The number refers to a typical daily menu. The numbers bear the following meanings:

   0 = No information   1 = Partial information   2 = Complete information

Nutrition facts:

_2_	Calories total	_2_	Protein %	_2_	Carbohydrate %
_2_	Total fat %	_0_	Saturated fat %	_0_	Trans fat %
_0_	Calories from fat	_0_	Cholesterol %	_1_	Sodium %
_1_	Potassium %	_1_	Minerals	_1_	Vitamins

Amounts of:

_2_	Red meat	_2_	Poultry	_2_	Seafood
_2_	Vegetables	_2_	Fruits	_1_	Dairy products

Comments: Too much red meat – hamburgers, hot dogs, sausages. More green vegetables would be desirable. A nice variety of fruits is included. Many of the beverages are healthful ones, but the sodas are high in sugar and caffeine so they should be replaced. The menus seem to be nicely varied from one day to another.

Figure 10.2. Checklist for One-Week's-Menus Assignment.

In a prison food-preparation course, students were assigned to plan healthful, appealing meals (three each day) for a seven-day period. At the outset of the assignment, the instructor provided each student a copy of the checklist and explained that it would be used to evaluate how well they completed the task. She then explained each item on the list. Therefore, as the students worked on the project, they would be clearly aware of the standards to be used in judging their menus.

ASSESSMENT PROBLEMS AND SOLUTIONS

The six problem situations analyzed in the following pages concern (a) students' fear of tests, (b) cheating, (c) predicting inmates' test success, (d) reporting students' progress, (e) varied lengths of time that students are in a class, and (f) tracking students' progress.

Frightened of Tests

The problem. A 31-year-old woman inmate who had correctly answered only 38 percent of the questions on a math test complained to the instructor, "Having to write tests scares me. I really know the math, but I get so nervous taking tests that I can't think straight."

Analysis. Clearly, some students become so emotionally distraught in testing situations that they fail to reveal their actual skill and knowledge. Usually the source of their debilitating distress can be traced to painful testing experiences in the past. In childhood, the 31-year-old woman may have been punished for doing poorly on a test, or her inadequate command of English had left her confused about the meaning of the test problems, or she had faced tests for which she lacked adequate preparation. In any event, each new test situation would now reignite her past fear and doom her to failure.

Solution. The instructor allowed the woman to substitute an interview for the written math test. That is, while the rest of the class was busy with workbook assignments, the instructor took the woman aside and posed math questions orally. The student was asked to say aloud her way of thinking about each question, and she was permitted to use pencil and paper to do whatever written calculating she needed. If she failed to grasp the intent of a question, the instructor rephrased the question. Through such a process, the instructor was able to estimate which math functions the student had mastered and which she still needed to learn.

Test Cheater

The problem. Mr. X, a 20-year-old prison inmate periodically pulled up his left sleeve in order to glance at his bare arm during the time the class took a weekly spelling test. The instructor suspected that Mr. X had a list of spelling words hidden in his sleeve.

Analysis. In many, if not most, correctional programs, inmates sign behavior contracts that identify rules to be followed and consequences to be borne for breaking the rules. Therefore, a student caught cheating on a test can expect to be disciplined. A teacher who suspects that an inmate is cheating can order the inmate to produce any forbidden notes or other devices being used illicitly. The instructor's attempting to wrest a cheat-sheet from a student in a prison classroom is rarely advisable. Instead, if the inmate refuses to hand over the requested item, the instructor is best advised to summon a custody officer who can remove the inmate from the classroom. The apparent cheater can then be escorted to an office where he or she will be interviewed and searched if necessary.

But if the student does promptly hand over the cheating device to the instructor, the instructor has several factors to consider. One is the importance placed on the test being taken. Tests that are designed merely to check for a student's competency in a specific skill, such as the ability to add and subtract fractions or capitalize proper nouns, may not be considered as significant as a comprehensive test used for determining whether the student should be promoted to the next higher class. A second factor is the student's classroom-behavior history. Inmates who have violated rules in the past may have strained the teacher's patience enough to warrant an official written report or a request that the student be dropped from the class. But if the student has usually been cooperative and has not seriously misbehaved in the past, a lesser punishment – such as a verbal reprehend or removal of a minor privilege – can be applied.

Solution. In the case of the inmate caught cheating on the spelling test, the teacher first ordered him to hand over the slip of paper he was suspected of hiding in his shirtsleeve. The inmate immediately complied. Once the teacher thus verified that the student was cheating, she admonished him in front of the class as a way of cautioning others against similar transgressions. She then advised the cheater that he would receive a written warning that would be placed in both his education file and his prison-behavior-history record. The instructor also informed the student that he would face more serious disciplinary consequences if he tried the same trick again and that he would be subject to checks for cheat-sheets during future tests. The student then had to retake the spelling test individually under the teacher's direct supervision. In response, the inmate appeared contrite and vowed not to cheat in the future.

Predicting Test Success

The problem. An instructor of a GED class was asked to submit a list of the students he believed were adequately prepared to take the official General-Education-Development test battery.

Analysis. The official GED exam includes five sections – social studies, writing skills, reading, mathematics, and science. Each section is assessed by a separate test. The entire examination process normally takes two full days and is costly because trained proctors must monitor the test administration at a specific site, and then the answer sheets must be sent to a central location for scoring. Therefore, it is important that teachers be as accurate as possibly in predicting which students are likely to pass the examination series.

Solutions. There are a number of methods that can be used to identify which students are likely to pass the GED tests. One indicator is an inmate's TABE results. Students who have scored between a 9.0 and 12.9 grade-level equivalent (with 12.9 the highest possible) on the mathematics, language, and reading sections of the TABE are often capable of passing the GED exams. Another gauge of a person's test-readiness is his or her progress in completing materials designed to prepare learners for each of the five areas of the battery. A third predictor is how well the inmate has succeeded on teacher-prepared lessons and evaluation procedures.

However, the most accurate indicator is a student's success on timed practice tests that simulate the actual examination process. Such tests can be purchased from textbook companies and are often included in the professionally developed workbooks described in Chapter 9. The simulated testing procedure gives students a chance to experience what the official testing is like and, in the process, can reduce the anxiety they may feel about the actual examination. Another advantage of using replicate tests is that the instructor can evaluate the test results with the same scoring procedure used for the official exam. A good method for estimating an individual's readiness to attempt the actual GED battery is to make sure the student has achieved at least a minimum score of 410 on each of the five constituent tests and a minimum average of 450 on the five tests combined.

The accuracy of prediction that the simulated-tests approach can achieve can be illustrated with the scores earned by students in a prison GED class within one academic year. Among the individuals who were recommended to take the official GED battery on the basis of their scoring above the minimum averages (410 and 450) on simulated preparation tests, seven out of the 10 students passed the entire official battery the first time they tried it (Table 10.1). Students 2 and 9 failed. Student 2 did not pass because his reading score was below 410, although his overall average of 462 was above the passing mark of 450. Student 9 fell short of the required 450 because his writing performance was inadequate (390). Student 7 received an incomplete because he had failed to finish the writing exam.

Table 10.1
Students' Scores on a GED Practice Test

Name	Writing	Social Studies	Science	Reading	Math	Stat	Avg.
	GED TEST SCORES: MAY 2007						
Student 1	410	440	480	560	420	P	462
Student 2	460	420	460	570	400	F	462
Student 3	520	410	530	540	460	P	492
Student 4	530	500	470	620	420	P	508
Student 5	410	510	480	500	430	P	466
Student 6	570	510	540	590	430	P	540
Student 7		510	470	450	420	INC	
Student 8	700	650	750	730	530	P	672
Student 9	390	550	540	600	440	F	504
Student 10	520	540	550	600	540	P	550

Report-Card Time

The problem. In a prison ABE3 (junior-high-level) program, the instructor faced the task of reporting the progress of two class members. One student was about to be paroled. The other was a regular class member being evaluated at the end of the current academic quarter.

Analysis. Virtually all correctional-education programs use standard forms – report cards – for recording each student's progress. In some prisons, the form is referred to as a *grade chrono*, for it offers a brief chronology of the student's recent achievement. If an inmate is leaving a program, the form is called a termination chrono.

Figures 10.3 and 10.4 illustrate one version of a report form used in California state prisons. The contents of the form include:

- The location of the school and the type of education program in which the student is enrolled.
- The number of study units (*certification units*) in the program and how many of those units the student has completed during the most recent academic or vocational quarter.
- A behavior assessment that addresses the student's adaptability, conduct, cooperation, dependability, and initiative.
- The student's initial enrollment date and, if the student is leaving the program, the reason for leaving.
- Subject fields in which grades are given.
- The student's name, prison identification number, and dormitory.
- The instructor's comments about the student's overall demeanor. The comments may focus on regularity of attendance, level of effort and productivity, willingness to participate in learning activities, ability to stay on task without prompting, and the subjects the learner has studied most recently.

State of California	**TERMINATION CHRONO**		
Department of Corrections			
CDC 128-E (Rev 4/02)	**EDUCATION PROGRESS REPORT**		Period Covered 07-01-07 to 09-30-07

BEHAVIOR/ASSESSMENT			CERTIFICATION UNITS IN COURSE	TOTAL	COMPLETED PRIOR TO THIS QUARTER
Adaptability	S☒	U☐	Vocational Title: _____		
Conduct	S☒	U☐	Academic Title: ABE-III	25	11
Cooperation	S☒	U☐	Adult High School Title: Central Coast Adult School		
Dependability	S☒	U☐	General Education Development		
Initiative	S☒	U☐			

LIST SPECIFIC CERTIFICATION UNITS COMPLETED THIS QUARTER BY NAME: INMATE DOUGH HAS COMPLETED 3 CERTIFICATION UNITS THIS QUARTER AND 14 CERTIFICATION UNITS TO DATE.:
Arithmetic and Mathematics: Measurement and Geometry: Writing: Writing Strategies: Written and Oral English Language: Sentence Structure

DATE INMATE ENROLLED	DATE INMATE TERMINATED	TERMINATION CODE	REASON FOR TERMINATION:
2/10/2007	7/20/2007	2P	Paroled

COMMENTS SPECIFIC TO COURSE: Inmate J. Dough, Z-10000, 38-07L, was an enthusiastic and industrious learner who attended class regularly and on time. He applied himself to assigned learning tasks while in the classroom without being prompted. At the time he was placed on pre-parole status, Inmate Dough was studying: Probability Concepts in the Math unit; improving his comprehension ability in Reading unit; studying Writing Strategies in the Writing unit; learning to organize and deliver information orally in the Listening and Speaking Skills unit; and studying proper grammar usage in the Written and Oral English Language unit.

VOCATIONAL EVALUATION OF EMPLOYMENT						
(X)	OCCUPATION JOB TITLE	DOT CODE NUMBER		(X)	OCCUPATION JOB TITLE	DOT CODE NUMBER

DATE OF REPORT	QUARTER GRADE	INSTRUCTOR/TEACHER (PRINT NAME AND SIGN)	SUPERVISORY REVIEW INITIALS _____
07/20/07	A	J. Smith	

INMATE NAME (LAST, FIRST, MI)	DORM	CDC NUMBER	INSTITUTION
Dough, John R.	38-07L	Z-10000	CMC-WEST

DISTRIBUTION: WHITE-CENTRAL FILE; CANARY-EDUCATION FILE; PINK-ORIGINATOR; GOLDENROD-INMATE

CMC-VE-002 (05/02) 0918

Figure 10.3. Student Report Form – Termination.

State of California
Department of Corrections
CDC 128-E (Rev 4/02)

QUARTERLY CHRONO

EDUCATION PROGRESS REPORT   Period Covered 04-01-07 to 06-30-07

BEHAVIOR/ASSESSMENT			CERTIFICATION UNITS IN COURSE	TOTAL	COMPLETED PRIOR TO THIS QUARTER
Adaptability	S☐	U☒	Vocational Title:		
Conduct	S☐	U☒	Academic Title: _____ ABE-III	25	0
Cooperation	S☐	U☒	Adult High School Title: Central Coast Adult School		
Dependability	S☐	U☒	General Education Development		
Initiative	S☐	U☒			

<u>LIST SPECIFIC CERTIFICATION UNITS COMPLETED THIS QUARTER BY NAME:</u> INMATE DOUGH HAS COMPLETED 5 CERTIFICATION UNITS THIS QUARTER AND 5 CERTIFICATION UNITS TO DATE.:   Orientation   <u>Classroom Safety</u>
<u>Arithmetic and Mathematics:</u> Number Sense   <u>Writing:</u> Writing Strategies   <u>Written and Oral English Language:</u> Sentence Structure

DATE INMATE ENROLLED	DATE INMATE TERMINATED	TERMINATION CODE	REASON FOR TERMINATION:
5/22/2007			

COMMENTS SPECIFIC TO COURSE: Inmate J. Dough has been enrolled in the ABE-III class for a little more than one month. During that time period, he has proven to be a capable learner when he applies himself. However, Dough is frequently late to class, is easily distracted, and must be reminded regularly to stay on task and complete academic assignments. Dough received a CDC 128-A counseling chrono on 6/18/07 for failing to meet the minimum academic work completion quota for three consecutive weeks. He has been advised that if he does not improve his attendance record and effort in the classroom during the upcoming academic quarter, he will be subject to further disciplinary action. Currently, Dough is studying: Measurement and Geometry in the Mathematics unit; Literary Response and Analysis in the Reading unit; Writing Strategies in the Writing unit; the Speaking Applications section of the Listening and Speaking unit; and comma usage as part of the Written and Oral English Language Conventions unit.

VOCATIONAL EVALUATION OF EMPLOYMENT					
(X)	OCCUPATION JOB TITLE	DOT CODE NUMBER	(X)	OCCUPATION JOB TITLE	DOT CODE NUMBER

DATE OF REPORT	QUARTER GRADE	INSTRUCTOR/TEACHER (PRINT NAME AND SIGN)	SUPERVISORY REVIEW INITIALS
07/02/07	D	J. Smith	

INMATE NAME (LAST, FIRST, MI)	DORM	CDC NUMBER	INSTITUTION
Roe, Richard V.	36-41L	Q-10000	CMC-WEST

DISTRIBUTION: WHITE-CENTRAL FILE; CANARY-EDUCATION FILE; PINK-ORIGINATOR; GOLDENROD-INMATE

CMC-VE-002 (05/02) 0918

Figure 10.4. Student Report Form – End of Quarter.

Solution. Figure 10.3 shows how the instructor of the ABE3 class completed a *termination chrono* for a class member who was being paroled from prison. Figure 10.4 shows how the progress of a continuing class member was reported on a *quarterly chrono*.

The Time-in-Class Dilemma

The problem. The teacher of a prison class must fill out end-of-the-academic-quarter evaluations for 27 students. Only two students who were in the class at the start of the quarter were still there at the end, and the three students who were most recently enrolled had just been assigned to the class during the final week.

Analysis. As has been discussed throughout this book, correctional-education programs operate year-round with a fluid pattern of enrollment. The student membership of a class may change several times during a given year. Also, the class members have different levels of skill and knowledge in the subjects they study. Therefore, conventional grading procedures used in public schools — where the same students attend class together for nine months at a time — are not appropriate for correctional settings.

One difficulty is that whole-class instruction, in which class members use the same textbook and proceed chapter-by-chapter, is virtually impossible in a prison or juvenile-detention facility. Instead, each learner's progress must be judged individually, based on the needs of the student as compared with how successfully he or she learns.

Of course, what it takes to be "successful" can be defined various ways. In regular public and private schools outside of prisons and juvenile centers, success is frequently determined by scores on subject-matter tests taken by all students in a class, with the scores based on the percent of correct responses to the test items. However, in penal institutions students typically start at different junctures of the course of study and learn at different speeds, so it makes better sense to test them individually at the level at which they are working in a particular subject field.

The second premise is that each student should be evaluated according to his or her level of academic effort, as opposed to the speed with which a student is able to master a skill or body of information.

Solution. To judge students' progress in the present case, the teacher focused on his own estimate of each inmate's learning potential in relation to the inmate's performance in the sequence of evaluations. The instructor estimated that particular student's level of effort to learn, both in the classroom and on homework assignments. The instructor then used the combination of learning potential and effort for grading the student at the end of the quarter. Thus, no matter how long an inmate had been in the class or at which level of skill and knowledge he was working, the quarter grade reflected a match between the student's estimated potential (apparent ability) and effort (diligence). Therefore, students received accolades and high marks if they reported to class regularly and on time, displayed industriousness, were enthusiastic about learning, stayed on task in the classroom without being prompted, and appeared to be working as hard as possible to master the curriculum. In contrast, students received written admonishments and low grades on report cards if they were frequently late or absent from class, appeared apathetic or resistive, were often observed off-task, were unproductive, and seemed not to take their educational opportunity seriously.

Tracking Students' Progress

The problem. The instructor of a prison academic class became concerned about two issues related to what his students were studying and how much they were accomplishing. First, he believed that some class members were not completing a reasonable amount of work in each subject area. Second, he noticed that certain members appeared to spend too much time on subjects in which they were most proficient at the expense of areas in which they needed the most improvement.

Analysis. The education program's open-entrance/exit-enrollment policy – combined with the averaging of math, reading, and language TABE scores to determine the proper class placement for students – not only makes it difficult for instructors to decide how much individual learners should be accomplishing, but also makes it desirable to identify exactly what individuals should focus on most. One way to determine how much work a student should reasonably complete is to utilize academic-production tracking forms. Such forms can be developed for individual learners or an entire class and may include columns for assigned subjects as well as for different time intervals when academic work is to be evaluated.

When using a work-production tracking system, the instructor can assess for a number of factors. For instance, it is easy to compare how much work a student has completed in a specific amount of time if the subjects in the curriculum are studied for set time-periods throughout the school day, such as 45 minutes for math, 30 minutes for reading, and 30 minutes for language usage. Also, if students are allowed to determine which subjects they will concentrate on, the amount of work completed in specific areas allows the teacher to speculate about which subject fields a student prefers compared to ones that he or she finds difficult, unappealing, or unimportant. Once a pattern of preferences is recognized, the teacher can interview underachieving students to get a clearer idea of why they are not producing the amount of work expected. The teacher can then respond with an appropriate strategy.

When initiating a tracking system in which students' work is evaluated weekly, the instructor can record the results for all students over several weeks and then decide what an average acceptable amount of progress can reasonably be in each of the subject areas. This average becomes the basis for quotas that students are to meet each week. Rewards and sanctions can then be used to motivate students to complete the expected amount of work.

After establishing class averages and resultant quotas, the instructor is better able to identify students who are either struggling or working at a level below their true ability. By means of interviews with individuals and the analysis of their test results, the teacher can decide whether an under-performing student's current study resources (textbooks, workbooks, encyclopedias) are too advanced or whether the student is merely negligent.

As an example, if a student is not completing a sufficient number of assignments in a reading workbook, the instructor can have the student read passages out loud and attempt to answer related questions. Additionally, the teacher can administer a reading-vocabulary test that identifies approximate reading grade levels. If the assessment indicates that the student is being asked to work above his or her ability level, the individual can be issued more appropriate learning materials, or the quota of work the student is expected to complete in the original workbook can be reduced. On the other hand, if it appears that the student is producing less than could reasonably be expected, it may be necessary for the instructor to apply disciplinary measures that encourage the learner to perform up to full potential. That is, the student initially can be warned to be more conscientious or face unpleasant consequences. As another approach, underachievers can be issued forms specifying production quotas for each subject field and that include the number of assignments or pages to complete.

The tracking system can also be used to reward students who meet or exceed work quotas. Rewards can be in the form of certificates of achievement, having one's name posted on an honor roll that is displayed on a wall, or stationery items such as a pen or pad of note paper, providing that it is made clear that such materials are performance awards and not gifts or gratuities that are prohibited in the prison.

Solution. The first step the teacher took in this case was that of interviewing the underachieving class member. During the consultation, the student revealed that Spanish was his primary language and that he was having difficulty understanding the vocabulary in the English-language reading material he had been assigned. The instructor then had the student read a section of the textbook aloud. The inmate read in a halting manner and mispronounced several words whose meanings he could not explain. The teacher, to double-check his impression of the source of the learner's problem, gave the student a vocabulary test and concluded that the reading material routinely assigned to class members was indeed above the struggling inmate's ability level. As a result, the teacher provided a lower-level reading-development workbook, which he verified was suitable by having the student again read aloud.

PART III

POSTSCRIPT

The single chapter in Part III (a) opens with recent trends in the field of corrections that suggest what may be expected in the years ahead, then (b) turns to what correctional education will need to accomplish its mission under the future's likely conditions.

Chapter 11

A LIKELY FUTURE

In this final chapter, we speculate about what might be expected of correctional education in the years ahead by reviewing trends in the practice of imprisoning offenders and by estimating correctional education's needs.

RECENT TRENDS

Two trends of particular import for correctional education's future concern (a) the numbers of lawbreakers under government supervision and (b) a new direction in the treatment of imprisoned offenders.

A Continually Rising Tide

As noted in Chapter 2, the number of people in prisons, jails, and juvenile facilities continues to grow, with the pace of increase accelerating over the decades. The quantity of offenders on probation and parole has progressed at a similar rate. Likewise, a rising number of juveniles guilty of delinquent acts attend alternative schools.

The United States has more imprisoned and supervised felons than any nation in the world. During the quarter century 1980-2005, the number of adult prisoners, probationers, and parolees increased 260%, from 1,842,100 to 7,056,000. If that pace continues, the quantity of adult Americans under the control of the justice system could rise to 18.3 million by 2030. In 2007

more than one in a hundred American adults were living behind bars, with the numbers even higher in the southern states. . . . In some neighborhoods and in some racial and economic categories, more young men now go to prison than go to college; and in many states, since the 1990s, more tax dollars have been diverted to the criminal-justice system than to public universities. In the post-World War II era, the GI Bill massively expanded access to higher education and fundamentally transformed the American economy and job market, creating the conditions for a dramatic increase in prosperity and access to middle-class lifestyles. More recent legislation, such as the 1986 Anti-Drug Abuse Act and the 1994 Omnibus Crime Bill, has had the reverse effect, ramping up popular involvement with the criminal-justice system, paving the way for large-scale and overwhelmingly negative economic changes. (Abramsky, 2007, xvii-xviii)

The rise in the number of people incarcerated has been accompanied by a dramatic increase in the cost of locking-up lawbreakers. The $12 billion needed for operating the nation's state prisons in 1990 rose to $22 billion by 1996, an 83 percent increase, while the prison population rose 52 percent (Kaplan, 1999). In 2001 the cost had reached $38.2 billion, an average of $22,650 annually per inmate ($62.05 a day) (Stephen, 2001). A study in 15 western states showed that in 2002 the average expense per student for one year in a first-rate public university (tuition, fees, room, board) was $9,454 compared to $24,809 per inmate in a state prison (Cost of college, 2002). By 2007, the annual cost per inmate in California state prisons had reached $42,000 (Russo, 2007).

In sum, rapid growth in the number of people imprisoned can be expected in the years ahead, and the cost per inmate is bound to rise at a similar pace.

Charting a New Course

As explained in Chapter 2, the last three decades of the twentieth century produced such *get-tough-on-crime* policies as "three strikes, you're out" and "lock up the bad guys and throw away the key." But in the twenty-first century, policy-makers increasingly have realized that punishment alone deters fewer than half of the offenders from law-breaking after their release from confinement. In effect, large numbers of former inmates are again caught in criminal acts and are once more locked up. By 2007 more than 70 percent of paroled felons in California had returned to prison.

At the same time, a growing body of evidence has suggested that recidivism declines significantly among inmates who were enrolled in educational programs while incarcerated.

> Once correctional education participants are released, they are about 10 percent to 20 percent less likely to re-offend than is the average released prisoner. One million dollars spent on correctional education prevents about 600 crimes, while that same money invested in incarceration prevents 350 crimes. Correctional education is almost twice as cost-effective as a crime control policy. (Bazos & Hausman, 2004, p. 2)

Therefore, recent years have witnessed greater interest among policy-makers in expanding correctional education so that penal institutions can become *correctional* and *rehabilitative* in practice as well as in name. This pro-education position shows up in recommendations that are taken seriously by state legislatures and justice systems.

California's current prison-reform program illustrates one state's attempt to rehabilitate prison inmates. A departure from past practice was first announced in January 2005 in Governor Arnold Schwarzenegger's state-of-the-state speech. The intention was to move the state

> away from an outdated, ineffective model of massive, remote prisoner warehouses that breed better criminals [and toward] a model in which smaller facilities and stronger rehabilitation programs prepare offenders for life outside prison. (Governor signs, 2007)

Steps to implement the reform led to the California legislature passing Assembly Bill 900 in May 2007, an effort to drastically reduce prison overcrowding which, by 2007, found 170,000 inmates in facilities designed for half that number. The legislation would fund smaller facilities than in the past to accommodate 53,000 inmates and would overhaul rehabilitation, substance-abuse, education, and job training programs.

During 2007, at least three other states mounted similar reform efforts.

• Pennsylvania legislators planned changes in the state criminal-justice system by which

> an estimated 6,000 people convicted of nonviolent crimes – mainly drug or property offenses – would have new opportunities to get out of prison early or to avoid a conventional prison term altogether. They would have to stay out of trouble and successfully complete

alcohol and drug treatment or other rehabilitation programs with proven track records. . . . Another proposal would allow an estimated 2,500 inmates a year to be sentenced to "intermediate punishment," which consists of at least a year in treatment programs that begin in special therapeutic prison units and progress to less secure settings closer to the offenders' homes. (Jackson, 2007)

• Michigan's state senate Republicans urged the reduction of recidivism through more education and job-training skills so as to facilitate prisoners' re-entry into the workforce (Senate Republicans, 2007).

• Washington state lawmakers passed an Offender Re-Entry Act intended to reduce recidivism by addressing the major reasons offenders violate the terms of their release and end up back behind bars – mental illness, lack of job skills, illiteracy, and lack of drug rehabilitation (MacTaggert, 2007).

In effect, increasing correctional education and the non-imprisonment treatment of perpetrators of non-violent crimes (drug abuse, child-support default, and the like) have been seen as ways of curtailing the rise in jail and prison populations and in costs.

Implications

Three consequences that the foregoing trends imply are that (a) the costs of imprisoning and supervising offenders will continue to rise rapidly, (b) far more correctional teachers and administrators will be required than in the past, and (c) effective teaching in correctional settings can help reduce recidivism by equipping inmates with skills and attitudes that enable them to live crime-free lives after they are freed from jail, prison, juvenile centers, and alternative schools. What correctional education will need in order to fulfill that mission is the matter we next consider.

CORRECTIONAL EDUCATION'S FUTURE NEEDS

In the years ahead, how schooling contributes to individual offenders' lives and to the welfare of the American public will depend to a great extent on (a) educational facilities, (b) funding, (c) inmate incentives, (d) course offerings, (e) educational personnel, and (f) measures of success.

Educational Facilities

As jails, prisons, and juvenile facilities in so many regions of the nation have overflowed with inmates in recent times, buildings traditionally used for education or recreation have increasingly been converted into housing for offenders. Thus, there is a critical need for:

(a) building more prisons, jails, and juvenile facilities to lodge inmates so that classrooms and vocational shops that had been converted to dormitories can be returned to their educational function and

(b) constructing more well-equipped classrooms and vocational shops so that larger numbers of inmates can attend school.

The need for more educational facilities has been reflected in national surveys of the numbers of prison, jail, and juvenile-center inmates enrolled in schooling. According to a Re-Entry Council report,

> Just over half of all state prisoners participate in educational programs at some point during their incarceration, a proportion that has been decreasing over time. About one-third of prisoners participate in vocational programs at some point during their incarceration. At any given time, however, the percentage of prisoners engaged in educational and vocational programs is far lower than these figures suggest. While all federal prisons, 91 percent of state prisons, 88 percent of private prisons, and 60 percent of jails offer some type of educational program, the relatively low number of available program slots often limits rates of program participation. Demand for programming often exceeds supply, resulting in waiting lists for many programs. In Maryland, 1,500 state inmates were on waiting lists to participate in educational or vocational programming in 2001.
> While comparable participation rates are not available for jail inmates, the Bureau of Justice Statistics reports that secondary education classes are most commonly available, offered in 46 percent of jail jurisdictions. Vocational program availability is very limited for jail inmates, with only five percent of jail jurisdictions offering vocational training. Many jail jurisdictions (33 percent) offer no educational or vocational training at all. (Re-Entry Policy Council, 2006)

Studies of recidivism suggest that the rate at which offenders return to prison will drop in relation to the proportion of inmates who complete education programs. Thus, the best chance of reducing the number of released offenders who are again arrested can be expected if prisons adopt a policy of requiring all inmates to enroll in schooling through the GED (high-school graduation) level or through a series of vocational classes leading to a certificate. If such a goal is to be achieved, a major expansion of prison-education facilities is needed.

Sufficient, Trustworthy Funding

Correctional education can be adequately funded only if

- lawmakers (Congress, state legislatures, county boards, city councils) are convinced that substantial justice-system money will be saved by educating offenders to become law-abiding citizens rather than by just locking them up and
- funds intended for education cannot be siphoned off for other uses.

The first of these two tasks is a lobbying effort that confronts legislatures with the facts about the money-saving results of reducing recidivism – a reduction especially vital during an era of rapidly rising costs to keep prisoners locked up.

The second task involves stipulating at the federal, state, or city level the amounts of a prison, jail, or juvenile-center budget that must be assigned to educational programs. The budgets that prison wardens, jail officials, and juvenile-justice supervisors are assigned should not permit those individuals to shift money around at their own discretion, because such discretion can harm education programs, particularly in facilities under the authority of "hard-nosed" officials who consider schooling opportunities for prisoners to be little more than the overindulgent mollycoddling of felons.

Inmate Incentives

A significant barrier to enrolling more inmates in educational programs has been offenders' lack of interest in schooling. One widely used way to guarantee that inmates enter programs is to make school attendance mandatory, at least until offenders complete the equivalent of high-school graduation. Federal prisons have such a mandatory policy, as do many states, as illustrated by the 2007 Florida Criminal Procedures and Corrections Statutes requiring all state penal institutions to

> Ensure that every inmate who has 2 years or more remaining to serve on his or her sentence at the time that he or she is received at an institution and who lacks basic and functional literacy skills attends not fewer than 150 hours of sequential instruction in a correctional adult basic education program. . . . Upon completion of the 150 hours of instruction, the inmate shall be retested and, if a composite test score of functional literacy is not attained, the department is authorized to require the inmate to remain in the instructional program. (State Correctional System, 2007)

Other methods of encouraging participation in academic and vocational courses include such incentives as certificates, graduation ceremonies, the shortening of inmates' sentences, special consideration for parole, preferential consideration for employment within the prison, pay for attending class, and opportunities for more advanced education (such as enrolling in college classes after earning a GED certificate). The Florida program not only mandated 150 hours of schooling but added the incentive of reducing an inmate's sentence by six days for actively participating in 150 hours of formal study. An additional six-days' credit was awarded for those who earned a GED or vocational certificate.

The practice of providing incentives is nothing new. In 1987, prisons in 21 states offered reduced sentences to inmates. Sixteen states paid enrollees a modest amount of money for attending classes, nine states allowed parole boards to include inmates' schooling in parole considerations, and five states required boards to do so (National Institute of Corrections, 1987).

Throughout the 1990s and into the twenty-first century, an increasing number of states expanded their incentive programs. In 2000, Arizona enacted reverse-incentive legislation that required inmates to forfeit early-release credits if they failed to earn a GED certificate while in custody. The following year West Virginia began awarding 60 days release credit to inmates who earned a high-school diploma. Illinois adopted a similar policy in 2005 (Education Commission of the States, 2007).

Course Offerings

The content of academic programs that stress literacy, numeracy, computer use, and citizenship are useful to inmates who are released into the general society, no matter what occupations they enter. However, the vocational training provided in penal institutions often does not fit the job opportunities in the community to which parolees return. Thus, an important need is for jails and prisons to investigate the job markets their inmates will likely enter and to give preference to offering vocational courses suited to those markets.

Bernard LoPinto, a long-time supervisor of education at a New York State penal facility, has proposed that first-rate correctional-education programs are ones that include:

- A learner-centered approach, recognizing the different learning styles, cultural backgrounds, and multiple illiteracies,
- Post-release services to re-enforce skills that can easily be lost,
- Special education services that meet the needs of all handicapped students regardless of age,
- English-language-development and bilingual instruction for all inmates who need it, and
- "Live work" programs, providing hands-on experience for the students while saving money for the department. (LoPinto, 2007)

Educational Personnel

As noted in Chapter 3, the teachers in correctional education are drawn chiefly from public schools and the occupational world. Rarely have teachers been specifically prepared for their jobs by completing a teacher-training program designed for correctional settings. Instead, the instructors that staff prison, jail, or juvenile-center academic classes have usually finished regular teacher-training programs and hold state teaching credentials. In contrast, instructors in vocational programs are often hired for their expertise in a particular occupation – computer repair, carpentry, plumbing, drywall construction, auto repair, and the like – without having had formal preparation for teaching. Consequently, the particular attitudes and skills needed for successfully teaching in penal institutions must be learned on the job.

Although it is possible to prepare for a correctional-education career in a few colleges' criminal-justice departments, the number of such opportunities is very small, indeed. An example of such a program is the one offered in the Center for the Study of Correctional Education, created in 1991 at the California State University, San Bernardino. The Center is designed to help "veteran and prospective teachers who work in local, state, federal, and private correctional facilities by providing training, historical perspectives, and teaching methods and showing them how to deal with prisoners in the classroom" (Gutierrez, 2005). In the years ahead, as many more teachers and administrators will be needed in penal facilities, the quality of new teachers entering the profession could well be improved by having more correctional educators coming from such programs. In effect, program expansion appears warranted.

Because most personnel in correctional education are obliged to learn the intricacies of their profession while on the job, inservice training becomes a significant determinant of the quality of correctional programs. The most common form of such training consists of staff members attending lectures about teaching and administrative skills, either during staff-improvement sessions within a given penal facility or during presentations at regional adult-education conferences. However, such sessions are of questionable value for improving teachers' classroom practices, because participants are merely passive listeners who are not required to demonstrate what they are expected to learn. Far greater benefits can be expected from inservice experiences that require staff members to (a) create lesson plans for using an improved teaching method and (b) apply those plans in classroom practice. Such "hands-on" learning can be provided through mentorship, apprenticeship, and demonstration/application programs. A mentorship or apprenticeship involves a less-experienced teacher being guided by a more-experienced teacher in applying an effective instructional method. A demonstration/application approach consists of a skilled teacher performing a method before a group, either directly or via a videotape taken in a correctional-education classroom. Following the demonstration, each member of the audience is assigned to prepare a lesson of the same type and to tryout that lesson, either in a classroom or with the audience assuming the roles of students in an imaginary class.

It is also the case that a penal institution's success recruiting and retaining high-quality teachers is increased when teachers' salaries are comparable to the pay received by teachers in public schools of the region in which the correctional facility is located.

Finally, I believe it is fitting that – as senior author of this book – I complete this discussion of correctional-education's personnel needs by voicing my own feelings about what it means to select teaching in a prison as a career.

Under any circumstances, the job of teaching is a challenging one. But, certainly most people who choose teaching as a profession do not enter the trade with the intention of teaching in a prison. In fact, I know only one person during my 28 years in correctional education who sought a teaching credential in order to become an instructor in a prison, and that person had previously worked at the prison as an office assistant. Instead, most of my colleagues took prison-teaching positions out of desperation, because there were no other jobs in their field of instruction available in the community.

I imagine an important reason that teachers are reluctant to choose a career in correctional education is the negative image of prison inmates often portrayed in television and newspaper accounts. However, the truth is that, quite unlike such a stereotype, the typical prisoner who enrolls in a schooling program is more mature, goal-oriented, and appreciative of the opportunity to get an education than is the average adolescent in the public-school system. In contrast to the problem in public schools of teachers having to tolerate indifferent and bothersome students, prison instructors can expediently remove any class members who are not serious learners. Hence, correctional-education teachers need not abide unruly or indifferent scholars. Another benefit of teaching in a prison is that the prisoners who work as teaching assistants in classrooms are often bright, talented, and dedicated individuals who provide a variety of essential services, thereby considerably reducing the teacher's workload. In short, it's my impression that the advantages of teaching in correctional settings may be the best-kept secret in the nation's teacher-education programs.

I have had a great many positive experiences in the prison classroom during my career, whether it has been teaching U.S. history and political science for students pursuing a degree at a nearby community college or teaching in my current assignment as an ABE3/GED instructor. I never tire of seeing the expression on a student's face as he masters a new concept or skill, and I appreciate the sincere gratitude that students express for my having helped them. In all, I believe the job of prison educator makes a great social contribution by arming inmates with knowledge and skills they can apply following their release. Schooling in prison offers undereducated felons their only viable opportunity for leaving prison with the chance of becoming honest, tax-paying citizens. Thus, it is my hope that some readers of this book will choose to enter the field of correctional education and achieve the same sense of fulfillment I get each day in my classroom.

Measures of Success

Two approaches to assessing the outcomes of correctional education are the *instructional* and the *societal.* Improvements are needed in both approaches.

Instructional evaluation answers the question: How well did the students learn what the educational program was supposed to teach them? Answers to this question are found through use of the assessment methods described in Chapter 10 – standardized tests (TABE, GED), teacher-made tests, teachers' observations of students' actions (speech, vocational skills), and teacher's judgments of students' products (written assignments, vocational-class projects). Many teachers in correctional programs have had little or no training in classroom assessment techniques. Therefore, the quality of instructional evaluation can be upgraded through teachers participating in workshops that provide practice in creating, applying, and interpreting the results of classroom evaluation techniques.

Societal evaluation answers the question: What effect does correctional education have on the communities which inmates enter following their release from custody? The most easily calculated and convincing indicator of societal effects is the rate of recidivism. Therefore, correctional-education programs can profit from analyzing studies of the lifestyles adopted by parolees from prisons, jails, and juvenile centers. The follow-up studies can be designed to compare recidivists with non-recidivists in terms of (a) the kinds of educational programs in which inmates participated during their incarceration, (b) how long they were in such programs, (c) their ages, and (d) their occupational histories after their release. Such information may help correctional educators fashion their programs in ways that help improve the chance that parolees will lead crime-free lives.

CONCLUSION

As suggested in this chapter, the nation's penal institutions can expect marked growth over the coming years in numbers of inmates and in their opportunities for education. To accommodate such growth, penal systems will require far more educational facilities, trustworthy funding, incentives that encourage offenders to pursue schooling, course offerings that prepare inmates for a law-abiding future, efficient teachers, and accurate measures of the results of correctional programs.

In closing, we should note that our intent in writing *Effective Teaching in Correctional Settings* was to contribute in a modest way toward the success of such a likely future.

Appendix A

ESSAY WRITING

Chapter 8 included a description of one way to apply a diminishing-aid method in teaching essay writing. This appendix extends the description by displaying a completed guide-sheet and the resulting essay.

Step 1: Present the topic.

How are consumers negatively influenced by the advertising they see?

Step 2: Write a topic sentence to explain the main idea of the essay.

Use the following topic sentence: Advertisers often use exaggeration and false promises to convince consumers to buy their merchandise.

Step 3: Identify 3-to-5 specific reasons that support your opinion of the subject you are writing about.

Use the following concepts as evidence to support your main reason. Notice that the reasons are numbered in the order in which they should be discussed in the body of the essay.

Advertisers suggest that users of their product:

4. Appear more attractive to the opposite sex.

1. Acquire a skill.

2. Become physically fit.

3. Get a large quantity of a certain product.

Step 4: Write the essay's introductory paragraph.

Begin the essay with the following paragraph.

Advertisers often use exaggeration and false promises to convince consumers to buy their merchandise. For example, some companies claim that a person using their product will develop a certain skill or ability. Others lead customers to believe they will become physically fit in a short time period. Still other companies' advertising makes people think they are getting a large quantity of a commodity at a low price. But perhaps the most misleading proclamation is that a product will make users attractive to the opposite sex.

Step 5: **Prepare notes that explain in greater detail each specific point you cited at Step 3 to support your essay's main idea. Remember to list the support ideas in the order in which they will appear in your essay.**
First support idea: Physical skills – basketball shoes, energy drinks.
Second support idea: Fitness – athletes as models, fancy machines.
Third support idea: Product amount – chip package, cereal box.
Fourth support idea: Sex appeal – cigarette, cologne, clothing, car.

Stop!: **Do not attempt to write the final essay before you show the teacher or teacher's aide the results of your work so far.**

Step 6: **Write the paragraphs that will make up the body of your essay. Remember to begin each paragraph with a topic sentence.**
(See final essay below.)

Step 7: **Develop a concluding paragraph for your essay, making sure that you remind the reader of the main point of the essay.**
Giving consumers false ideas about the benefits of purchasing certain products is an age-old practice. In some cases, the government has passed laws to either reduce or control the problem of false advertising. Even so, many companies still defraud customers by lying about the benefits of what they are selling.

Step 8: **Write the final version of the essay.**

How Consumers Are Influenced By Advertising

Advertisers often use exaggeration and false promises to convince consumers to buy their merchandise. For example, some companies claim that a person using their product will develop a certain skill or ability. Others lead customers to believe they will become physically fit in a short time period. Still other companies' advertising makes people think they are getting a large quantity of a commodity at a low price. But perhaps the most misleading proclamation is that a product will make users attractive to the opposite sex.

Some companies make you believe you will magically develop better physical skills or powers. As an example, some basketball-shoe companies claim that by wearing their shoes, you will be able to play as well as professionals. One energy-drink company gives people the impression that they can actually fly through the air after consuming one of their drinks.

Numbers of physical-fitness-equipment companies advertise their products using young athletes as models to convince customers that they, too, can look like a model after only a few short weeks. Such products as the Thigh Master and the Boflex machine are supposed to trim fat and build muscles quickly.

Another misleading advertising scheme is intended to make customers think they are getting more of a product than the amount actually in the packages. Potato-chip bags are often much larger than needed to hold the contents, with air pumped into the bags to make the bags look full. Also, many cereal boxes are actually only half full.

The most deceiving method some advertisers use, however, is to say that by using their product, a person will immediately develop sex appeal. A man is led to believe that by smoking the right brand of cigarette, using the proper cologne, wearing a certain brand of clothing, or owning the right car he will automatically attract beautiful women.

Giving consumers false ideas about the benefits of purchasing certain products is an age-old practice. In some cases, the government has passed laws to either reduce or control the problem of false advertising. Even so, many companies still defraud customers by lying about the benefits of what they are selling.

Appendix B

INSTRUCTIONAL BOOKS

As an example of the kinds of instructional reading materials used in typical correctional-education classes, the following list identifies the titles of a limited sampling of books from one state prison's education department. The items in the sample have been chosen to illustrate the diversity and difficulty-levels of reading matter in various courses.

The list is divided according to the kinds of classes for which the reading materials have been adopted. The first section describes books for academic programs. In that section, the abbreviation *ABE* stands for *Adult Basic Education*, and *GED* stands for *General Educational Development*. The second section identifies materials for vocational programs.

Readers who wish to learn the source of a particular item can find the publisher's address and the publication date by entering the book title into an Internet search engine, such as Google or Ask.

Additional instructor-created materials can be found on the Rob Thomas website at – http://web.pages.charter.net/rgtcorrectionaled.

Academic Programs

Most of the items in this section are textbooks, workbooks, study guides, novels, or teacher's manuals. A few items are audiocassettes that accompany the listed books.

ABE1 – Primary-Grade Level

Absolutely Essential Words
Achieving TABE Success (Level E language, math, reading)
Amazing Facts (three-book set: famous people; places and events; outstanding
    Americans.

Basic Sight Words
Challenger Adult Reading Series (Levels 1–3)
Checkbook Math
Famous Celebrity Readers
Following Directions
Funbook of Creative Writing
Grammillionaire
Hands on Math Games
High Points (reading, language levels A, B, C)
Inference
Life Skill Lessons
Longman Dccionario Mexican
Math Skills Games
Of Mice and Men (novel)
Openers for English Classes
Parts of Speech
SRA Math Skillbuilder (Levels: gold, brown, red, orange, yellow)

ABE2 – Upper-Elementary-Grade Level

Achieving TABE Success (Levels E, M, D for language, math, reading)
American Lives (Books 1, 2, 3)
Anne Frank; Diary of a Young Girl (student book, study guide, teacher's manual, audiocassette)
Basic Skills Puzzles
Challenger Adult Reading Series (Books 1–6)
Complete Check Writing Kit
Descriptive Writing
Diagramming Sentences
Encarta Premium
Encyclopaedia Britannica
Expository Writing
Grammar for You (nouns in context, verbs in context)
Literature: Timeless Voices (Levels: copper, brown)
Maps, Globes, and Graphs (Books 1–3)
Patterns in Spelling
Raisin in the Sun (novel)
Roget's Thesaurus in Dictionary Form
Three-in-One Science Kits (chemo-electro, PH fun)
Twenty Thousand Leagues Under the Sea (student book, study guide, teacher's manual, audio cassette)
Two Hundred Words You Need to Know

Vocabulary Connections (Books 3–6)
Writing and Gramma: Communication in Action (Levels: brown, silver)

ABE3 – Junior-High Level

Achieving TABE Success (Levels M, D, A for language, math, reading)
Challenger Adult Reading Series (Levels 6–8)
Critical Reading for Proficiency (Levels: 1–3)
I Can Read It, But I Don't Get It (reading comprehension)
Language Exercises (Levels: D, E, F, G)
Literature: Timeless Voices, Timeless Themes (Level: brown)
Number Power Math Series (Levels: 2–8)
Pre-Algebra
Saxon Math Homeschool (Levels: 4/5, 6/7)
Scope English Anthology (Levels: 4–6)
Writing and Grammar: Communication in Action (Levels: brown, silver)

ELD/ESL – English Language Development

English Action Pictures
English Picture Dictionary
Everyday Situations in English
Fundamentals of English Grammar
High Point – Basics
Longman Diccionario Ingles Basico
Word by Word

GED – Senior-High or High-School Diploma

Assessment Program for the GED
Calculator Power for GED
Complete GED
Contemporary's Complete GED
Essential GED
GED Connection Workbook (math)
GED Model Test
GED Satillite Series (math, reading, science, social studies, writing)
Math Exercises (algebra, data analysis, decimals, fractions, geometry, measurement, percents, pre-algebra, problem solving, money)
Top 50 Skills for GED Success (math, reading, writing)

DDP – Developmental/Disabled Program

Basic English Composition Student Text
Basic English Grammar Student Text
Countries of the World
Game: Life Skills, Money Skills
Game: Life Skills, SocialSkills
English to Use (student text)
Let's Talk About Life Skills
Native Peoples Classroom Library
World Geography for You
World History Student Text

Plato – Computer-Assisted-Learning Laboratory

Math Spectrum
Number Power 10 (pre-algebra)
Vocabulary Connections
(Many computer programs in various subject fields.)

Various Classes

Merriam-Webster's Collegiate Dictionary
Spanish-English Dictionary
Encarta Encyclopedia
Encyclopaedia Britannica

Vocational Programs

The total number of vocational programs in prisons is very large, indeed – far too many to include here. Thus, for the purpose of identifying typical vocational reading materials, we have confined the examples to books and computer programs for six courses.

Automotive Body Repair and Refinishing

Auto Body Repair Technology, 4th Edition
Car Certification System

Business-Office Services

Alphabetic Indexing Rules
Business Communications and Study Guide
Calculators: Printing and Display 4E
Century 21 Computer Keyboarding Lessons
Job Preparation – Getting a Job Process Kit
Microsoft Power-Point 2003
Microsoft Word 2003, Specialist
Proofreading at the Computer

Construction-Industry Trades

Building Maintenance
Carpentry
Electrical Construction
Foundations and Flooring
Heating, Ventilation, Air Conditioning
Metal Trades – Sheet Metal
Metal Trades – Welding
Plumbing

Electronics

Foundations of Electronics: Circuits and Devices
Paynter's Introductory Electronic Devices and Circuits

Landscape Maintenance

Landscape Training Manuals (3 books: installation, irrigation, maintenance)
Retail Nursery Professional Training Manual
University of California Master Garden Book

Eyewear Manufacturing

Exam Preparation for Spectacle Dispensing
Exam preparation for Contact Lens Dispensers
Opthalmic Fabrication and Dispensing
Technical Options for Professional Services

Small-Engine Repair

Briggs and Stratton Parts Look-Up (CD)
Outdoor Power Equipment
Practical Problems in Mathematics for the Automotive Technician
Small Engines
Small Engine Technology
Small Gas Engines
Tecumseh Service Manual

Transmission/Transaxel Service

Automotive Service, 2nd Edition
Automotive Service Workbook, 2nd Edition

REFERENCES

Abramsky, S. (2007). *American furies*. Boston: Beacon.

Adams, K. (1994, December). A large-scale multidimensional test of the effect of prison education programs on offenders' behavior. *The Prison Journal, 74* (2), 433–449.

Aging facts answers. (2007). Available online: http://cas.umkc.edu/cas/AgingFacts Answers.htm.

American Council on Education. (2007). *GED sample test items*. Available online: http://www.acenet.edu/AM/Template.cfm?Section=TestTaersInfo&CONTENT ID=5691&TEMPLATE=/CM/HTMLDispla y.cfm.

Anderson, N. D., Craik, F. I, & Naveh-Benjamin, M. (1998, September). The attentional demands of encoding and retrieval in younger and older adults: 1. Evidence from divided attention costs. *The Psychology of Aging, 13* (3), 405–423.

Bazos, A., & Hausman, J. (2004, March). *Correctional education as a crime control program*. Los Angeles: University of California at Los Angeles, School of Public Policy and Social Research.

Boulder County Sheriff's Department. (2007). *Jail education programs*. Available online: http://www.co.boulder.co.us/sheriff/jail/jail_edu. Htm.

Bureau of Justice Statistics. (2005). *Summary findings*. Available online: http://www.ojp.usdoj.gov/bjs/glance/tables/corr2tab.htm.

California code of regulations title 15, section 3043.4. (2007). Sacramento: California Department of Corrections and Rehabilitation.

Class expectations and standards. (2007). San Luis Obispo: California Men's Colony Education Department.

Correctional Service of Canada. (2006, February 9). *Literacy training and reintegration of offenders*. Available online: http://www.csc-scc.gc.ca/text/pblct/forum/e03/e031j_e.shtml.

Crook, T. H., & West, R. L. (1990, August). Name recall performance across the adult life-span. *British Journal of Psychology, 81* (3), 335–349.

Cost of college vs. cost of prison. (2002). *WICHE factbook*. Available online: http://www.wiche.edu/Policy/FactBook/tables/tbl_44.pdf.

Custody data. (2003). *Frequently asked questions about juveniles in corrections*. Available online: http://ojjdp.ncjrs.org/ojstatbb/corrections/ faqs.asp.

Davis, H. P., et al. (2003, September-December). Acquisition, recall, and forgetting of verbal information in long-term memory by young, middle-aged, and elderly individuals. *Cortex, 39* (4–5), 1063–1091.

Education Commission of the States. (2007. *Corrections education.* Available online: http://www.ecs.org/html/issue.asp?issueID=28.

Fine, M., et al. (2001). *Changing minds: The impact of college in a maximum security prison.* New York: Graduate Center, City College of New York. Available online: http://www.changingminds.ws/.

Fischer, R. G. (2005). Are California's recidivism rates really the highest in the nation? *UCI Corrections,* vol. 1. Available online: http:// ucicorrections. seweb.uci.edu/pdf/bulletin_2005_vol-1_is-1.pdf.

Gaes, G. G., Wallace, S., Gilman, E., Klein-Saffran, J, & Suppa, S. (2001, March 9). *The influence of prison gang affiliation on violence and other prison misconduct.* Available online: http://72.14.253.104/ search? q=cache:MPAkDpCLKiIJ: www.bop.gov/news/research_projects/published_reports/cond_envir/oreprcri m_2br.pdf+gangs+in+prison&hl=en&ct=clnk&cd=7&gl=us.

Gee, J. (2006, December). Education in rural county jails: Need versus opportunity. *Journal of Correctional Education, 57* (4), 312–325.

Geraci, P. M. (2003, June). Promoting positive reading discourse and self-exploration through a multicultural book club. *Journal of Correctional Education, 52* (2), 54–59.

Governor signs prison agreement. (2007, May). Office of the governor. Available online: http://gov.ca.gov/prisonreform/.

Gutierrez, J. (2005, Spring/Summer). Barring an education. *Cal State Bernardino Magazine.* http://magazine.csusb.edu/05spring/cover/ index.html.

Henry, S. (2003). *On the effectiveness of prison as punishment.* Available online: http://www.is.wayne.edu/stuarthenry/Effectiveness_of_Punishment.htm.

Hultsch, D. F., Hertzog, C., & Dixon, R. A. (1990, September). Ability correlates of memory performance in adulthood and aging. *Psychology of Aging, 5* (3), 356–368.

Human Rights Education Associates. (2007). *Basic principles for the treatment of prisoners.* Available online: http://www.hrea.org/erc/Library/display.php?doc_id =592&category_id=767&category_type=2.

Jackson, P. (2007, August 30). Pa. considers prison reform. *The Sentinel.* Available online: http://www.cumberlink.com/articles/2007/08/30/ news/news497.txt.

Juvenile detention. (2007). Available online: http://www.accesskent.com/Courts AndLawEnforcement/JuvenileDetention/jd_index.htm.

Kaplan, S. (1999, August 24). State prison costs up 83 percent in six years, report shows. *Stateline.org.* Available online: http://www.stateline.org/live/View Page.action?siteNodeId=136&languageId=1&contented=14612.

Klein, S., Tolbert, M., Bugarin, R., Cataldi, E. F., & Tauschek, G. (2004). *Correctional Education.* Washington, DC: U.S. Department of Education.

Learning disabilities. (2007). Available online: http://www.kidshealth. org/teen/diseases_ conditions/learning/learning_disabilities.html.

Legislative Analyst's Office. (2006, February). *Adult corrections – Who is in prison?* Available online: http://www.lao.ca.gov/analysis_2006/crim_justice/ cj_05_anl06.html.

Leone, P. E., Meisel, S. M, & Drakeford, W. (2002, June). Special education programs for youth wih disabilities in juvenile corrections. *Journal of Correctional Education, 53* (2), 46–50.

LoBuglio, S. (2001). Time to reframe politics and practices in correctional education. *Review of Adult Learning and Literacy,* Vol. 2. Available online: http://www.ncsall.net/?id=560.

Long, J. (2007, April 25). California Vocational Education Programs. Personal communication.

LoPinto, B. (2007). How schools in prisons help inmates and society. *Prison education.* Available online: http://adulted.about.com/cs/prisoneducation/a/prison_ed.htm.

Macallair, D. (2000). *America's One-Million Nonviolent Prisoners.* Available online: http://www.cjcj.org/pubs/one_million/onemillion.

Mageehon, A. (2006, June). What makes a "good" teacher "good." Women in transition from prison to community reflect. *The Journal of Correctional Education, 57* (2), 145–157.

National Center for Juvenile Justice. (2006). *Juvenile offenders and victims: 2006 National Report.* Available online: ojjdp.ncjrs.org/ojstatbb/nr 2006/index.html.

National Institute of Corrections. (1987). *Quarterly Survey Questions.* Available online: http://nicic.org/Library/period41.

Piccone, J. E. (2006, September). Administering the Test of Adult Basic Education at intake: A biased marker of offender ability. *The Journal of Correctional Education 57* (3), 239–248.

Price, L., Said, K., & Haaland, K. Y. (2004, June). Age-associated memory impairment of logical memory and visual reproduction. *Journal of Clinical Experimental Neuropsychology, 26* (4), 531–538.

Prison and jail inmates at midyear 1996. (1996). *Bureau of Justice statistics.* Washington, DC: U.S. Department of Justice. Available online: http://www.ojp.usdoj.gov/bjs/abstract/pjimy96.htm.

Prison break. (2002, October 9). *New Republic.* Available online: http://www.tnr.com/doc.mhtml?i=20021021&s=editorial102102.

Prison statistics. (2005). *Bureau of Justice statistics.* Washington, DC: U.S. Department of Justice. Available online: http://www.ojp.usdoj.gov/bjs/ prisons.htm.

Re-Entry Policy Council. (2006). *Report of the Re-Entry Policy Council.* Available online: http://www.reentrypolicy.org/reentry/PS16.aspx.

Report: U.S. prison growth could cost $27.5 billion over next 5 years. (2007, February 15). *Salem-News.* Available online: http://www.sal em-news.com/articles/february152007/usprisongrowth_021507.php.

Rice, L. (1997, December 15). Civility explored behind prison walls. *The Gazette, 27* (15). Available online:http://www.jhu.edu/~gazette/octdec97/dec1597/15civil.html.

Ross, R. R., & Fabiano, E. A. (1985). *Time to think: A cognitive model of delinquency prevention and offender rehabilitation.* Johnson City, TN: Institute of Social Sciences and Arts.

Russo, F. D. (2007, April 26). Prison bill passes legislature and goes to governor. *California Progress Report.* Available online: http://www. californiaprogressreport.com/2007/04/prison_bill_pas.html.

Ryan, T. A. (2006, February 9). *Literacy training and reintegration of offenders.* Available online: http://www.csc-scc.gc.ca/text/pblct/ forum/e03/e031j_e.shtml.

Senate Republicans oppose governor's sentencing guideline changes; outline $200 million in real reforms. (2007, July 19). *Michigan Senate Republicans.* Available online: http://www.senate.michigan.gov/gop/readarticle.asp?id=631.

Shuler, P. (2004, April 4). Educating prisoners is cheaper than locking them up again. *City Beat.* Available online: http://www.citybeat. com/2002-04-04/statehouse.shtml.

State Correctional System. (2007). *The 2007 Florida Statutes, Title XLVII, Chapter 944.* Available online: http://www.leg.state.fl.us/Statutes/index.cfm?App_mode= Display_Statute&Search_String=&URL=Ch0944/Sec801.HTM.

Stephan, J. J. (2004, June 15). *State prison expenditures 2001.* Available online: http://www.ojp.usdoj.gov/bjs/pub/pdf/spe01.pdf.

Thomas, R. G. (2003). The revolving door. *Journal of Correctional Education.*

Thomas, R. G. (2007a). *Education program contract ABE III/A – Classroom 377A.* San Luis Obispo: California Men's Colony Education Department.

Thomas, R. G. (2007b). *Students' reasons for enrolling in class.* Unpublished raw data.

United Nations. (1948, December 10). *Universal Declaration of Human Rights.* Available online: http://www.un.org/Overview/rights.html.

U.S. prison population sets record. (2006, December 1). *Washington Post.* Available online: http://www.washingtonpost.com/wp-dyn/content/article/2006/11/30/AR2006113000912.html.

Walker, R. (2007). *Gangs or us.* Available online: http://www. gangs orus.com/prisongangs.html.

Wiggelsworth, G. L. (2007). *Jail education program.* Available online: http://www.ingham.org/sh/education.htm.

Youngjohn, J. G., & Crook, T. H. (1993, July). Learning, forgetting, and retrieval of everyday material across the adult life span. *Journal of Clinical Experimental Neuropsychology, 15* (4), 447–460.

Zaro, D. (2007, March). Teaching strategies for the self-actualized educator: The inside person vs. the outside person. *The Journal of Correctional Education, 58* (1), 27–41.

Zelinski, E. M., Gilewski, M. J., & Schaie, K. W. (1993, June). Individual differences in cross-sectional and 3-year longitudinal memory performance across the adult life span. *Psychology of Aging, 8* (2), 176–186.

INDEX

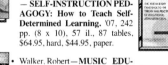

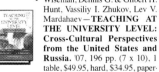

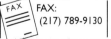